# Shamanic
# Worlds

# Shamanic Worlds

## Rituals and Lore of Siberia and Central Asia

Marjorie Mandelstam Balzer, Editor

NORTH CASTLE BOOKS

*An imprint of M.E. Sharpe,*INC.

Armonk, New York
London, England

This North Castle paperback edition is a revised and expanded version
of the collection *Shamanism: Soviet Studies of Traditional Religion
in Siberia and Central Asia* published by M.E. Sharpe in 1990.
Translations were previously published in the journals
*Soviet Anthropology and Archeology/Anthropology and Archeology of Eurasia*
and *Shaman: Journal of the International Society for Shamanistic Research.*

**Library of Congress Cataloging-in-Publication Data**

Shamanic Worlds : rituals and lore of Siberia and Central Asia /
edited by Marjorie Mandelstam Balzer.
p.   c.m.
Originally published: New York : M. E. Sharpe, 1990.
Includes bibliographical references and index.
ISBN 1-56324-973-1 (pbk. : alk. paper)
1. Shamanism—Russia (Federation)—Siberia. 2. Rites and ceremonies—Russia (Federation)—Siberia. 3. Folklore—Russia (Federation)—Siberia. 4. Turkic peoples—Religion.
5. Siberia (Russia)—Religious life and customs.
BL2370.S5L35   1997
299'.43—dc20       96-28497
CIP

**Cover: The cover art is adapted from a drawing by Vasily Parnikov, Sakha (Yakut)
artist, one of the first to portray shamans in a positive light in the Soviet period.
"Udagan (Female Shaman)," 1981.**

Printed in the United States of America

The paper used in this publication meets the minimum requirements of
American National Standard for Information Sciences—
Permanence of Paper for Printed Library Materials,
ANSI Z 39.48-1984.

| BM (c) | 10 | 9 | 8 | 7 | 6 | 5 | 4 | 3 | 2 | 1 |
| BM (p) | 10 | 9 | 8 | 7 | 6 | 5 | 4 | 3 | 2 | 1 |

## Dedication

This book is dedicated to the Evenk shaman
Matriona Petrovna Kurbeltinova,
whose life spanned the twentieth century
and whose wisdom and kindness spans the ages.

# Contents

# About the Editor and Contributors

MARJORIE MANDELSTAM BALZER (Ph.D., anthropology, 1979) is Research Professor at Georgetown University in the Sociology Department and the Center for Eurasian, Russian, and East European Studies (CERES), where she coordinates the CERES program "Social, Regional, and Ethnic Issues." She is editor of the M.E. Sharpe journal *Anthropology and Archeology of Eurasia* and of the books *Culture Incarnate: Native Anthropology from Russia* (1995); and *Russian Traditional Culture* (1992). She has done several years of fieldwork in the former Soviet Union, beginning in 1975, especially in western Siberia (with the Ob-Ugrian Khanty, 1976, 1991) and the Far East (Sakha Republic, Yakutia, 1986, periodically each year 1991–95). She writes on religion, nationalism, and gender in the former Soviet Union.

VLADIMIR NIKOLAEVICH BASILOV is a well-known Russian ethnographer, head of the Section of Central Asian and Kazakhstan Research in the Miklukho-Maklai Institute of Ethnology and Anthropology, Russian Academy of Sciences, Moscow. Basilov's main field sites are in Central Asia, with focus on Uzbekistan and extensive comparative knowledge of Kazakhstan and Siberia. He is author of many books and articles, including *Shamanstva u narodov Srednei Azii i Kazakhstana* [Shamanism Among the Peoples of Central Asia and Kazakhstan] (Moscow: Nauka, 1992); and editor of *Nomads of Eurasia* (Seattle: University of Washington and Natural History Museum of Los Angeles County, 1989).

NIKOLAI ALEKSEEVICH ALEKSEEV is a senior researcher at the Academy of Sciences, Siberian Division, Institute of History, Philology, and Philosophy in Novosibirsk. A Sakha (Yakut) ethnographer, Alekseev has done meticulous fieldwork for many years in the Sakha Republic (Yakutia) and in the Altai mountains, among the Turkic peoples of Siberia. Widely known as a scholar of shamanism, he has published numerous books and articles on Turkic, especially Sakha, religion, including *Traditsionnye religioznye verovaniia Iakutov v XIX–nachale XX vv.* [Traditional Religious Beliefs of the Yakuts in the XIX–early XX centuries] (Novosibirsk: Nauka, 1975); *Traditsionnye religioznye verovaniia tiurkoiazychnykh narodov Sibiri* [Traditional Religious Beliefs of the Turkic-Speaking Peoples of Siberia] (Novosibirsk: Nauka, 1992).

MONGUSH BORAKHOVICH KENIN-LOPSAN is a senior researcher in the Tuvan Academy of Sciences and head of the Scientific Center for the Study of Shamanism in the Tuvan Museum of Regional Studies "Aldan-Maadyr" (Sixty Heroes). He is president of the Society of Tuvan Shamans. Candidate of Historical Sciences and People's Writer of the Republic of Tuva, he is author of many articles and books, including *Magiia tuvinskikh shamanov* [The Magic of Tuvan Shamans] (Kyzyl: Novosti Tuvy, 1993).

ANATOLY ALEKSEEV is the founder of a business center at Yakutsk State University, and avid collector of the folklore of his people, the Even (Lamut). Featured in the film "Siberia After the Shaman" (by Graham Johnson and Piers Vitebsky, UK, ITEL, 1991), he is well known for efforts to revive the reindeer-breeding culture of Even communities.

DMITRI ANATOL'EVICH FUNK is head of the Section on Peoples of the Far North and Siberia, Institute of Ethnology and Anthropology, Russian Academy of Sciences, Moscow. Candidate of Historical Sciences, his ethnographic fieldwork has focused especially on the Teleut of southern Siberia. Readers are referred to his *Teleuty* [The Teleut] (Moscow: Rossiiskaia Akademiia Nauk, 1992, 2 vols., in the series "Narody i Kul'tury," XVII).

ELENA SERGEEVNA NOVIK is professor of folklore in the Russian State Humanities University of Moscow, having spent many years as a senior researcher in the Folklore Division of the USSR Composers Union, in Moscow. Her extensive field experience ranges from western Siberia (with Ob-Ugrians) to the Far East (Sakha Republic and Chukotka). In the 1980s, she was a founding member of a famous folklore, ethnography, and film team (with Eduard E. Alekseev and Andres Slapinš) that produced notable ethnographic films, including "Time of Dreams," on shamanism. She is the author of numerous articles on folklore and ritual, and editor, with S. Iu. Nekliudov, of *Ot mifa k literature: sbornik v chest' semidesiatipiatiletiia Eleazara Moiseevicha Meletinskogo* [From Myth to Literature: Collection in Honor of the 75th Birthday of E.M. Meletinskii (Moscow: Rossiiskii universitet, 1993).

NADEZHDA YAKOVLEVNA BULATOVA is senior researcher in the Institute of Linguistics of the Russian Academy of Sciences in St. Petersburg, and a professor in the Division of Northern Peoples of the Herzen Pedagogical Institute in Saint Petersburg. An Evenk scholar originally from the Far East, she is also affiliated with the Institute of the Problems of the Minorities of the North in Yakutsk. She is author of *Govory evenkov Amurskoi oblasti* [The Speech of Evenki of the Amur Region] (Leningrad: Nauka, 1987).

# Introduction

## Marjorie Mandelstam Balzer

A Sakha (Yakut) friend tells a rather racy story about a female shaman, Alykhardaakh, that has circulated widely in the Viliuisk area of north-eastern Siberia since the 1930s. It is worth recounting not to shock, but to communicate the lingering power, into the 1990s, of the ancient belief and medical system called shamanism, as well as the complex nature of Soviet and post-Soviet approaches to shamanism.

> Before Alykhardaakh died there was a lot of pressure on her to stop shamanizing and to confess that she was a charlatan. But she was not, and she insisted that she would prove her strength to the Yakut men who were running the village soviet. She invited them all to her hut and they sat on benches. First she stood by the fire and started dancing and calling to spirit helpers. She began her séance, in front of these men, dancing and drumming herself into trance. She called forth water, so that the men's ankles were covered with water, before she commanded that the water flooding her hut should stop. Then she called forth a pike and caught it for the men to show them her strength. Finally she told the men to take their pants off, and all of them did. She asked them to hold their male organs and then she came out of her séance and commanded them to notice what had happened, that they were all still sitting there with their pants off. They begged her forgiveness for doubting her power, and bowed low to her, vowing never to bother her again.

Most shamans in the Soviet period were neither so powerful nor so lucky as to be spared public denunciation, confiscation of property, and persecution. They were branded as practitioners of fraudulent medicine and perpetuators of outdated religious beliefs in a dawning age of science and logic. They were sometimes jailed as conservative leaders of anti-Soviet activity. By the 1980s most shamans of Siberia and Central Asia had indeed been discredited with their people by Soviet officials and doctors. Some parents even avoided telling their children that they had shamanic ancestors. Many of the most powerful shamans died without passing on their esoteric knowledge or the de-

xiv MARJORIE MANDELSTAM BALZER

tails of their rituals. Yet stories of their strength abound to this day, and a few shamans still practice, no longer in secret, for devoted believers.

Former Soviet scholars of shamanism often explain the power of shamans like Alykhardaakh as the ability to hypnotize susceptible believers. This position, not fully sympathetic to the talents of traditional shamans, nonetheless places shamans in a social and psychological context. Other scholars, especially those from the non-Russian cultures featured here, come closer to giving credibility to traditional beliefs in spirit powers by stressing shamanic cures. Whether discussing shamanism as faith healing, psychiatry, or spirit power, contemporary scholars of the former Soviet Union are taking the practice far more seriously than writers in the Stalin era, who saw shamans as malicious deceivers and rich exploiters of their people. Until the collapse of the Soviet Union, a blatantly negative portrayal persisted in many museums, where wild-eyed, life-sized mannequins of shamans looked insane and frightening (see photo p. xv). But at the end of the twentieth century, Siberian and Central Asian children are no longer frightened by obsolete Marxist-Leninist projections of shamans as religious devils. Rather, some are exploring a shamanic heritage that their proud parents no longer hide.

Dramatic changes in attitudes toward shamans and shamanism in Siberia and Central Asia have occurred within the past decade as part of wider societal changes that made all religious faith valid again, after many years of repression. More specifically, the changes were caused by multicultural intellectual leaders, who opened the way for multiple approaches to shamanism. The authors whose works are translated here are such leaders. They come from Russian, Sakha (Yakut), Even (Lamut), Evenk (Tungus), and Tuvan backgrounds. All, as inquisitive multilingual ethnographers and folklorists, have experienced the pain and fascination of learning their own and other cultural traditions at a time when those traditions were under siege. Brought up when Soviet ideologies dominated, they have each in their own way transcended Marxism-Leninism through in-depth study of shamanism. Their works reveal that traditional shamans provided psychotherapy, cures, and leadership for their communities, along with poetry and entertainment.

## Debates about shamanism

Debates in the vast ethnographic and historical literature about shamanism reveal differences between and within Western and Soviet-

This typical image of a terrifying shaman was featured for decades in the Yaroslavsky Museum of Yakutsk, Russian Federation. Photo M.M. Balzer, 1991.

influenced Russian traditions. The first debate is definitional: who are shamans and what is their purpose? Many writers would agree that shamans are medical and spiritual practitioners. Disagreement comes as people struggle to understand the political, mystical, and religious roles shamans played and sometimes still play in communities no longer easily defined as "traditional."

Western historian Mircea Eliade defined the shaman as a "psycho-pomp" and "technician of ecstasy," emphasizing shamanic communication with sacred celestial spirits. Russian ethnographer Vladimir Basilov refutes Eliade's stress on celestial worlds and points out that shamans believed themselves to be in communication with spirits on multiple levels of the universe, above, on, and below the ground. Elena Novik views shamans as mediators between social and spiritual worlds, having a full range of good and bad attributes, as well as benevolent and evil relations with people. Sakha colleague Nikolai Alekseev sees at least some shamans as more ready to curse than cure, being preoccupied with power and deception. This contrasts with Evén Anatoly Alekseev, who stresses genuine shamanic successes in curing human and animal ills, and with British social anthropologist Ioan M. Lewis, who focuses on shamanism and spirit possession as a path of social protest.[1]

The eminent émigré scholar of Siberian shamanism Sergei Shiro-kogoroff depicted shamans as part of a "psychomental complex," helping small communities cope with illness, change, and stress. He was thus a precursor of such anthropologists as Jean Comaroff and Lola Romanucci-Ross, who have interpreted traditional healers as helping to cure the body politic, as well as individual body-minds.[2] Many writers choose among the multiple functions of shamans, although historically many shamanic roles, including fear-generating and awe-inspiring ones, have coexisted.

Shamans are clearly more than the sum of their functions. They can be men and women, old and young, sympathetic and tyrannical, strong and weak, oriented toward good ("white") and bad ("black") spirits. To understand shamanism, one must explore the art and symbolism inherent in many shamanic ritual performances: an enactment of usually sincere beliefs in shamanic ability to be sacred intermediaries between human and supernatural worlds.[3] Are shamans crazy to believe themselves such intermediaries? This too has been a raging debate. As Vladimir Basilov points out, writers in both the East and West have seen shamans as deluded at best, dangerous deviants at worst. This view fits especially well with the Soviet historical campaign to discredit shamans, and persists among some ethnographers today. Nikolai Alekseev considers shamans to be suffering from a "neuropsychological illness" that is controlled during séances. This contrasts somewhat with Eliade's view that shamans are cured psychotics—cured through their shamanizing. It contrasts considerably with Basilov's carefully reasoned claim that shamans were in full control during their séances and trances, behaving in culturally patterned ways. Basilov's view converges with much Western scholarship.[4]

Just as shamans have long existed, so too scholars have long speculated about their historical origins and development. Even the origin of the word "shaman" is hotly disputed, though often attributed to Siberian, especially Evenk, culture. Clues to specific cultural roots and interrelations are also sought in examination of shamanic drums and dress.[5] The greatest divide probably comes between those who see shamanism as stemming from humanity's most archaic and therefore archetypical levels of spirituality and symbolism and those who trace more specific cultural trends.[6]

The tradition in Soviet scholarship of studying ethnogenesis makes many ethnographers amenable to hunting specific culture traits. Nikolai Alekseev's work on Turkic shamanism is a good example, with priestly shamanism seen as a relatively late development in Siberian Turkic history, postdating hunting and clan cults. His position contrasts with those, such as French structuralist Roberte Hamayon, who argue that earlier hunting-based Siberians had one of the most ancient variations of shamanism. Evidence of shamanism from as far back as the paleolithic Lascaux caves, and from pictographs on cliffs, can be used to argue multiple theories. Unfortunately, many of the arguments about pre-written-history sorcerers, shamans, and priests must remain unresolved.[7]

Another kind of historical approach, arguing for refined studies of the sociopolitical and syncretic context of shamanic traditions, is advocated by Caroline Humphrey and Nicholas Thomas. In a similar spirit, Michael Taussig calls shamans "the shock absorbers of history."[8] Sensitivity to political and historical context is illustrated here by Russian ethnographer Dmitri Funk, writing on the southern Siberian Teleut.

The heart of shamanism, the shamanic séance, has been variously portrayed, depending on the cultural context of the séance and the perspectives of observers. Alekseev provides new data on the séance itself by giving samples from the poetry of Turkic shamanic chants—enough to tempt readers and researchers to delve more into shamanic texts. A wealth of such texts is also provided by the Tuvan scholar Mongush Kenin-Lopsan and others in this volume.[9]

Séances are intense emotional dramas, usually involving trance, of the shaman and sometimes others, with drumming, dancing, and audience involvement. As explained by shamans themselves, their goals include recovery of a patient's lost soul, exorcism of spirits manifest in a patient's body, escorting the soul of a deceased person, plus various spirit consultations on multiple cosmological levels for specific problem solving.[10] While most observers depict shamans of Siberia and Central Asia as using autosuggestion and drumming rather than narcotics or alcohol to induce trance states, some evidence points to archaic use of the mushroom *amanita muscaria* or of smoke from hemp (*cannibis*) as well.[11] Techniques of trance, and the degree to which séances, were dramatic and diverting, are intriguing subjects with no single answer, especially since during Christianization and Sovietization campaigns some curers became subdued, secretive, and focused on problem solving without fancy display.

The most controversial aspects of shamanic séances are what is reported to be their "miracles." For example, eyewitnesses claim shamans, while in trance, have produced spirit voices in odd places, walked on hot coals, withstood cold, stabbed themselves without leaving scars, disappeared and reappeared, escaped the bonds of ropes, found lost objects and people, and even induced or controlled floods, winds, and storms. Some of these talents, celebrated in Siberian and Central Asian lore, probably involved sleight-of-hand tricks, ventriloquism, and hypnosis, as suggested here by Basilov and Alekseev. Other behavior, including rapid curing, is less easily explained by current scientific knowledge.

This leads to the ultimate debate, concerning the significance of shamanism. Is it merely an outdated and quaint backwater of religious history? Can shamans and shamanism teach us anything? Does the remarkable persistence of shamanism indicate some human need to reach deep, mythic, spiritual levels within ourselves? Or does it exist because some spiritual and supra- or hypernatural dimension of the universe is more real than scientists admit? Although these latter views are more common, even faddish, in the West, some post-Soviet citizens also are drawn to mystical and psychotherapeutic aspects of shamanism.[12] Even before the current boom in alternative medicine in Russia, and the popularity of healers called "extrasenses," one Russian linguist and many native Siberians have suggested privately to me that shamans were indeed tapping into a real spiritual realm. At least three of the authors here, Mongush Kenin-Lopsan, Anatoly Alekseev, and

Nadezhda Bulatova, represent this view. Shamanism may be in its historical "twilight," as Basilov explains, but that twilight has lasted an extraordinary time, despite Christian, Lamaist, and Soviet agitation against shamans (see photos pages xx and xxi).[13]

## Perspectives from life and tradition

Delving into the interpretive realm of shamanism has led many researchers into flights of fancy almost as complex as the mystical journeys of shamans themselves. Material on traditional religious mysteries invites a degree of creative explanation unwise in other dimensions of ethnography, and unusual individuals often are attracted to the subject. Nonetheless, ethnographers' interpretations (like shamans') are wedded to their own intellectual backgrounds and cultural contexts. The writing featured here is no exception, yet it also represents a broadening and deepening of Soviet and post-Soviet thought on traditional religious life. Most significant, each author shows a healthy respect for the importance of collecting detailed data.

The core of this volume consists of native Siberian scholars writing  about their own cultural traditions in diverse ways. In his survey of shamanic practices and beliefs, Sakha (Yakut) scholar Nikolai Alekseev uncovers both Turkic and Mongolic roots of Sakha culture, today located in the Far East of the Russian Federation. He combines standard historical categories of Marx and Engels with sensitivity to native concepts. He signals skepticism with quotes around words such as "purification," and "miracles." Yet he also reminds his readers that shamanic séances "at times were poetic productions of high art."[14]

Tuvan ethnographer Mongush Kenin-Lopsan has become the beloved dean of shamanic studies in his republic, and is today closely associated with the revitalization of shamanism in a folk medicine clinic in Kyzyl, the capital of Tuva, on the edge of Mongolia in the Sayan mountains. Descended from a long line of shamans, he masked his spirituality for many years through "salvage anthropology" folklore collection. Although he once wrote obligatory phrases about "religious superstition," his long-term understanding of the beauty, style, and power of shamanic poetry is what has made his work enduring (see photo page xxii).[15]

The Evén author Anatoly Alekseev grew up in a reindeer-breeding community in Yakutia, where he absorbed Soviet-style respect for education, along with the value of honoring spirits and ancestors. His

Sakha (Yakut) elder Yakim Izbekov was a shaman's assistant in his youth, and later became a well-known choreographer. He is at his homestead here, with shamanic helper bird images. The 1989 photo was a gift to M.M. Balzer from Aisen Doidu.

Yakut National Theater actor Afanasii Fedorov playing the shaman at an opening of art with shamanic themes. In the 1990s, he has become interested in shamanic curing and the curative aspects of ritual performance. Photo M.M. Balzer, 1992.

A Tuvan (or Soyot) shaman of Altai Region, ca. 1900. Photo in archives of the Hamburgishches Museum für Völkerkunde.

sensitive descriptions of shamanic healing show the attention shamans paid to symbolic precision, as well as to what anthropologist Victor Turner has termed "multivocal meanings."[16] Alekseev's people, sometimes called Lamut in historical sources and anthropological literature, were once spread more widely in the Far East, and distinguish themselves from the related Evenki.

Evenk scholar Nadezhda Bulatova has written a poignant description of the warm ritual reception that the Evenk shaman Matriona Kurbeltinova accorded her and two Evenk colleagues in 1987. The ritual recorded here with attention to linguistic nuances is called *alga*, meaning "blessing." Matriona, before her death in 1996, was renowned through Siberia and beyond as one of the last great shamans of the twentieth century. Her knowledge of shamanic cosmology, her unexplained telepathy, her wisdom and empathy, and her kindness to guests had made her a legend. Featured in the film "Time of Dreams," Matriona adapted Evenk shamanic tradition to such exigencies of contemporary life as the purification of her Soviet soldier grandson when he returned from the Afghanistan war.[17]

The Evenk, like the Even, are a Tungusic people whose widespread reindeer breeding historically crossed many political boundaries, bringing them into contact with diverse Siberian peoples. Scholars of Siberian shamanism such as Arkady Anisimov and Sergei Shirokogorov touted the elaborate Tungusic shamanism as influencing many other Siberian groups, much as their reindeer nomadism had.[18] It is thus appropriate that the final chapter here, and the volume itself, honors Matriona (see photo page xxiv).

## Wedding theory to field data

Like Nadezhda Bulatova, Dmitri Funk confirms the living adaptation of shamanic rituals in everyday Siberian life. He also explores classic problems in anthropology, discussing issues of spirit possession and exorcism.[19] The southern Siberian Teleut of the Altai mountains considered such problems common enough to warrant treatment by spiritual practitioners who need not be full-fledged shamans to cure in familial settings. They used, and still use, shamanic incantations called *chymyr*—one of the many strategies for dealing with combined biological-spiritual crises. Some of the incantations are written and serve as "crib notes" or instructions for ritual results.

Acknowledging that he missed being able to question fully a key ritual practitioner before she died, Funk has nonetheless collected one of the longest recorded exorcism incantations. His respect for the material is evident in the way that he presents it (originally in Teleut and Russian, here in Teleut and English) and in the way that he reminds us of its effectiveness. Sensitive to methodological concerns, Funk mentions difficulties of reading incantations in an ethnographic, information-seeking context rather than a curative one.

Testing information-age communications (e-mail), I asked Dmitri Funk for clarifications and an article update. His answers were so compelling that they have become an appendix to his chapter. They elaborate on his field situation, the correlation of living rituals with Teleut identity, and the history of repression of shamanism among the Teleut.[20] While not blatantly representing a particular theoretical position, Funk is one of the younger post-Soviet scholars whose priorities are concern for indigenous categories and ideas.

Elena Novik attacks the problem of integrating indigenous meanings with academic theory through structural analysis. Her structuralism owes much to Estonian, Russian, and French traditions, and to the

Matriona Petrovna Kurbeltinova, Evenk shaman famed for healing those who sought her help through the twentieth century. Photo by the late Latvian film-maker Andres Slapinš, 1982, courtesy of Elena Novik and Mihály Hoppál.

influence of Vladimir Propp, Eleazar Meletinskii, and Claude Lévi-Strauss.[21] She builds her categories primarily on informant distinctions, some of which are so subtle as to have been noticed by only the most sensitive of fieldworkers. Examples include distinctions of folklore genres on the basis of degrees of fantasy and reality, and differentiations of shamanic behavior according to multilayered insider/outsider perspectives.

Novik compares shamanic folklore with shamanic ritual to see how the two interrelate in various cultures, without assuming a priori that they relate in a single way. Thus her structuralism, a search for consistent patterns, "blocs," and transformations, is open-minded—generative in the most flexible sense. She theorizes that underlying the relations structuring ritual and folklore are three forms of communicative exchanges: of information, power, and values.

Novik provides insights into the depth and breadth of shamanic cultures and values. She warns of the folly of reading too much into ostensibly historical legends about the evolution of a given people. For example, the presence of a strong heroine-shaman in an Amur River Nanai folktale does not necessarily prove that the Nanai once had matriarchy. Stories of incest among ancestors may reinforce taboos against incest but do not prove incest occurred. Interestingly, certain tales pertain more to the point of view of spirits than humans, and therefore can be read as inverted morality tales.

In comparing shamanic tales and rituals, Novik finds that tales can reflect the diversity of human life more realistically than rituals. Tales can end badly and can reveal a full gamut of emotion, from love to enmity or competition between interlocutors (humans and spirits, for example). Rituals, while reflecting or transforming tales and containing fragments of them, are more likely to end well. They are programmed positively for results that relate directly to the everyday life of their participants. A shaman attempts to build confidence during a séance by creating an atmosphere in which multiple cultural symbols coalesce and enable belief in spiritual aid to become a self-fulfilling prophesy. But two legends can be about two shamans, one successful and one not. Within both the legend and the séance, spirit voices and views are heard, producing a dialogue between shamans and spirits. This enables cultural participants to feel part of an interaction, a dialogic, similar to that described by Mikhail Bakhtin.[22]

Novik negotiates between generalizations about Siberian, including so-called paleo-Asiatic, structures, and specific cultural constructs.[23] Within the shamanic tradition, remarkably similar ideas of souls, illness, fire, spirit incarnations, revenge, gender relationships, and relations with animals prevail. One of the most widespread concepts involves the sacredness of the bear, for whom special rituals are performed throughout the North.[24] Beliefs about the bear, including those mentioned by Nadezhda Bulatova, help put human-animal relations in ecological context. The bear is logically a powerful intermediary for shamans, associated with linkages between human and spirit levels of the cosmos, but the bear's allegiance must be bought (exchanged for rituals and services) and a bear's revenge for misconduct can be devastating.

A story I was told in Yakutia (now the Sakha Republic) in 1986 dramatizes the significance of bears as cosmic intermediaries. The original storyteller was the protagonist, a Sakha bear hunter.[25] Living his adult life in the Soviet period, he had ignored traditions stipulating ritual respect for shamanic beliefs and for the bear. He had killed over twenty bears in his lifetime, returning unceremoniously with their carcasses to the local collective. Elders, including shamans, warned he would have to pay for his disbelief, and indeed he began to feel he was followed while he was in the woods. Dismissing the idea that a hunter could be stalked by his prey, he shrugged off his fears yet kept himself well-armed and alert. One day, checking traps in the taiga, he let his guard slip; he had also left his hunting knife at home. That was the moment a huge bear picked to attack him, knocking his rifle out of his hands, mauling his face and body and leaving him blind. He became a masterful singer of traditional improvisational poetic songs, and was convinced that the bear knew exactly whom he attacked.

## Acknowledgments

I am grateful to all at M.E. Sharpe who have helped bring this book together, especially Leslie English, Ana Erlic, and Patricia Kolb; and to all who have tried to help me understand shamanic worlds—they know who they are.

## Notes

1. Compare Mircea Eliade, *Shamanism: Archaic Techniques of Ecstasy* (Princeton: Princeton University Press [Original in French 1951], 1972); Ioan M.

Lewis, *Ecstatic Religions: An Anthropological Study of Spirit Possession and Shamanism* (Middlesex: Penguin, 1971). On shamanic curing, see Jane M. Murphy, "Psychotherapeutic Aspects of Shamanism on St. Lawrence Island," *Magic, Faith and Healing*, ed. Ari Kiev (New York: Free Press, 1964); Arthur Kleinman, *Patients and Healers in the Context of Culture* (Berkeley: University of California Press, 1979); M. Mandelstam Balzer, "Doctors or Deceivers? The Siberian Khanty Shaman and Soviet Medicine," *The Anthropology of Medicine*, eds. Lola Romanucci-Ross, Daniel Moerman, and Lawrence Tancredi (New York: Bergin [1983] 1991), pp. 56–85. For debate within Soviet ethnography on religion, see *Soviet Anthropology and Archeology*, Winter 1979–80–Spring 1982 (vols. 20–22) for S.A. Tokarev's article "Religion As a Social Phenomenon" and his critics' responses. For classic Soviet propaganda on shamanic deception, see I.M. Suslov, *Shamanstvo i bor'ba s nim* (Moscow: Izdatel'stvo Komiteta Severa, 1931); N. Ankudinov, A. Dobriev, and K.S. Sergeeva, *Shamany obmanshchiki* (Leningrad: Glavsemorputi, 1939).

2. Sergei Shirokogoroff (Shirokogorov), *The Psychomental Complex of the Tungus* (London: Routledge and Kegan Paul, 1935); Jean Comaroff, "Medicine, Symbol and Ideology," in *The Problem of Medical Knowledge. Examining the Social Construction of Medicine*, eds. P. Wright and A. Treacher (Edinburgh: Edinburgh University Press, 1982), pp. 49–65; Lola Romanucci-Ross, Daniel Moerman, and Lawrence Tancredi, eds., *The Anthropology of Medicine: From Culture to Method* (New York: Bergin [1983], 1991); Libbet Crandon, ed., "Beyond the Cure: Anthropological Inquiries in Medical Theories and Epistomologies," *Social Science and Medicine*, 1987, vol. 24, no. 12, pp. 997–1118.

3. Supernatural is used here in the sense of beyond the ordinary. See M. Mandelstam Balzer, "Shamanism," *Encyclopedia of Cultural Anthropology* (New York: Henry Holt for Human Relations Area Files, 1996), pp. 1182–1190; Taegon Kim and Mihály Hoppál, eds., *Shamanism in Performing Arts* (Budapest: Akademiai Kiado, 1995); Carol Laderman and Marina Roseman, eds., *The Performance of Healing* (New York: Routledge, 1995); Anna-Leena Siikala and Mihály Hoppál, *Studies on Shamanism* (Helsinki: Finnish Anthropological Society; Budapest: Akademiai Kiado, 1992); Piers Vitebsky, *The Shaman* (London: Macmillan, 1995). For early sources on Asian shamanism, see Andrei A. Popov, *Materialy dlia bibliografii russkoi literatury po izucheniiu shamanstva severoaziatskikh narodov* (Leningrad: Institut Narodov Severa, 1932); V.M. Mikhailovskii, *Shamanstvo* (Moscow: Izvestiia Imperatorskogo obshchestva liubitelei estestvoznaniia, antropologii i etnografii, 12, 1892).

4. E. Ackerknecht, "Psychopathology," *Bulletin of the History of Medicine*, 1943, no. 14, pp. 30–67; J. Silverman, "Shamans and Acute Schizophrenia," *American Anthropologist*, 1967, no. 69, pp. 21–31; L. G. Peters and D. Price-Williams, "Towards an Experiential Analysis of Shamanism," *American Ethnologist*, 1980, no. 7, pp. 98–418; Joan Halifax, *Shaman: The Wounded Healer* (New York: Crossroads, 1982); R. Noll, "Shamanism and Schizophrenia," *American Ethnologist*, 1983, vol. 10, no. 3, pp. 443–59; Roger Walsh, *The Spirit of Shamanism* (Los Angeles: Tarcher, 1990).

5. On linguistics, see Berthold Laufer, "Origin of the Word Shaman," *American Anthropologist*, 1917, no. 19, pp. 261–78; Robert Austerlitz, "Shaman," *Ural-Altaic Yearbook*, 1986, no. 58, pp. 143–44. On drums and dress, see Vilmos

Diószegi, *Tracing Shamans in Siberia* (New York: Humanities [1960], 1968); E.E. Prokof'eva, "Shamanskie kostiumy narodov Sibiri," *Sbornik Muzeia Antropologii i Etnografii*, 1971, no. 27, pp. 5–10.

6. Compare Jane Monnig Atkinson, "Shamanisms Today," *Annual Review of Anthropology*, 1992, no. 21, pp. 301–30; and Åke Hultkranz, "Introductory Remarks on the Study of Shamanism," *Shaman*, 1993, vol. 1, no. 1, pp. 3–14. For discussion of archetypical roots of shamanism, with a sensitivity to specific traditions, see Paul Radin, *Primitive Religion: Its Nature and Origin* (New York: Viking, 1937). Sources comparing Native American and Asian shamanism include Waldemar Bogoras (V. Bogoraz) 1930, "The Shamanistic call and the Period of Initiation in Northern Asia and Northern America," *Proceedings of the 23rd International Congress of Americanists*, pp. 441–44; J. Grim, *The Shaman: Patterns of Siberian and Ojibway Healing* (Tulsa: University of Oklahoma Press, 1994); Gary Seamans and Jane Day, eds., *Ancient Traditions: Culture and Shamanism in Central Asia and the Americas* (Denver: University of Colorodo, and Denver Museum of Natural History, 1994).

7. Roberte Hamayon, *La chasse à l'âme: Esquisse d'une théorie du shamanisme sibérien* (Nanterre: Societe d'etnologie, 1990). Compare Andreas Lommel, *Shamanism: The Beginning of Art* (New York: McGraw-Hill, 1967); Peter Furst, *Stones, Bones and Skin: Ritual and Shamanic Art* (Toronto: Arts Canada, 1977); André Leroi-Gourhan, *The Dawn of European Art* (New York: Cambridge University Press, 1982); Mihály Hoppál, "On the Origin of Shamanism and the Siberian Rock Art," *Studies on Shamanism* (Helsinki: Finnish Anthropological Society; Budapest: Akademiai Kiado, 1992), pp. 132–49.

8. Michael Taussig, *Shamanism, Colonialism and the Wild Man* (Chicago: University of Chicago Press, 1987), p. 237; Caroline Humphrey and Nicholas Thomas, eds., *Shamanism, History and the State* (Ann Arbor: University of Michigan, 1994); Caroline Humphrey with Urgunge Onon, *Shamans and Elders: Experience, Knowledge and Power Among the Daur Mongols* (Oxford: Oxford University Press, Clarendon, 1995). See also Frank Salomon, "Shamanism and Politics in Late-Colonial Ecuador," *American Ethnologist*, 1983, vol. 10, no. 3, pp. 413–28. Clifford Geertz's famous statement in *Islam Observed* (Chicago: University of Chicago Press, 1968, p. 1) that in religion, "old wine goes as easily into new bottles as old bottles contain new wine" is relevant to issues of syncretism, but needs further refinement in light of much data, including Central and North Asian, on religion.

9. This includes Dmitri Funk and Nadezhda Bulatova. Another excellent example is Gregory G. Maskarinec, *The Rulings of the Night: An Ethnography of Nepalese Shaman Oral Texts* (Madison, WI: University of Wisconsin Press, 1995). See also Margaret Nowak and Steve Durrant, *The Tale of the Nišan Shamaness* (Seattle: University of Washington Press, 1977); and Joan Halifax, *Shamanic Voices* (New York: Dutton, 1979).

10. For rich descriptions of séances and shamanic feats see the classic monographs of the *Jesup North Pacific Expedition*, for example by W. Bogoras and W. Jochelson, *American Museum of Natural History Memoirs* (1904–1909), nos. 11 & 13; Kustaa F. Karjalainen, *Die Religion der Jugra-Volker* (Porvoo: Finnish Academy of Sciences, 1927); and Anna-Leena Siikala, *The Rite Technique of the Siberian Shaman* (Helsinki: Academia Scientiarum Fennica, 1978). For Native

American comparisons, see Franz Boas, "The Religion of the Kwakiutl," *Columbia University Contributions to Anthropology*, 1930, vol. 10, no. 2; A. Irving Hallowell, *The Role of Conjuring in Salteaux Society* (Philadelphia: University of Pennsylvania Press, 1942); Åke Hultkranz, *Shamanic Healing and Ritual Drama: Health and Medicine in Native North American Religious Traditions* (New York: Crossroad, 1992). See also Michel Matarasso, ed., "Chamanes et chamanisme au seuil du nouveau millénnaire." *Diogène*, 1992, no. 158, pp. 1–163.

11. My fieldwork and research on Ob-Ugrian Khanty shamanism indicates their use of *amanita muscaria*, which is also well known among the Itelmen of Kamchatka. For a summary of arguments on narcotic use in Siberia and North America, see Peter Furst, ed., *Flesh of the Gods: The Ritual Use of Hallucinogens* (London, New York: Praeger, 1972). The theory of R. Gordon Wasson in *Soma: The Divine Mushroom of Immortality* (New York: Harcourt, Brace, Janovich, 1960) that the "soma" of the *Rig Veda* was *amanita muscaria* relied heavily on Siberian data, and is still debated. See also my editorial note "b" of the lead chapter here by Vladimir Basilov.

12. The increased popularity of urban Russian "extrasenses" such as Kaspirovsky, Zhuna, and Slobodova illustrate this. Western authors searching for spiritual and psychological answers to contemporary problems include Steve Larsen, *The Shaman's Doorway: Opening Imagination to Power and Myth* (New York: Anchor, Station Hill, [1976] 1988); Michael Harner, *The Way of the Shaman: A Guide to Power and Healing* (New York: Bantam, 1982); Felicitas D. Goodman, *Where the Spirits Ride the Wind: Trance Journeys and Other Ecstatic Experiences* (Bloomington: Indiana University Press, 1990); and the controversial Carlos Castenada, e.g., *The Teachings of Don Juan, a Yaqui Way of Knowledge* (Berkeley: University of California, 1968). See also Larry G. Peters, *Ecstasy and Healing in Nepal: An Ethnographic Study of Tamang Shamanism* (Los Angeles: Undena, 1981); and C. Campbell, *The Way of the Animal Powers* (New York: Alfred Van Der Mark, 1983).

13. Since Basilov's book on shamanism was written for a wide audience, he provided only a few notes but referred to many authors. These have been traced and listed in the bibliography. See also Dmitri Funk, ed., *Shamanizm i rannie religioznye predstavleniia* (Moscow: Rossiiskaia Akademiia Nauk, 1995); Anna V. Smoliak, *Shaman: Lichnost', funktsii, mirovozrenie (narody nizhnego Amura)* (Moscow: Nauka, 1991); the Buryat ethnographer Taras Mikhailov, *Buriatskii shamanizm: istoriia, struktura i sotsial'nye funktsii* (Novosibirsk: Nauka, 1987); his edited *Sovremennye problemy buddizma, shamanizma i pravoslaviia* (Ulan-Ude: Akademiia Nauk, 1980); and a pathbreaking article by E.V. Revunenkova, "O lichnosti shamana," *Sovetskaia etnografiia*, 1974, no. 3, pp. 104–11. For translated works on shamanism from the former Soviet Union, see Henry N. Michael, ed., *Studies in Siberian Shamanism*, trans. Stephen P. Dunn and Ethel Dunn (Toronto: University of Toronto Press, Anthropology of the North, 4, 1963); Vilmos Diószegi, ed., *Popular Beliefs and Folklore Tradition in Siberia* (Bloomington: Indiana University Press, Ural-Altaic Series, 57, 1968); I.S. Vdovin "The Study of Shamanism Among the Peoples of Siberia and the North," in *The Realm of the Extra-Human: Agents and Audiences* (The Hague: Mouton, 1976), pp. 261–73; Vilmos Diószegi and Mihály Hoppál, eds., *Shamanism in Siberia* (Budapest: Akademiai Kiado, 1978); Mihály Hoppál and Keith Howard,

eds., *Shamans and Cultures* (Budapest: Akademiai Kiado, 1993).

14. For more on Sakha (Yakut) shamanism, see Gavril V. Ksenofontov, *Shamanizm: Izbrannye trudy* (Yakutsk: Sever-Iug, [1928–29] 1992); Anatoly I. Gogolev, *Istoricheskaia etnografiia Yakutov: Narodnye znaniia i obychnoe pravo* (Yakutsk: Yakutskii gosudarstvennyi universitet, 1983); Ekaterina N. Romanova, *Yakutskii prazdnik ysyakh: istoki i predstavleniia* (Novosibirsk: Nauka, 1994); M. Mandelstam Balzer, "Flights of the Sacred: Symbolism and Theory in Siberian Shamanism," *American Anthropologist*, 1996, vol. 98, no. 2, pp. 305–18.

15. I am grateful to Siberianist Boris Chichlo for first calling my attention to the work of Mongush Kenin-Lopsan, and to anthropologist William Brunton for providing an update on Kenin-Lopsan in 1993. Kenin-Lopsan was featured in David Brown, "Traditional Healing Returns to Tuva," *Washington Post Health*, 18 July 1995, pp. 10–11. Mongush Kenin-Lopsan is currently president of the Society of Tuvan Shamans. By 1995, over thirty-four shamans were registered, with over one hundred studying for certification. Tuvan shamanism has also been the focus of several recent films, for example Belgian ethnographer Dirk Dumon's "They Who Know: Shamanism in Tuva" (1992) and Tom and Tamia Anderson's "The Foundation for Shamanic Studies Expedition to Tuva" (1993). See also Tamara Budegechi, ed., *Shamanizm v Tuve* (Kyzyl: Gosudarstvennyi litsei respubliki Tuva, 1994).

16. Victor Turner, *The Ritual Process: Structure and Anti-Structure* (Ithaca: Cornell Press, 1977); Victor Turner, ed., *Celebration: Studies in Festivity and Ritual* (Washington, D.C.: Smithsonian Institution Press, 1982). On the Even (Lamut), see V.G. Bogoraz, "Lamuty. Iz nabliudenii v Kolymskome krae," *Zemlevedenie*, 1900, vol. 7, no. 1.

17. This remarkable 1982–86 film was shot by the famous Latvian camera-man Andres Slapinš, with ethnomusicologist Eduard Alekseev, and ethnographer Elena Novik, whose work is featured here. The film is at the Smithsonian Institution, with other films relevant to the 1990 Soviet-American exhibit, "Crossroads of Continents." At a crucial moment during filming, some of Matriona's protective kin feared that spirits would be disturbed by the camera and endanger Matriona. They thus asked Andres to stop, so that the film ends with only a still photograph of Matriona in trance. Parts of the "Time of Dreams" can be seen in Mihály Hoppál's 1994 film "Shamanism: Past and Present" along with other valuable historical and current footage. Another film of Matriona was made by the Sakha filmmaker Viacheslav Semenov in 1991.

Estonian filmmaker Lennart Meri's "Winds of the Milky Way" (1978) captured part of a séance of (western Siberian) Nganasan shaman Demnime. Rare footage of Inner Asian shamanic séances is available in the film "Shamans of the Blind Country" by Swiss ethnographer Michael Oppitz (available through Media Services, University of Texas, Dallas, 75083–0643). See also Laurel Kendall and Diana Lee, "An Initiation, *Kut* for a Korean Shaman" (in video format, distributed by Honolulu: University of Hawaii Press, 1991). A source for films on shamanism is Shamanic Film/Video Archives, Inc., founded by Burrill Crohn, P.O. Box 691, Bearsville, NY 12409.

18. Sergei Shirokogoroff (Shirokogorov), *The Psychomental Complex of the Tungus* (London: Routledge and Kegan Paul, 1935); Arkady F. Anisimov, *Religiia Evenkov v istoriko-geneticheskom izuchenii i problemy proiskhozheniia*

*pervobytnykh verovanii* (Moscow-Leningrad: Akademiia Nauk, 1958).

19. Another example of adaptation of shamanism concerns recent Buryat rituals for drafted young men likely to go to the Chechnya war (personal communication Natalia Zhukovskaia, June 1996). On problems of defining possession and spirit "manifestation," see Laurel Kendall, *Shamans, Housewives, and Other Restless Spirits: Women in Korean Ritual Life* (Honolulu: University of Hawaii Press, 1985); and her, "Korean Shamans and the Spirits of Capitalism," *American Anthropologist*, 1996, vol. 98, no. 3. Compare David N. Gellner, "Priests, Healers, Mediums and Witches: The Context of Possession in the Kathmandu Valley, Nepal," *Man*, 1994, no. 29, pp. 27–48.

20. For more on the Teleut, see Dmitri Funk, *Teleuty* (Moscow: Rossiiskaia Akademiia Nauk, 1992, 2 vols., in series, "Narody i Kul'tury," XVII). The Teleut of the Altai are a Turkic-language-speaking group who have mixed with the Altai people, and are related to the Telengit and Telesy. The Teleut were not officially recognized as one of the "twenty-six minority nationalities of the North" in the Soviet period. Questions of identity are thus particularly acute for them.

21. Novik cites these authors extensively in her references. See especially Claude Lévi-Strauss, *Structural Anthropology* (New York: Anchor, [1958] 1967); and his *The Raw and the Cooked* (New York: Harper and Row, 1975); Eleazar M. Meletinskii, "The Epic of the Raven Among the Paleo-Asiatics," *Diogenes*, 1980, no. 110, pp. 98–133; Vladimir Iakovlevich Propp, *Morphology of the Folktale* (Bloomington: Indiana University Press, 1968); and his "The Historical Bases of Some Russian Religious Festivals," in *Introduction to Soviet Ethnography*, eds. Stephen P. Dunn and Ethel Dunn (Berkeley: Highgate Road Social Science Research Station, 1974), pp. 367–410. Lévi-Strauss has credited influence by Russian and Estonian (the Tartu school of Iurii M. Lotman) structuralists. Novik's analysis, while unique, is akin to the structural interpretation of folklore and ritual in Eva Hunt, *The Transformation of the Hummingbird: Cultural Roots of a Zinacantecan Mythical Poem* (Ithaca: Cornell Press, 1977).

22. Mikhail Mikhailovich Bakhtin has become a folk hero of sorts for Western and Russian Federation intellectuals, who claim that his 1920s and 1930s writings preceded much postmodern literary criticism theory (although many in his circle in the 1920s discussed the same issues). See *Rabelais and His World* (Cambridge: MIT Press, 1965); *The Dialogic Imagination* (Austin: University of Texas Press, 1981); and Katerina Clark and Michael Holquist, *Mikhail Bakhtin* (Cambridge: Harvard Press, 1984.)

23. The term "paleo-Asiatic" is disputed as describing a valid cultural or linguistic group, because of the diversity of cultures within its usually conceived boundaries—e.g., Yukagir, Chukchi, Koryak, Kamchadal (Itelmen), Gilyak (Nivkh), Ket. The concept is useful, however, for some cultural correlations, if not linguistic ones. See Roman Jakobson, Gerta Hüttl-Worth, and John Fred Beebe, *Paleosiberian Peoples and Languages: A Bibliographic Guide* (New Haven: Human Relations Area Files Press, 1957).

24. This includes North America. On bear ceremonies, see A. Irving Hallowell, "Bear Ceremonialism in the Northern Hemisphere," *American Anthropologist*, 1926, no. 28, pp. 1–175. On connections between beliefs about the bear and shamanism, see Boris Chichlo, "L'Ours Chamane," *Études Mongoles*, 1981, no. 12, pp. 35–112; and "La Fête de l'ours aujourd'hui chez les Ougriens de

Sibérie," *Études Mongoles*, 1980, no. 11, pp. 47–62. See also Juha Pentikainen, ed., *Shamanism and Northern Ecology* (Berlin/New York: Mouton de Gruyter, 1996).

25. This story can be considered in Novik's category of a "memorate" or personal history. It comes from Igor Pantelevich Sleptsov of the Abyi region, via the Sakha linguist Natalia Popova, who was part of an Institute of Languages, Literature and History (Siberian Academy of Sciences) field expedition headed by E.I. Korkina in 1986. I am grateful to Natalia Popova for sharing the story.

# Part I.

# Debates, Definitions, and Indigenous Perspectives

# Chosen by the Spirits

Vladimir N. Basilov

## Is the Shaman Sane?

The occupation of shaman required vigorous health, as well as numerous skills. The Eskimos acknowledged only healthy persons as shaman. The Nenets shaman was expected to have a strong frame. And among the Saami in ancient times, only a person at the height of physical and mental health could be a shaman. A man older than fifty years, especially one who had lost his teeth, could not be a servant of the spirits.

But the life of a shaman involved a condition alien to healthy individuals. One thing about the shamans has always impressed observers: the incoherent exclamations and movements, the foaming at the mouth, vacant stare, and total loss of consciousness at one of the most critical moments of the ritual. In the nineteenth century, this was usually given a simple and obvious explanation: the shamans were adroit deceivers and swindlers, feigning possessions by ''demons'' in order to fleece their trusting tribesmen. At the beginning of our century, a different opinion prevailed: the shamans were persons of a disordered mind, neuropaths. While the suggestion is still very muted in V. M. Mikhailovskii (1892), by 1905 N. N. Kharuzin was proposing ''to recognize that the true shamans . . . are first and foremost neuropathic persons, in whom the nervousness has developed in a particular direction.'' V. G. Bogoraz asserted that, among the shamans known to him, ''many were almost hysterical, and some were literally half-insane.'' ''Shamanism''—he declared in 1910—''is a form of religion created by selection of the most nervously unstable persons.'' G. V. Ksenofontov published *The Cult of Madness in Ural-Altaic Shamanism* in 1929. D. K. Zelenin wrote in 1935 that a healthy individual could not even become a shaman: only a neuropath, whom ''the spirits are continually

Russian text © 1984 by Politizdat. *Izbranniki dukhov* (Moscow: Politizdat, 1984), pp. 138–69, 188–207. Published by arrangement with Basil Blackwell.

During the seance, the shaman consorted with spirits in a state of ecstasy. A special assistant maintained this state by chanting or accompanying on the drum. In the photo: a Nganasan shaman with his assistant (1978).

entering,'' could cure those suffering from ''spirit possession'' without risk to personal health. ''The shaman . . . is a neuropath, obliged by the community of the clan to assume a peculiar medical function— to personally absorb the demons of disease from the sick of the community''—writes Zelenin. Similar views prevailed in Western European scholarship. The Danish investigator A. Ohlmarks, for example, linked shamanism to the severe Arctic climate, which he claimed produced mental anomalies suitable to the development of shamanism.

We find the clearest and most concise argument in favor of regarding the shaman as a neuropath in S. A. Tokarev: ''All observers unanimously report that the shaman is most notably a nervous, hysterical person, prone to seizures, occasionally an epileptic. . . . The shamanic seance itself has much similarity to an hysterical attack.''[1]

The inherited character of shamanism (among most peoples) led to the belief that special mental qualities ''characteristic'' of shamans were passed on through heredity. A. V. Anokhin wrote in 1929 that shamans ''receive their predisposition to the shamanic vocation from their ancestors alone, through a nervous 'falling' sickness, epilepsy. Against this wearisome, often fatal disease, the natives have no recourse other than the seance. The seance offers the epileptic a release from illness. And observations show that while performing, the shaman is in fact not sick." A person becomes a shaman (in Anokhin's estimation) for "purely physiological" reasons.

L. Ia. Shternberg is more cautious: "In order to become a shaman, it is essential to have a particular morbid neural organization, extreme excitability, a tendency to ecstatic fits, a susceptibility to various kinds of hallucination, and so forth—in a word, to suffer from some degree of hysteria. And hysteria, we know, is easily transmitted by heredity." Shternberg emphasizes that the "shamanic illness," accompanied by fits, fainting spells, and hallucinations, usually occurs "in the so-called transitional years, at the onset of sexual maturity."

Thus, it was patently clear that shamans were persons with a deranged mind! And the hypothesis, never verified, triumphantly proceeded from one work to another. As frequently happens in science, an opinion once received is no longer doubted. Even the renowned neuropathologist S. N. Davidenkov in 1947 talked of shamanism as a "cult of hysteria," "a socially organized neurosis, taking a finished and stable form." (These remarks were based on information taken from the literature.)

The view of the shaman as mentally ill reigned in science for nearly half a century. True, S. M. Shirokogorov (1919), I. N. Kosokov (1930), and I. M. Suslov (1931) did not agree, but their objections went unnoticed. In the West, one of the first to reject this opinion was N. Chadwick in 1936, but this criticism did not result in abandonment of the former concept. Only in the past twenty or thirty years has a marked change occurred: the assertion that the mind of the shaman is characterized by deviations from the norm is no longer satisfactory to many scholars. However, the idea of the neurasthenic shaman is still alive today.

Is it correct? Is the shaman sane? It is time to have a clear answer to this question. The shaman is not a haphazard figure in the history of humanity. He is a person who has taken on the functions dictated by the norms of his culture. Today, the view of the shaman as a sick person is difficult to accept, as it is in conflict with a broad range of facts. Our purpose is to examine these facts. In order to refute the hypothesis of the neurasthenic shaman, we shall consult the identical materials giving rise to it—the observations of the ethnographers.

First of all, the ethnographic material does not support the "biological" basis of the "shamanic illness," which allegedly appears during the years of age-related changes in the organism associated with sexual maturation. To be sure, there are many reports of the illness beginning to perturb the future shaman at the age of puberty. But the literature also abounds in information on those who began to shamanize after the age of twenty, thirty, or even forty. "A Selkup who is to become a shaman would take ill at different ages, from fourteen to fifteen, but usually later, twenty or twenty-one," writes E. D. Prokof'eva. "The onset of the calling of shaman ranges between those six and fifty years of age. The largest percentage occurs in the twentieth year," we read in Anokhin. The number of such statements is huge. According to my materials, a good many Uzbek shamanesses underwent the "shamanic illness" well after marriage, already having one to three children. I met an Uzbek shaman to whom the spirits appeared when he was around sixty years old. Thus, "shamanic illness" is not necessarily and naturally linked to age-related changes in the body, and it may be presumed that it is caused by factors of a different quality.

It is more accurate to seek these factors in the particularities of the early forms of human culture. Beginning in remote antiquity, it was thought that insanity and nervous disorders occur by the will of the spirits. Granted this fact, a person in possession of the spirits should exhibit attacks, fainting spells, and behavior that is inexplicable to the sound mind. The necessity of the attacks and madness may have been suggested to the shaman by the traditions of his people. He who was chosen by the spirits would fall into a fit not because he had epilepsy or a neurosis, but because he knew from childhood that such attacks were inevitable and always happened to those who were destined to become the servant of the spirits.

Why does the chosen one recover after becoming a shaman? Perhaps because the neuropathological particularities of his organism abate? This is unlikely. Rather, the recovery is dictated by the traditional behavioral pattern of the shaman, according to which the illness is supposed to pass. We already know that the "shamanic illness" reproduces in hallucinations or dreams the ritual of initiation. The "illness" should have its end, just as the period of initiation also ends. Once it is ended, the person, now in a new status, returns to ordinary everyday existence.

That "shamanic illness" is the result of autosuggestion is also indicated by facts clarifying under which circumstances the future shaman becomes ill. V. I. Anuchin writes about the Ket in 1914: "The calling of the shaman in the majority of cases occurs unexpectedly, sometimes when the person has attained the age of twenty, never thinking that he was destined to become a shaman.'' But this opinion seems naive today. The future shaman would be thinking of his possible selection. He would know that the choice of the hereditary spirits might fall to him. He would not desire this, he would resist, yet still be internally prepared for the inevitable, anxiously awaiting the call of the spirits. In this anguished anticipation, much might be understood as a sign sent by the spirits. The very readiness of the person to undertake the service of the spirits was the cause of the illness.

These same Ket, as recently discovered by E. A. Alekseenko, were well ''aware in which family and in which generation the appearance of a new shaman could be expected.'' ''If there had not been a new shaman in a family or a family group for a long time, a special psychological mood of anticipation would arise. In an atmosphere of such mental preparedness, the demonstration of evidence of a calling by a particular person would be quite quickly deciphered by the others.'' Such a person would easily understand that the spirits had ''attached'' themselves to him; in cases of doubt, a shaman would be consulted.

The wider the circle of persons entitled to play the part of shaman, the more victims the ''shamanic illness'' had. According to the beliefs of the Evenk, after the death of a shaman his spirits became unmanageable and endeavored to find a new host among clan members; they wandered about, bringing sickness. The closest relatives of the shaman and young people of either sex were especially susceptible to the illnesses. S. M. Shirokogorov wrote: ''Those taking ill become pensive and confused, unable to work, not fit for ordinary employment; they sleep a lot, constantly mumble in their sleep, jump about on their bed; they avoid the company of people, sometimes running away to the forest and staying there a long time, usually refusing food and growing thin. Sometimes the illness is accompanied by hysterical attacks with all the typical symptoms of hysteria: convulsions, arching the body, insensibility, photophobia, and so on. Sometimes they are found in the forest, having climbed up a tree during an attack, or sitting among rocks or in a cave. . . . No treatment helps in such case.'' A new shaman is needed.[a]

It may be believed that the spirits have not settled on any of the ailing persons. In that case, ''the illness begins to befall other members of the clan, undergoing different modifications. Adults can become nervous and commit acts of unaccountable brutishness, even criminality; a general irritation and tendency to hysterical attacks will spread; there is increased mortality from the diseased state itself and from misadventures.'' Such condition may even threaten the clan with destruction. Everything returns to normal as soon as someone displays evidence of having been chosen by the spirits. He is scrutinized carefully. And indeed, it is confirmed with certainty. A day is appointed when the new shaman will make his first offering to the spirits, signifying his acknowledgment by the clan. The tension is relaxed. The advent of the new shaman "cures the other possible candidates for shaman, and a sense of ease gradually envelops the clan."[2] Thus, the "shamanic illness" was not unexpected, but manifested itself at a time when the people were in need of a shaman.

Children were often prepared for shamanic activity from an early age. According to the Shor, the future shaman was supposed to be born with a "mark" from the god Ul'gen—an "extra bone." This might be a prominence on the finger or toe, or even a dimple on the ear lobe. Elders, noticing the "mark," pointed it out to the parents, who consulted a shaman. A seance was held in order to learn from the chief spirit of the locality—the owner of the mountain—whether the child would become a shaman [kam]. "The spirit generally 'confirms' this, and it is instilled in the child from tender years that he is a future kam." I. D. Khlopina reported a youngster who began to shamanize while playing at the age of three. His "mark" was a thickness of the bone on the left ankle. "Instead of a drum, he took . . . a frying pan, a tray, or the like, instead of words he pronounced inarticulate sounds, and everyone was convinced that he was a future kam."

A similar case was observed by G. N. Gracheva among the Nganasan in the 1970s. "Before our very eyes"—she writes—"the primary 'schooling' took place in the form of a game of a young child, who already at the age of four had a small drum and a little shaman's cap. At the age of five, he was repeating the shamanic chants of his grandfather with astonishing accuracy. At the age of six, wearing his shaman's cap, he was tying himself to a pole in the tent and leaping like his grandfather, banging a stick against the hook for hanging the cauldron."

The people had need of a protector against misfortunes and diseases. Therefore, they usually welcomed possible candidates for shaman, guiding and encouraging them. The community's support helped in the formation of the shaman. The person's readiness for the "shamanic illness" and, on occasion, its very course depended largely on the attitude of the onlookers. At times, the community itself decided who was to become a shaman, and the evidence of the "shamanic illness" had no influence on the person's fate. One such case is reported by S. M. Shirokogorov.

At the beginning of the twentieth century, a certain Manchurian shaman died. After a couple of years, the members of his clan became troubled by continual failure in their affairs, as well as nervous ailments, which appeared especially strong in two persons—the young son and the mistress of the deceased shaman. Two positions emerged in the clan: one was reluctant for the woman to become the clan's shaman, the other supported her. At length, it was resolved to ''convene the entire clan, select a jury of three people, and settle the matter of which of the two should be shaman.'' The illness of the woman (who was thirty-six or thirty-seven years old) took acute forms—''she would disappear for several days in the forest and be found stuck among the branches of trees, exhausted and bruised. This was accompanied by hysterical fits.'' The twenty-two-year-old shaman's son only had mysterious dreams, and ''at night he would jump up and begin to shamanize without a drum.'' Nevertheless, on the day of the trial, held in the presence of sixty to seventy people, the woman did not succeed in placing herself in a condition of ecstasy, and the other candidate, even though the spirits at first ''did not want'' to ''join'' with him, gradually grew into the role and ''on the fourth night proved before all that he was in full mastery of the spirits.'' Why such an outcome? ''One of the reasons for the failure of the woman was, beyond doubt, the unwillingness of the majority to have her as shaman. She was handed a damp, bad-sounding drum, laughed at, and the like, which doubtlessly prevented her from concentrating.'' It was decided that she was not controlling the spirits, but the spirits her, and therefore could not become shamaness.

Such facts make us think that the willingness to experience the ''shamanic illness'' is suggested to the future shaman not only by himself: in the lengthy act of suggestion, his clan also plays a more or less significant part.

A good many authors have affirmed that the shamanic seance resembles a hysterical attack. ''That certain features of the shamanic trance are entirely consistent with hysteria is obvious to every neuropathologist,'' writes S. N. Davidenkov. This refers to those moments of the ritual when the shaman is twisting like an epileptic or loses consciousness. But would the seizures not disturb the progress of the complicated ritual performances? There was a reply to this: the shaman was endowed with ''tremendous power to control himself in the intervals between genuine attacks occurring during the ceremonies'' [Czaplicka, 1914]; ''the shaman, unlike a regular neurasthenic or hysteric, is able to artificially regulate the attacks of the illness'' [Tokarev, 1964].

We shall not digress to debate whether a hysteric may gain control over himself. The main point is that the ''attacks'' and ''fainting'' cannot be divorced from the ritual. They constitute an inalienable part of the ritual, logically connected with its purposes and substance. The shaman loses consciousness, thrashes in convulsions, performs ''wild'' leaps and all the rest because it is prescribed by the ritual. It is what must be done. He is not disrupting the ritual. And fellow tribal members know what his unusual behavior implies. If the shaman trembles from head to foot or flies into a rage, jumps up and screams, it means that the spirits have come into him or that he is fighting with hostile demons. If the shaman lies senseless, it means that the soul has left his body and is wandering in other worlds. Thus, during the seance, as during the period of the ''shamanic illness,'' the shaman behaved as demanded by the beliefs of his people.

The ritual fainting and attacks of the shaman come from the same source as his agonizing madness during the ''shamanic illness.'' Convinced of his connection with the spirits, the shaman expected of himself the behavioral characteristics that conformed to this connection. Having assumed the role, he would live it, no longer straying from the pattern. An important part of this role were the imaginary wanderings and encounters with the spirits during the seance. While conducting the ritual, the shaman was in the power of his visions. The spirits and scenes from other worlds would appear before him. He would experience all the details of his journey. For example, a Chukotka shaman in his hallucinations would fly through the air and shoot up to the stars, travel under the earth and beneath the water, change his form, encounter and converse with the spirits of his ancestors. It should be kept in mind that these hallucinations were not arbitrary, but connected with the purposes of the ritual.

It is customary to refer to the state in which the shaman is entranced by visions as ecstasy. The shaman was supposed to be able to achieve this state whenever his services were required by his community. Shamanic ecstasy is characterized by being induced deliberately, with an effort of will. S. M. Shirokogorov has defined the ecstasy as a state of willful loss of control over oneself. This judgment is not entirely accurate; it is best not to talk of a loss of control. The concentration of attention whereby the shaman finds himself in an imaginary world requires great mental exertion, which is possible only with strict self-discipline. Much closer to the truth is N. Chadwick, who writes about the ecstasy: "This strange, exalted, and supremely mental condition is not only consciously achieved, but may also be consciously and successfully controlled throughout, and in conformity with the traditional prescriptions." The foregoing warrants viewing the ecstasy as a condition programmed in advance (more or less consciously), which the shaman achieves by means of autosuggestion.

The shaman is not instantly transported to the world of his visions. The length of time required to attain an ecstatic state depends on the personal qualities and mastery of the shamans. Much depends on the shaman's mood, on internal preparation for the seance. "If the shaman wants to shamanize and is looking for an opportunity, it is easier for him, but if he is requested and compelled to shamanize, it is harder, since he must first place himself in a condition where he desires to shamanize." Failing this, he could not feel assured that the spirits have entered into him. According to the observations of Shirokogorov, the shaman sometimes needed more than an hour to reach ecstasy.

The experience of many generations of shamans led to procedures that hastened the attainment of ecstasy. Thus, the Ket shaman ate nothing on the day of the ritual (and therefore the seance would be arranged in advance). The Nganasan and Saami shamans fasted a full day before the ritual. Before the seance, some shamans would go off by themselves for a time to concentrate or, though staying among people, would meditate deeply. From the description by V. L. Seroshevskii (Sieroszewski) we have an idea of the conduct of a Yakut shaman just before the beginning of the seance. At times, he hiccoughs nervously, such that his entire body shivers strangely. His eyes do not shift about: either they are downcast or fixed immovably on a certain point, usually the fire. As the fire wanes little by little, darkness and quiet settle over the yurt. The shaman slowly removes his shirt and puts on his "magical kaftan," then takes up a lighted pipe and smokes a long time, gulping the smoke. The hiccoughing becomes louder, the shaking more excited. When the shaman has finished smoking, his face is pale, head hanging low and eyes half shut. Finally, taking a ladleful of cold water, he swallows several large gulps and with a slow and sleepy motion searches on the bench for the previously arranged whip or drum clapper.

The ambiance of the ritual itself was conducive to ecstasy. The seance was usually held at night, in a semidarkened room. Rhythmical beating of the drum and movements of the body heightened the shaman's excitement. The shaman usually shamanized with the eyes closed, so that the surroundings would not disturb the clarity of his visions. The shamans of the Nenets wore a special binding on the eyes or a headband with a fringe falling onto the face: only the "inner vision" could reach into the world of the spirits. Judging from the literature, the shamans of certain peoples made use of intoxicating substances and hallucinogens, especially *mukhomor* mushrooms and alcohol.[b] These reports, however, deserve careful confirmation. Inaccuracies and confusion are possible here. The intoxicating substances might not be used to attain ritual ecstasy. According to Iu. B. Simchenko, the Chukotka shamans, for example, liked to eat *mukhomor* to induce hallucinations, but not before a ritual. Earlier Shirokogorov, noting that certain Evenk shamans would smoke several pipes of tobacco in a row before the seance, declared: "Such practices are evidently harmful to the shaman, since they raise his energy for a moment, but then a reaction sets in. Consequently, experienced shamans avoid narcotics during the seance, and prefer to have a meal and sleep before shamanizing. If a shaman fails to attain ecstasy, he will begin the entire procedure from the start, after a little rest."

The condition of ecstasy is itself unstable, and improper conduct of the onlookers may dispel it. Therefore, those attending the ritual were forbidden to touch the shaman. The Selkup explained that the shaman during a ritual was a kind of spirit, a being of another world, and contact could injure both the prohibition violators and the shaman himself. But a practical motive is concealed behind this belief: contact might bring the shaman out of ecstasy and spoil the ritual. No extraneous noise was permitted during the seance. However, in some cases, ritual participants were expected to assist the shaman in chanting. The Nenets accompanied each striking of the drum by the shaman with shouts of "*goi! goi! goi!*" As the cries of the participants intensified and blended with the general noise, the shaman would begin to summon the spirits. Also among the Ket, certain portions of the shamanic songs were repeated by everyone present: "the chorus had not yet finished as the shaman sang further; the chorus would catch up with him, and thus the singing was uninterrupted." The Khakass shaman, setting off on the "distant journey,"[c] would invite seven boys and nine girls to chant at the seance.

S. M. Shirokogorov was apparently the first to realize the important role of the shaman's special assistant. Among the Evenk, anyone taking part in the ritual could be such an assistant, but usually the same person, accustomed to the shaman and the peculiarities of his behavior in ecstasy, would play this role. "The importance of the shaman's assistant is huge. It is his ability. . . that helps the shaman remain in the state that he has achieved." So long as ecstasy is not fully attained, the assistant chants after every stanza of the shaman, filling in the gaps in the song and providing a melodious background of sound. If the drum is at hand, the assistant passes it to the shaman. If the shaman is unable or unwilling to hold the drum, the assistant himself takes it and beats it, helping the shaman to feel in full spirit possession.

The shamans of many other peoples—the Nenets, Selkup, Ents, and Ket—also had special assistants. The Nganasan shaman had a "chanting helper." "No shaman will shamanize without one: he is the closest guiding companion of the shaman."[d] The assistant usually began the seance by chanting the "proper" song of a particular spirit. Those in attendance would join in. If the equanimity of the shaman indicated that the spirit was not coming, the assistant changed the melody, singing the song of a different spirit. When the shaman began to beat the drum, the assistant summoned the spirits with a recitative. During the ritual, he repeated the shamanic hymns, in this way sustaining both the shaman and his spirits. If the seance was being performed for an especially severe emergency illness, a relative or the shaman's wife could be the assistant.

After achieving the necessary concentration and reaching ecstasy, various shamans were engrossed by their visions to differing extent. Some could shamanize under any circumstances. The Altaian shaman [*kam*] Mampyi, for example, invited in 1909 to Tomsk by G. N. Potanin to participate in a "Siberian soirée," shamanized enthusiastically on a stage before a numerous audience of strangers. The evening's program had other features, and after a time the curtain was lowered, but Mampyi continued to shamanize: "they say he was hard to stop, and indignant about it." Other shamans were easily taken out of the state of ecstasy. One such Nganasan shaman was described to A. A. Popov: "The shaman was very timid and during his seance forbade everyone from coughing loudly, making noise, tossing aside a smoldering match after lighting a pipe, or the like, since his spirits would be startled and abandon him. If any other bystanders made noise, the shaman immediately began undressing and removing his ritual dress."

Visions appeared before the shaman "as in a dream." Some shamans in the state of ecstasy evidently lost all connection with the surrounding world. When the Evenk shaman falls into ecstasy, according to Shirokogorov, "his mind, his tongue, and his body are taken over by the spirit, he abandons himself absolutely, the image of the spirit, its desires and sufferings, take control of the shaman." The force of the visions, the sense of reality of the hallucinations, could be so great that the shaman could even die during the seance, if the dangerous journey to the world beyond led to an encounter with a powerful enemy, who, according to the beliefs of the people, could capture the shaman's soul and kill him. But more often, it seems, the shamans did not become totally estranged and were aware that those sitting in the tent were eagerly following their every movement. The explanations of the Nganasan shaman Diukhade, to whom a blacksmith-spirit revealed three extra body parts, are unusually interesting: "Because I have three extra body parts, I can be in three places at the same time . . . during the seance, as though I have three pairs of eyes, three ears, and so on. Even though I am still to this day arguing with my spirits that this is untrue, I am finally forced to admit the justice of their words, that I indeed exist in three states at the same time."[e]

The Chukchi believed it useful to appeal to their departed ancestors for advice in difficult situations. The shaman, reaching ecstasy, would summon an ancestor spirit and ask it questions. He delivered the answers in a changed voice—the "voice of the ancestor." Thus, in talking to the ancestor, the shaman was mindful of the fact that the conversation should be the property of everyone present. The Orochi shaman, placing himself in a state of trance by dancing, singing, and striking the drum, would sit down exhausted on the earthen floor of the dwelling and continue to sing in a low voice, still hitting the drum softly. Everyone knew that meant the soul was leaving him and setting off on a distant and difficult journey. In his song, the shaman told the hushed audience where his soul was flying and what it was seeing. Thus, the Orochi shaman also remembered that he was not alone.

It is appropriate to be skeptical of statements, found in the literature, that the shaman after the ritual does not recall where he has been and what he has done. This is reported as far back as I. G. Gmelin, who described his encounter with a Yakut shaman. The latter shamanized— beating the drum, "squirming," shouting, appealing to the spirits, rushing about the yurt, falling into a faint, reviving, and prophesying. When everything was over, the shaman took off the ceremonial dress and declared he could remember nothing.

Usually, however, shamans of different peoples did not claim to forget about everything during the ecstasy. An Altaian shaman, after holding a seance that represented his visit to the underground realm of Erlik, sat down and rubbed his eyes as though awakening from sleep. He was asked: "How was the journey? What outcome?" The shaman replied: "A good journey! I was well received." A Selkup shaman ended a seance abruptly, suddenly dropping to the floor of the hut. "Some assistants grab the drum, others the shaman himself and place him on the rug. No one disturbs the hushed silence. Only the crackling of the fireplace is heard. The shaman lies pale and apparently lifeless. After some time, he comes to and sits up. He removes the parka [kaftan—V. B.], the crown, and the breastplate. He smokes long in silence. He is given tea. He drinks and then tells of the results of his journey, the outcome of his dealings with the unseen world."[3]

Of course, we may surmise that local traditions determining a self-hypnosis program may cut off remembrance of the visions. If it has long been believed that the shaman entering ecstasy is oblivious, then he should so behave; and the belief that he in fact remembers nothing may be sincere. Even so, it is obvious that assertions of the shamans that they do not know what is happening during the ritual are inspired primarily by an ancient stereotypical explanation of ecstasy: the shaman is not responsible for his actions, since he is in the power of the spirits, fulfilling their will and pronouncing their words. I more than once heard Uzbek shamanesses say that they do not remember their ritual hymns, that all the words are "put into their mouths by the spirits." But it afterwards turned out that the shamanesses actually are well aware of which words they are supposed to sing. Tape recordings of their hymns, made during the ritual, were sometimes inaudible. The drum would drown out the person's voice. It was necessary to ask a shamaness to listen to the recording. The shamaness would be intrigued by the sound of her voice, but also could not make out the words. She would then say: "This is what I should have sung"—and begin to dictate. Thus, the texts of the hymns "put into their mouths by the spirits" are familiar to the shamanesses. Moreover, these texts are traditional—the hymns of different shamans and shamanesses living at different times and in different places are much alike.

If we compare the portions of text distinctly audible in the tape recording with that dictated by a shamaness, discrepancies are always found. Even the very same text, taken down as dictated by a shamaness at different times, is not entirely identical: the order of certain phrases is changed, individual phrases and "couplets" may be missing. But the ritual does not require a psalmody whose text is fixed once and for all. Infinite versions of the text are inevitable, since each particular seance has its own singularities. But the basis of the text is uniform, dictated by the content of the ritual, and therefore stable. And if the shaman in a state of ecstasy is capable of reproducing it, then we can hardly agree that he has lost all control and does not remember what he is doing. The ritual behavior of the shaman was supposed to be consistent with the purpose of the ritual. The shaman is "not responsible for his actions" only to the extent required by the ritual.

Ecstasy is one of the most vivid traits of the shaman's activity. It distinguishes the shaman from other categories of priest. This has been discussed on numerous occasions. Thus, S. A. Tokarev observed "the employment of methods of ecstatic intercourse with the supernatural world" is "the most typical characteristic of shamanism." M. Eliade gave his book *Shamanism* the subtitle *Archaic Techniques of Ecstasy*. (Incidentally, the main point here is not technique, but outlook. Ecstasy in the present case is not simply a form of ritual behavior, but a manifestation of faith in the chosenness of the shaman, his immediate connection with the spirits, which take possession of him or visit other worlds in company with his soul. Ecstasy is the principal concept of shamanism, embodied in action.)

The idea that ecstasy is a type of self-hypnosis was advanced as early as the beginning of the century (L. Ia. Shternberg in 1904, N. N. Kharuzin in 1905, S. M. Shirokogorov in 1919). It is customary to define hypnosis as a partial, incomplete sleep, during which some of the nerve cells of the brain are alert. The inadequacy of this definition is apparent when we consider the shaman in seance. The dancing, leaping, loud ejaculations, and exercises with a white-hot iron are difficult to associate with a sleeplike condition. Furthermore, it is obviously not only a question of certain portions of the cerebral cortex "not sleeping": these portions acquire tremendous power over the activity of the organism, such as does not occur in the ordinary state. In other words, the activity of these portions is intensified. Therefore, probably closer to the truth are those who explain hypnosis as an altered state of consciousness, induced by great concentration of the attention on certain specific tasks, thereby making possible a detachment from reality. The activity of the person may be either depressed or heightened in this process.

Everything that we know about shamanic ecstasy is consistent with such understanding of hypnosis. Once ecstasy is attained, the shaman is able to employ such capabilities of the human organism as are not exhibited in the ordinary state.

The most vivid example is the demonstration of unusual physical strength in the state of ecstasy. "At such time the shaman is capable of displaying energy totally inconsistent with his physical profile. Thus, weak female shamans have as much strength as several grown men and cannot be restrained, if such is required. Old women and men become limber and youthful," reports Shirokogorov. The latter once had occasion to observe an Evenk shaman "more than eighty years old, who was blind and no longer able to move about without assistance; when he was dressed in the costume, weighing well over thirty pounds, and when the spirit had taken possession of him, he began to jump to a height of at least one meter, beating the drum, and danced with an ease absolutely unfathomable for his decrepitude." A similar situation amazed V. I. Anuchin, investigator of the Ket: "It is hard to imagine how a seventy-year-old shaman in apparel weighing around fifty pounds could dance for two hours straight."

An interesting story is told by S. I. Vainshtein, who persuaded the Tuvinian shaman Shonchur to shamanize a little. The elderly shaman appeared very weak. A relative and his wife placed the heavy kaftan on him with difficulty. "It seemed that the costume and drum were heavy for the old man, and I was forced to wonder whether Shonchur could move in this attire. . . . All of a sudden, the shaman . . . jumped up. Almost in a dance, he made several movements, greatly surprising me by their ease and freedom. . . . Using the drum like a shield, he ran and hopped lightly around the yurt, chasing an evil spirit, but without opening his eyes; and strange as it may seem, without running into any of those attending. . . . The shaman made quick, adroit, and unexpectedly sharp movements. He leaped and finally caught his foe. A struggle ensued. The adversaries fell down and rolled along the floor of the yurt. The shaman pressed the drum tightly against the evil spirit." But the ritual ended here. "After several strides around the yurt, Shonchur in deep exhaustion sank heavily to the floor and opened his eyes only several minutes later—we again beheld an old, crooked, and very tired man."

Sometimes a seance lasted all night—from sundown till sunrise. The shaman was in a state of very strong arousal for several hours straight. We are correct in speaking of the exceptional endurance of the shaman during the seance. Even a shaman of advanced age, once in ecstasy, is capable of extraordinary bodily exertion and mobilization of force.

The state of ecstasy makes possible alterations in the functioning of the sense organs that are astounding to onlookers. The organism may not react to very strong stimuli and not experience the sensations customary to the normal state. If the shaman is convinced that he is possessed of a spirit that does not fear pain, he is able to bear stabbing, cutting, and hitting without feeling pain. Shirokogorov relates that he "often had occasion to observe the extraordinary insensitivity of shamans when this group of spirits would come into them. Moreover, cuts and stab wounds received during the seance, according to the testimony of many, heal much more quickly. . . . When the fire spirit is embodied, the shamans walk with bare feet into a pile of burning coals, manipulate white-hot iron, lick burning Chinese smoking candles and place them in their mouth, and are generally unafraid of high temperatures." (Recall that the art of walking over white-hot coals or stones is familiar not only to the Siberian shamans. In the past, it was practiced in Asia Minor, Europe, and Japan; even today, it is mastered by the Fiji Islanders, the Indians, and the Nestor Bulgarians. Scientists explain this ability as a classic example of the power of autosuggestion prevailing over the stimulatory processes of the nerves.)

Shamans may lose the sensation of cold during a seance. Evenk shamans sometimes spent hours half-clothed outside the dwelling in bitter frost. Nganasan shamans also displayed insensitivity to cold. Thus, on one of the days of the "pure tent" festival, the shaman in seance imagined himself in the sky, traveling past the dwelling of an awful deity. He laid aside the drum and went out of the tent. Under his direction, a ring of men and women executed three circles in the direction of the solar path. With this operation, the shaman magically "enclosed himself," so that the deity was not able to capture the soul of any attending the ritual. A. A. Popov wrote:

"The weather was extremely cold, down to −50 degrees, with a slight, but unpleasantly piercing breeze. One had to admire the toughness of the shaman, who wore only a costume of thin leather over a naked body. On his head, in no way protected from the freezing cold, was an open fur cap. . . . The circle continued dancing for 20 minutes. Whereas nothing happened to the shaman from the freezing cold, I managed to get frost-bitten fingers while taking pictures."

On the other hand, it seems ecstasy also enables an extreme sharpening of the sense organs. We should be very cautious with conclusions of this sort—the observer may be mistaken, after all, and his impressions cannot be verified. Even so, we cannot simply ignore reports suggesting a heightened sensitivity of the sense organs of the shaman in an ecstatic state.

For example, A. A. Popov told an interesting account of a "testing" of the shaman on the first day of the "pure tent" festival. A special binding was placed on the shaman's eyes, a staff was placed in his hand, and he was led out into the field so that he could find his own way to the "pure tent." "They bound the eyes of the shaman in order to demonstrate to the onlookers his miraculous ability to move correctly along the indicated path with eyes closed, thereby confirming the reality of his supernatural calling." It was believed that "during the ceremony, the shaman does not require ordinary human eyes, but acquires special vision. . . . As the shaman was led onto the path, he was turned around to disorient him, and placed with his back to the 'pure tent.' But he at once took the correct direction and walked to the 'pure tent.' Along the way, everything was done to confuse him, grabbing him from various directions and leading him toward the bushes, the sleds, or other objects. Yet the shaman did not bump into these objects, but stopped a certain distance from them, as though he could see. One of the bystanders crept up behind him with a club in his hands and took a swing, pretending to strike him. The shaman, as though seeing this, ducked. Along the way, two saplings grew at some distance from each other. When the shaman drew near them, a reindeer lasso was noiselessly stretched between them. Without running into it, the shaman stopped short, proceeding further only when the lasso was removed." The shaman successfully found the "pure tent," opened the door, and disappeared inside.

Popov assumed that the shaman in this test was amazing the bystanders with "more or less adroitly performed stunts." But a different understanding of the actions of the shaman is also possible. It is quite probable that he was not peeking from beneath the blindfold, but had given himself entirely to his feelings, picking up signals as to both the movement behind his back and the obstacles in his path. There is nothing impossible about this. Our organism receives much more information about the surrounding world than we notice. We do not always understand even a marked change in sensations (thus, the relation between how a person feels and the whims of the weather is not immediately apparent). And certain sensations may go totally unnoticed by the conscious mind.

The state of ecstasy probably allows the shaman to concentrate his attention on signals of the sense organs that are usually unperceived.

Such an explanation may account for the seemingly strange ability of the shaman to locate lost people and animals far from home.

This ability is reported by many authors, although briefly and in passing. Only A. A. Popov, it seems, recorded a sufficiently detailed account of a case when a shaman (our now-familiar Diukhade) located a member of his tribe who became lost in the tundra. The Nganasan told Popov that a man had gotten lost in a heavy blizzard just before his arrival. The relatives had waited two weeks, and only then requested Diukhade to begin a search. Diukhade resisted, but after long negotiations said: "I saw in a dream that the lost man still lives. Very well then, let me see what I can do. . . . I will try to locate him. Prepare me three reindeer." He shamanized for three days. This was an unusual seance. He did not beat the drum in the tent, but wandered through the tundra. He was followed by two men on reindeer, harnessed to dog-sledges. Diukhade himself related: "I put on only the shamanic costume over a naked body, caused my eyes to be bound, and wandered through the tundra for three days and three nights. . . . The stalks of withered grass and the bushes around my tent had no knowledge and could tell me nothing about the lost man. Finally, I asked the (spirit) owner of the brook, and on the third day he showed me, and I came upon the man, completely covered with ice. He was still alive, and my companions took him immediately to the tent." The shaman's insensitivity to cold tells us that he was in a state of ecstasy: "Although I had on only the shamanic parka over a naked body, I did not freeze, but I did take a good chill, which I felt when I arrived back at my tent."

This ability of the shaman to locate objects and discover thieves astonished both the members of his tribe and outside observers. Popov himself watched as Diukhade discovered who in a group had concealed in their shirt the ritual objects required for a ceremony. "After a certain time, the shaman entered the tent, took his seat, struck the drum several times, and listened with his ear applied to the skin of the drum. He then stood up and, bending over, began to sniff the trail, exactly like a dog." This led the shaman to his goal. Standing before the person who had concealed the ritual object and staring him in the face, Diukhade struck the drum three times.

There is no need to suspect fraud on the part of the shaman in this case. A person who hides an object from the shaman and knows he will come under scrutiny usually experiences agitation. The heart beats faster, and the eyes change their expression. I may add that I myself experienced all of this when playing the exciting "ring" game of the

Turkomen. The game is played as follows. The players are divided into two groups. The leader of one group unobtrusively places a small object (not necessarily a ring, it may be a penknife or the like) into the hand of one of his teammates. The other group is supposed to find who has the object. This game is a competition in power of observation and self-control. It is based on the fact that the person handed the object is seized with sudden excitement. (I was amazed at my own agitation as I felt the leader place the knife in my hand.) An experienced player, regulating his breathing, may conceal the agitation. But it is hard to mislead an observant opponent. They usually look at the "vein" in the neck—a quickened pulsation reveals the agitation. But they may also scrutinize the face, especially the eyes.

The ability of the shaman to discover a concealed object or "sniff out" thieves appears to depend on his ability to sense certain features in the condition of others. Ecstasy is evidently not necessary for this, but ecstasy makes it possible to concentrate on the senses. Perhaps in this way shamans are able to sense the condition of a sick person and know whether a cure is possible. Let me emphasize once more that many of the "miracles" or "feats" of the shaman are based on heightened receptivity of the sense organs, intensified by ecstasy.

Shamans themselves, of course, believed otherwise. The sensations discerned by the conscious mind were couched in traditional images permeating the entire worldview of the shaman. Signals from the sense organs were interpreted as the voices of spirits, animals, and plants. Diukhade . . . thought that the blacksmith-spirit had removed his eyes and put in other ones.

"I myself don't know where these new eyes are, I think they are under the skin. When I shamanize, I don't see anything with my natural eyes, I see with these new ones. When they make me find some lost object, they bind up my natural eyes, and I see with the other eyes much better and more sharply than with my natural ones." The spirit also "drilled ears for him" and gave him the ability to understand "the speech of plants."

"Even I am amazed. A little mound in the swamp, with grass growing at the top, will give a warning, like a person, and when I am walking with bound eyes, so I don't go astray, it shows the trail of the person I am seeking." According to accounts of several Uzbek shamans, the spirits show them the diseased areas of the patient's body, which appear black. Sometimes the patient appears to their inner gaze

During the seance, not only the shaman fell into ecstasy. The photo shows one of the participants at the seance of an Uzbek shamaness, in ecstasy. Author's photograph (1979).

wrapped in a shroud or lying on a burial stretcher; in this case he is incurable and doomed to die.

Important to an understanding of the nature of ecstasy is the fact that it may affect not only the shaman, but also other participants of the ritual. A report from the early nineteenth century describes quite graphically how Nenets were caught up in the seance of their shaman: "Faces frozen in a grimace, bloodshot bulging eyes, taut, foam-flecked mouth, flat nose with flaring nostrils, black hair standing on end. . . ."*f*

The ethnographer A. L. Troitskaia in 1925 attended a shamanic ritual in Uzbekistan. The seance was performed on behalf of a woman who could not have children following a miscarriage. Under the sound of the drum and the singing of the shamaness, the patient quickly fell into ecstasy. She "began raving, hopping up and down, shaking her head and flailing her arms, shouting, and sometimes just screaming, as though pushing away someone or something in horror." When the ritual was over, Troitskaia asked the patient why she carried on so during the seance. She replied that she "saw every manner of monster and animal attacking her, and she defended herself. At times, a man of frightful aspect seemed to be taking control over her. For this reason, surrounded by such apparitions, she did not recall what she had said and done." (But she did indeed recall, since she described the monsters menacing her.) The words of this woman clearly characterize her ecstasy as a state of suggestion. According to the observations of Troitskaia, the patient "very rapidly came to. . . . Perhaps, she was not able to achieve the proper state, being embarrassed. She afterwards admitted this to me."

In the 1970s I was present on several occasions at seances of Uzbek shamanesses. Several of the participants of the ritual fell into ecstasy, but this state generally did not last long, and did not appear to grip them with the proper force. One day, I mentioned this to the women. They explained that my presence made them bashful. Usually, when no men were around, they reached ecstasy more quickly and abandoned themselves entirely to their visions.

Thus, the state of ecstasy is not confined to the shaman alone. It was also possible for the other participants of the seance to experience it. This fact indeed runs counter to the view that ecstasy is a manifestation of the shaman's mental derangement.

By interpreting the ecstasy as a result of autosuggestion, we may better understand the matter of the shaman's training. By what means did the shaman grasp the secrets of his complicated craft? It seems difficult to imagine that the novice shaman could begin practicing without first undergoing an apprenticeship from an experienced master. N. N. Kharuzin wrote: "The shamanic practices were more or less rigidly elaborated among each people. Hence, the shaman required special training." Nonetheless, ethnographers have gathered little information confirming the existence of a "school" of shamans. Among the Buryats, the novice would be taught by an experienced master; the Nenets, also, appeared to have a kind of shamanic "school." In the latter half of the nineteenth century, among the Nenets, an adolescent would be "abducted" and taken to the family of a shaman-teacher. Here, he would be taught to handle the drum, "dissemble, perform tricks, recite incomprehensible words, howl like all the animals, imitate the hissing of the snake, mimic in sound the ambling of the bear through brushwood and the scurrying of the squirrel along branches." And among the Selkup, "a shaman who agreed to teach (a beginner) would often remain in the tent of the young shaman's family and live there a certain time, less commonly taking the pupil to his home."

However, among many peoples no traditions of direct teaching are found. For example, the Nganasan "oppose the view that a shaman school exists, or that the shaman is taught by anyone." According to the Nganasan, the shaman is supposed to do what the spirits and deities tell him. Central Asiatic shamans also made do without teaching. How can the absence of a shamanic "school" be explained? Perhaps the very fact of the teaching is held in strict secrecy from outsiders? No. Quite simply, the "school" is not the only, compulsory form of learning. Knowledge necessary to a shaman could be gained independently. The ideas regarding the organization of the world and the spirits were known by the entire community, and each member of the shaman's tribe interested in the subject was well informed on the details of the shamanic rites. As for the skills, these come with practice. Kharuzin himself stressed this fact. "The actual instruction involves not only mastering the rituals, but also developing the essential qualities of the shaman," he wrote. A person who is willing to become a shaman "will develop and perfect these qualities during a preparatory period. He will strive to increase the number and clarity of his visions and dreams, have more frequent attacks, and place himself in a stimulated state."

The beginning shaman seeks solitude. Away from the eyes of others, he tries his powers in singing and in the art of mastering the drum. M. N. Khangalov reported that the young man chosen by the spirits among the Buryats "goes away into the forest or the mountain and, lighting a fire there, begins to shamanize, summoning the gods with a loud unnatural voice, and frequently falling into a faint. . . . Such isolation is rather effective, as the neophyte begins here to exercise himself in the bodily motions, the intonation of the voice, the facial expressions, that he may begin his future career fully prepared, skillful, adept, and resourceful." The future shaman among the Selkup also resorted to the forest or an empty tent and sang in solitude. The Selkup said that "he is learning to sing, learning to walk the paths of the shaman by himself." The shamans of the Tadzhiks and Uzbeks stayed home for forty days in ritual isolation. Alone with himself, the shaman learned his new role. Not only did he learn to sing and perform the ritual, but most especially he developed an ability to fall into ecstasy and to contemplate the spirits. He was expected to master the technique of self-hypnosis, and this was done by continual practice.

The training of the shaman did not end with the preparatory period. According to the ethnographer G. D. Verbov, one night was usually sufficient for the future shaman to learn the basic techniques, but many years were needed to achieve mastery. The training of the Nenets shaman, according to L. V. Khomich, lasted as many as twenty years. The long and arduous process of professional growth was reflected in the costume and attributes of the shaman. As already stated, the shaman did not receive all parts of the costume, the drum, and the other ritual objects at once. Tribal members, convinced that the shaman was perfecting his art, let him know when the time had arrived to acquire yet another shamanic attribute. He himself, certainly, was aware of this. His confidence in his powers created the soil for hallucinations or dreams to grow, in which he would see the spirits telling him to make a drum or a kaftan.

There is another matter involved in the discussion of ecstasy. Many peoples had a belief that the shaman's "power" declines with age. The Ket, in particular, believed that the shaman's helping spirits ("sky people") suffer from the agedness of their host and ask him to give them a "young human bone." The shaman search for his replacement, but if he did not hasten to select a successor, the spirits gradually abandoned him. The ethnographer E. D. Prokof'eva nearly became a shaman's successor. She knew the Selkup language, and a sixty-three-year-old Selkup shaman had adopted her. He gave her the honor of drying the drum at the fire (i.e., functioning as his assistant), and after the seance said: "You should come to me next spring! I have become old, the spirits are tormenting me, I received them from my mother and have no one to give them to. You will come, I will give them to you and be free. If you do not want to come, he will bring you!" With these words, the shaman removed a pendant in the shape of a human figure (the likeness of the Yakut spirit-protector *emeget*) and gave it to her. "To my great regret"—writes Prokof'eva—"the trip in 1934 (next year) did not come off."

It is not difficult to understand why an aging shaman did not "befit" the spirits. The shaman's own feelings would appear to him in the form of the spirits. He would be burdened with the responsibility of serving the spirits. It would be harder now to concentrate on his visions and transport himself to the imaginary world. Ecstasy would require a tremendous effort of the nervous system, and not every person would be capable of such outlay of force in advanced age.

Is the shaman sane? To fellow tribal members, there was no doubt. Of course he is. The "shamanic illness" was regarded as an ailment, but the shaman then recovered, in the opinion of those around him. Everywhere the shaman was clearly distinguished from the neuropath, and this must be emphasized to avoid distortion in evaluating the traditional culture of the native peoples of Siberia and the Far North.

The "children of nature"—reindeer breeders, hunters, fishermen—were quite sober and practical people and by no means eager to trust their fate to the random individual who shook in a frenzy and howled at night. They wanted to be sure that an illness caused by the spirits had made the person a shaman. Among some peoples (such as the Eskimo), virtually every adult male considered himself capable of shamanism, but these claims would be rejected. The shaman was expected to receive the recognition of those around him. For this, he would be tested by tribal members. The trial and its result, the recognition, were indispensable prerequisites of the shaman's activity.

The Nganasan examined the potential candidate for shaman as follows. "For the trial, a blindfold is sewn from wild reindeer skin, and with eyes bound he is required to find various objects, step over a trip rope [khorei] placed on the ground, walk through the tundra without bumping into bushes, without falling into pits, and going around obstacles." Among the Khanty, the future shaman after dreaming that the supreme god Torum had commanded him to begin telling fortunes and healing would keep his vocation a secret for some time, afraid of being thought insane. He would arrange his own trial. Over a period of two or three years, he was supposed to determine for himself whether he correctly indicated the fishing spots and whether his hunting advice proved right. "Luck in the hunt was considered a true sign of a genuine calling." If the chosen one proved successful and his counsel was a help to others, he would tell them of his calling.[g]

The trial also called for a testing of the shaman's ability to fall into ecstasy. When a shaman declared himself among the Kazakh, the people demanded that he "walk through the snow barefoot and bareheaded in a strong frost and lick red-hot iron objects with his tongue. If he remained unharmed after such trials, it would mean that good spirits were protecting him."

It happened that the community might not recognize the claimant's shamanic abilities and would accuse him of imposture. This is reported by investigators of the Ket and Khanty. The Khanty considered such an unlucky one merely insane. According to their ideas, if he ventured to begin shamanizing he might suddenly vanish, carried away by the spirits.

Testing of the shaman also took place after he had shown his worth and gained experience, and continued throughout his life. Among the Ul'chi, the shaman was tested during great memorial feasts [*pominki*], when he was conducting the souls of the departed to the "other world." Usually the shaman was brought in from another village. During the seance, he was expected to "see" these souls. "A good shaman will divine how many have died, what they were wearing, what was the sequence of their death, when they died, by day or by night. If the shaman made a mistake . . . , the memorial would be considered a failure. It was here where the shaman was supposed to confirm his right to practice shamanism. If he made a mistake, he was scolded and even beaten."

The Nanai had an identical custom. During a seance, the shaman would look for the soul of the deceased in the universe. And he would "find" it. But was it the right soul? To check, the shaman addressed questions to the relatives of the deceased, placing himself in ever-mounting ecstasy by uniform beating of the drum. He asked: "Is it true that this person died when his son was not at home?" "True," responded the relatives in a chorus. "Is it true that when the coffin was made there was one board ruined by nails?" "True." "Is it true that, on the point of death, he called all his relatives to bid them farewell, and the eldest son was not home at that time?" "True," they replied to the shaman. "An inept guessing of the signs would displease the family," reported P. P. Shimkevich. He suggested that the shaman's assistant, "using every resource, discovered in advance all the particulars about the burial of the departed, the guessing of which would strengthen the shaman's reputation." His impressions are very interesting. "One had to see how the family, trembling and excited, observed the process of the shaman's guessing. After several failures, the shaman nevertheless managed to prove to the family that the soul placed in the *fania* [image—V. B.], according to the signs, did belong to the appropriate corpse. The elder son of the deceased, by the way, told me: 'It is a good thing that he found the soul, or else I would have beaten him half to death. A splendid shaman: his memorials are always successful.'" This trial was hard on the shaman: "Worn out, his whole body trembling with excitement, the shaman sat down to catch his breath."[h]

Testing of the shaman took different forms among the varied peoples, but its meaning was always the same: the shaman had to demonstrate in practice that the spirits were rendering him aid. The authority of the shaman, his "career," depended on successful healing, predictions coming true, accurate counsel. Failure meant that the shaman had lost power over the spirits. The community would lose confidence in him and no longer ask his help.

Let us summarize. The frenzy of the shaman during the "shamanic illness" and the seizures during the seance should not be regarded as symptoms of a particular hereditary ailment. The "bizarreness" of the shaman's ritual or everyday behavior depended on the nature of the role he was living with all his being. This role was exemplified by various people. Some were not able to fully personify the model and in the best of cases made do with only partial performance of shamanic duties. Others took up the task, but desired with advancing years to "rid themselves of the spirits" and pass their role to a younger person. Still others carried the burden of the shaman's office to their final breath.

It is important to recognize that the shaman lived a very intense inner existence. P. I. Tret'iakov has left us an excellent description of an Evenk shaman: "Abandoning himself to the representations of his imagination, he became anxious, apprehensive, especially at night, when his head was filled with various dreams. As the day appointed for shamanizing drew near, the exorcist would lose sleep, become absent-minded, and stare fixedly at an object for several hours. Pale, fatigued, with a sharp penetrating gaze, this person made a curious impression." S. M. Shirokogorov agreed with such a characterization: "Expending much energy on the seance, overtaxing themselves greatly, always willing to receive the spirits and, thus, always in a state of great nervous tension, the shamans never have a healthy, untroubled appearance, but are usually emaciated, gaunt, always pensive and withdrawn. The extremely complex mental existence of these people . . . , who are always, even in sleep, under the influence of (faith in) the spirits and are constantly using their sleep to consort with other shamans and spirits, leaves a special mark on them." With good reason, a Nanai shaman told L. Ia. Shternberg: "It is hard to shamanize, very hard. It is easier to chop wood than to shamanize." And Shternberg himself wrote: "The shaman's talent is not a gift, but a burden."

Not everyone, it appears, could withstand the stress. A person might lack the strength and self-confidence, the nerves might give out. This is most likely what occurred when a shaman died during a seance, having persuaded himself of defeat in the struggle with hostile spirits. The shaman might also convince himself that the spirits, angered by his disobedience or some other fault, require his death or punishment with sickness. It might happen that the spirits, after "punishing" the shaman, would "abandon" him to spend the remainder of his life an invalid. Seroshevskii wrote of an old Yakut, who became convinced of the "sinfulness" of shamanism under the influence of the Christian faith and ceased shamanizing: "the spirits became angry and blinded him."

But a good many shamans approached the end of their life in good health and sound mind, enjoying the respect of their community. A. V. Anokhin wrote of one Altaic shaman: "Sangyzak lived to a great age and often fell unconscious. The Altaians were very fond of his shamanizing and often carried him, enfeebled with age, on an ox hide to their villages [*ails*]." V. I. Anuchin reported on the Ket: "A great shaman is a very rare occurrence, and is always someone extremely aged." According to E. D. Prokof'eva, among the Selkup "there were also very old shamans, who retained great shamanic strength until death." As long as the shaman properly performed his difficult and important role, he was healthy. His fainting and seizures were demanded by the logic of the role allotted him. While entirely under the sway of his belief in the spirits, at the same time he controlled his imagination—otherwise he could not remain within the bounds of the model that he was supposed to personify with his whole being, with every thought and gesture. As soon as the shaman lost control over his visions, he would become a neuropath. But having lost control over himself, he would no longer be a shaman.

These conclusions are based on the ethnographic data. Lamentably, medicine and ethnography have not joined forces in this area. Soviet medicine has paid little attention to shamanism. Instead of conducting investigations along with ethnographers, medical doctors have mainly commented on their works. There have been a few observations by medical doctors—when the Altaian *kam*, Mampyi, visited Tomsk in 1909, he was examined by the physician V. V. Karelin, who concluded: "Mampyi is perfectly normal in physical as well as mental and psychological respects, with quite a good development."

Concluding the discussion of health, let us look at shamanism in general. In trying to comprehend the surrounding world, humanity arrived at a belief in spirits. The belief in powerful spirits diminished humans, oppressed their willpower, and inspired a feeling of inadequacy and weakness. But people refused to live in perpetual dependency on the spirits and "invented" a means of protection against them. They learned to "control" them. This enabled our ancestors to maintain their spiritual equilibrium in the difficult struggle with nature.

## The Twilight of Shamanism

As already noted, shamanism probably arose in the Stone Age (possibly the Paleolithic) and was known to all peoples in the early stages of their history. Like any other historical phenomenon, it did not come into being at once, but went through various stages in its development.

It has often been declared that originally, in deep antiquity, anyone was able to shamanize. It is believed that the first explorers of Kamchatka in the eighteenth century observed this initial form of shamanism. But the matter of the Kamchadal is not entirely clear. It is likely that their shamans practiced in secret, hiding from the severe persecutions of the Orthodox church. Nevertheless, the existence of a collective shamanism in the early stage is probable.

We have already mentioned that among many peoples there was no abrupt boundary separating the shaman from other tribal members. Almost every Eskimo and Orochi considered themselves privy to the shaman's practice. Among the Chukchi, according to the observations of V. G. Bogoraz, "almost every third or fourth person claims to be able to shamanize." The involvement of clan members in the shamanic ritual was deemed beneficial, even among those peoples whose shaman was a clearly differentiated individual.

The further society progressed in its development, the more the shaman was separated from his kinsmen. Hence, in the early stage of history, the shaman may not have been a special figure. At that time, probably any person was held capable of consorting with spirits, and the most important rituals were performed collectively. The establishment of shamanism as a profession evidently followed the same path as the formation of many other professions: as more complex skills developed, an occupation formerly open to everyone was taken over by specialists. For a majority of the peoples of Siberia, shamanism was the only specialized occupation. Was it not also the first profession in the history of humanity? Did not the social division of labor start with this?

The philosophical outlook of ancient people encouraged the development of shamanism into a profession. Weakness in the face of nature was perceived as a dependency on the spirits. The ability to come to terms with the spirits was viewed as a vitally important matter, and those able to accomplish this were valued highly. This ability was evidently associated with certain special talents (even in later times, any given talent would be regarded as a sign of favor, a gift of the spirits). Gradually, the inescapable conclusion emerged that not every-

Shamanism survives in places even today. This photograph was taken in 1983. The Tuvinian shamaness shamanizes with a jew's harp [*vargan*], which emits a dismal, droning, "otherworldly" sound.

one could successfully deal with the spirits. The issue of shamanic specialization was handled in a very practical way. Ordinary experience showed that a single shaman was sufficient to meet the needs of many people. Experience must also have taught that having two shamans was not only superfluous but even harmful, for ambitious rivalry between them could bring discord into the life of the people.

Shamanism had long existed deep within the clan system. (It is perhaps even older than the clan. There were shamans among Australian aborigines, who are generally considered as not having reached the clan stage of organization.) Ritual traditions preserve the memory of a link between shamanism and the most archaic cults of the clan. As mentioned, the ritual costume once signified the animal-spirit from whom the shaman was descended. At an early stage, this was the same animal (totem) from whom the entire clan traced its origin. Subsequently, the relationship between the clan and the animal was gradually forgotten, but the image of the ancestor-animal continued to live on in shamanism for some time. (We may mention, incidentally, that the belief in the clans' origin from different animals did not vanish entirely in Siberia and was preserved among certain peoples until the turn of the twentieth century.)[i]

The appointment of one person to perform cult duties does not mean that this person is set apart from the collective. The shaman ministered to clan members, and the protector-spirit of the shaman also acted as the protector of the entire clan.

As social relations develop and grow more complex, the figure of the shaman acquires new attributes. When the boundaries of the clan become restrictive, "strong" shamans extend the sphere of their activities: maintaining their connection with the clan, they minister to the entire tribe. In this stage, the shaman is no longer confined to the clan spirits, but has a vast army of the most diverse spirits. He may attribute his origin to several animal-spirits.

With the decay of clan and tribe relationships, the shaman acquires a more aloof position in society. He becomes a specialist dealing with the spirits, who ministers to the surrounding population. His clientele include other neighboring peoples. Even his spirits may belong to a different people, and the shaman must negotiate with the spirits in the language of his neighbors. Shamans encourage the growth of concepts about their supernatural power and special relations with higher forces not accessible to the ordinary mortal. Social control over the activity of the shamans weakens. "Princely" shamans and wealthy shamans are clearly differentiated from tribal members, even in opposition to them.

This must have been the period when the concept of the malevolent shaman was formed. In the early stage, a hostile shaman always belonged to a different clan, and the local shaman would protect his clan against such machinations. With the breakdown of the pillars of clan society, the shaman assumed greater independence and could set himself against his community. Shamans thus come to be accused of misdeeds. The Orochi, for example, were convinced that some of the professional shamans had taken to eating people's souls. They believed that the Orochi were formerly very populous, but their numbers diminished due to the shamans' need to eat the souls of the people. The legends of the Nanai abound in references to people-eating shamans. Speaking of an old man, a "great" shaman, the people warn the hero: "One month he eats ordinary food, and the next month he lives on human meat." The heroine of another legend, a maiden (apparently a shamaness), swims to shore, where an enormous poplar is growing. The ground all about is strewn with human bones. It appears that a certain "big" shaman always devours his prey in this tree of the "great" shamans. He alights here in the form of a huge bird with iron feathers, holding a person in his talons.

Community ties did not deter an evil shaman. According to a Nanai legend, a child in one village suddenly took sick and died. The parents, suspecting foul play, decided to watch over the body at night, without lighting a fire. All at once the door opened, a white dog ran into the house and began to drink the blood of the infant. The father sank a harpoon into it, and the dog vanished. In the morning, a man in the same village, a ''great'' shaman, took ill. When examined, a harpoon wound was discovered in his stomach. He died the same day. Such legends reflect an increasing estrangement of the shaman from society.

Shamanism was essentially intended to meet the needs of comparatively small groups of people, united by the bonds of family and, later, community. As the social structure becomes more complex, religious ideas grow in complexity and new cults arise. The distance between deities and humans increases. The stratification of society, resulting in formation of classes of the exploiters and the exploited, instills in many people a dissatisfaction with life, which is mitigated by the expectation of bliss in another world. From that point, religious dogma incorporates the idea of retribution beyond the grave.

The appearance of the state, which took on itself the management of society, was the decisive stage in the process of suppression of shamanism by other forms of religion. The age of the inspired favorite of the spirits or deities had passed. A king has no need of an independent priest, surrounded by the aura of supernatural election. He would rather concentrate in his own hands such affairs as relationships with deities. Under monarchical rule, society is persistently accustomed to the idea that the king is the successor of the gods and their chief priest. In the ancient religions of the Mediterranean, for example, we find the figure of the priest-king, who is pictured as a god. The ruler takes on the mediating function of the shaman, predicated upon personal contact with the deities. (He also retains several external attributes, such as the ritual cap. Why do the crowns of European monarchs bear a remote resemblance to the shaman's metallic cap? Perhaps because the shamanic ''crown'' was once the prototype of the regal crown. It is no accident that the crowns of the Korean rulers of the early Middle Ages have the same symbolism as the shamanic headdress, and are similar in shape.)

Even though the king is the closest to the gods, the affairs of religion are handled by the priests. Under the new conditions, an organized priesthood was necessary to support a regular established cult. The new priesthood not uncommonly formed from the ranks of the shamans. Such was the case, for example, in the early days of the Mongol empire. Guillaume Rubruc, who visited the headquarters of Mangu-khan in the middle of the thirteenth century, writes: "The soothsayers, as the khan himself admits, are their priests, and everything they advise is performed without delay. . . . There are many soothsayers, and there is always a chief among them, a kind of pope . . . , who always has his dwelling near the main palace of Mangu-khan, at a stone's throw in front of it. The carriages bearing their idols are under the protection of this priest. . . . The other soothsayers live in back of the courtyard, in their appointed places; people from the various countries of the world, trusting in their skill, have recourse to them."[j]

These "soothsayers" are shamans. They even preserved the old Turkic word for shaman, *kam* (*kham* in Rubruc). Certain of these would summon the spirits. At night, in the presence of those "who wished to have answers from the demons," the shaman "begins to pronounce his incantations and, holding a drum, strikes it forcefully against the ground. At length, he begins to rage, and they begin tying him up. The demon then appears in a haze, the *kham* gives him meat to eat, and the demon answers questions." But these are quite different shamans. They live at court, servants of an official cult, united into a corporation. They keep the people in a state of fear and can destroy whomever they please with accusations of sorcery. Rubruc tells of a case where a wife of the khan, at the instigation of the "soothsayers," commanded that innocent people be killed. The enraged khan meted out swift justice to those who had committed the murder and his wife fell into temporary disfavor, but nothing happened to the "soothsayers," so far as may be inferred from the text.

The development of religious philosophy took different paths in various societies. Each produced its own dogma, its own type of priesthood. And the relationship between shamanism and the new cults, ideas, and entire religious systems was also of various types. But alongside this diversity, a uniform process—the decline of shamanism—was occurring everywhere. It had long since ceased to be the major cult and was being pushed ever further from the stage of social existence into the dark corners of daily life. And the bright colors of its ritual attire had also faded.

Even so, the ideas and myths characteristic of shamanism exerted great influence on later religions. In the religions of antiquity, for example, the cult of the dying and resurrecting gods of fertility held an important place. The Phoenician-Greek Adonis was such a god. According to the myths, after the death of Adonis, Aphrodite (Astarte) freed him from the subterranean realm of the dead. It was the will of Zeus that he spend the winter in the nether regions and return to earth in the spring. (This myth reflects the annual death and rebirth of nature.) But we recall that the shaman also visited other worlds and on occasion returned the dead to life. It is possible that the myths of the gods of fertility took their origin from shamanism.

The figure of the prophet, familiar to virtually every religion in the world, is also connected with shamanism. In the prophet—the chosen of god, who proclaims to the people revelations heard from the deity itself (or an angel)—it is not hard to recognize the shaman, divested of ritual guise. In an altered appearance, in new societal circumstances, the former shaman continued to assert himself in the ancient role of mediator between humans and a godhead. He had retained something from the inheritance of the shamanic epoch. Thus, the Old Testament prophets would be possessed by the spirit. "And when he [God—V. B.] spoke to me, the spirit came into me," we read in the book of the prophet Ezekiel (Ez. 2:2). The prophets experienced visions that chilled them to the marrow. The same Ezekiel on more than one occasion felt himself transported to other places: "He [God—V. B.] stretched out what seemed to be a hand and took me by the hair; and the spirit lifted me between earth and sky, and took me . . . to Jerusalem . . ." (Ez. 8:3). In the legendary lives of the founders of the new religions, the principal theme of the "shamanic illness" is preserved in a changed form—the "re-creation" of the shaman. The crucifixion and resurrection of Christ, as well as the rationale for his painful death—can be traced back to the shamanic "re-creation." This theme has been retained more clearly in Islam. According to the legends, Gabriel and the other angels cut up the body of the prophet Muhammed and purify it of filth to render it perfect. The legend of Muhammed's ascent into the sky riding a fantastic beast, from which he was shown heaven and hell, is also of a shamanic nature.

Different types of priests indeed bore shamanic attributes for a long time. This is readily apparent in the case from antiquity of the Greco-Roman priesthood. Ecstasy as temporary insanity and ability to prophesy, caused by the inspiration of deity, are both present. Through the lips of the Greek prophetess Cassandra (in the words of Cicero) "god enclosed in human body speaks." Enamored of Cassandra, Apollo bestowed on her the ability to see the future, which appeared to her in frightening pictures: "I see as though in a bloody haze. There, they are strangling children. . . . They fry them and give them to the father for dinner. . . .'' Drums and tambourines were widely used as a means of inducing ecstasy. Priests talked to the gods in a special language. The priestly vocation and the gift of prophecy were passed on by inheritance.

The preservation of traditions from early antiquity in religions is a universal law. Every new ideology, supplanting an older one, employs former models and ideas for its own uses. ''Once created, religion always preserves a certain stock of ideas, inherited from former times . . . ,[4] according to Engels. In time, the ancient philosophy gradually expires. When the official cult came to power in the ancient world, shamanic practices continued to survive only among the lesser clergy (sorcerers, diviners, curers). But later on, in the Middle Ages, ideas once associated with shamanism had such great influence on the life of the peoples of Europe that the Christian inquisitors considered them a threat to the existence of the Church. They tortured and immolated sorcerers and witches for their imagined cohabitation with the devil and their flights to demonic gatherings. Beliefs in various kinds of sorcerers and sorceresses can be traced back in large measure to shamanism. In these beliefs, we find special circumstances of birth as a sign of election, association with the spirits, ecstasy, and journeying of the soul. It is no accident that a Nanai shaman, transformed into a dog, is similar to the evil stepmother and witch in Gogol's story ''May Night, or the Drowned Woman.''

Various phases in the development of shamanism produced by changes in the life of society can also be glimpsed in the religions of the peoples of Siberia and the European North. In particular, we may trace the development of the community priesthood from shamanism. In southern Siberia, this process led to differentiation of shamans into ''black'' and ''white.'' Among the Yakuts and Buryats, ''black'' shamans were servants of evil spirits, ''white'' of good spirits. (This distinction was not always observed in practice. Shamans who served both good and evil deities and spirits were found among the Buryats.)

The categories of ''black'' and ''white'' shamanism formed gradually. At their heart, they are related to the conceptions of the ''upper'' and ''lower'' worlds, which the shaman was supposed to visit. Among the Altaians, a *kam* who did not perform prayers to the sovereign of the underground realm, Erlik, was considered a ''white'' shaman. He would appeal to the celestial deities and the ''pure'' spirits of earth. A ''black'' shaman was able to consort with various spirits. Nonetheless, the ''black'' shamans were not believed apt to occasion harm.

Tuvinian traditions show quite clearly that the "black" shaman was originally a specialist in relations with the "lower" world, and a "white," with the "upper." As V. P. D'iakonova shows, among the Tuvinians it is scarcely possible to "differentiate the shamans by function into those who shamanize only to the pure spirits and those only to the black (evil). The 'greater' shamans shamanized to both." The relation between the shaman and the spirits of the "upper" or "lower" world was denoted by color. For the journey to the sky, a red cloak, a headdress with eagle feathers, and a red drum would be made for the shaman. For the "black path" (to the underground world), a black cloak, a cap with raven feathers, and a black drum would be made. One of the principal spirits of the underground spheres among the Tuvinians, as well as many other peoples, was the bear. For this reason, Tuvinian shamans would most often personify a bear during the seance to the "lower" world. At the same time, the conviction that the "black" shaman is predominantly evil had already formed among southern Tuvinians: "He who had destroyed at least one human being usually became a shaman with the black path." Such shamans could no longer cure the sick or protect livestock. If the Tuvinians suspected that a shaman with the "black path" was causing harm, they appealed for help to a shaman with the "white path," who would enter into battle with the evil shaman. Sometimes the clash would end in the death of the rival.

With the breakdown of the clan and tribe system, concepts regarding other worlds were revised in southern Siberia in light of understanding about good and evil. Since the "lower" world was the realm of evil spirits, a shaman associated with it became evil. He was a destroyer of people. The good spirits and deities concentrated mostly in the sky, and their servant, the "white" shaman, assumed the role of a good shaman. Such contrast could not have formed in the clan society. What need has the clan for an evil shaman?

The "white" shamans could hardly be called shamans at all. They were a priesthood of tribal or community cults, formed from the ranks of the shamans. The new priesthood did not require all of the old traditions. As N. A. Alekseev has convincingly shown, the "white" shaman of the Yakuts lost many of the characteristic shaman features: "The duty of the white shaman was to appeal to the (good) deities, the *aiyy*. While performing the rituals, they would be assisted by 'pure' boys and girls. The white shamans did not fall into ecstasy, nor did they have helping spirits [this should be confirmed!—V. B.]. They were not able to deal with the evil spirits. Furthermore, they were supposed to observe ritual purity (not touch corpses, and so on). The white shamans of the Yakuts . . . were basically priests of the tribal cult of tutelary deities (aiyy).'' It is significant that the ''white'' shamans of the Altaians also gave up certain external tokens of their profession. Of the ritual costume, they kept only the cap, made of white sheepskin, whereas the ''black'' shaman also had a special cloak.

(Since M. Eliade's book *Shamanism* has gained much celebrity and has also received high acclaim in our country, it is advisable to call the reader's attention to one of the conclusions with which I cannot agree. Eliade considers the relationship with a celestial deity as the hallmark of shamanism. But we have found that, historically, shamanism is equally associated with both the ''upper'' and the ''lower'' worlds. Only with the growth of religious ideas does the service to the celestial gods become the chief function of the cult. And it is the servants of the celestial gods who are most deprived of characteristic shamanic features.)[k]

Among some peoples of Siberia, probably in ancient times when transitory tribal leagues, kingdoms, or states arose, shamanism was raised time and again to the status of an official cult. It is likely that shamanism was the official cult of the ancient Turkic state. But with the fall of weak political unions, the religious life again resumed its previous forms.

The independent process of transformation in shamanism was interrupted among many peoples of our country by the world religions—Islam, Buddhism, Christianity. These religions had a well-organized clergy and enjoyed the support of the authorities. All of them tried to do away with shamanism.

Islam was introduced into Central Asia by the Arabs in the eighth century and was definitively established soon after the conquest of the territory by the hordes of Jinghiz Khan. We have no historical sources describing the struggle between Islam and shamanism, but the mere spirit of the Muslim fanaticism of the Middle Ages suggests that the eradication of heathenism would have been conducted with implacable dedication. Thus, even in the late nineteenth century, the faithful of Karakalpakia, incited by the clergy, threw stones at shamans dressed in female garb.

The Kalmyks adopted Lamaism in the sixteenth century. As an echo of the struggle with shamanism, a law adopted by the Kalmyk feudal lords in 1640 has come down to us: ''Whoever calls a shaman or shamaness to him, let the horse be taken from the person calling and the horse be taken from the shamaness who arrives; if one should see this and not take (a horse from each), let his horse be taken from him.'' Lamaism began to penetrate to the Buryat from Mongolia in the seventeenth century. The Lamaist clergy, aided by the authorities, destroyed ancient shrines and organized persecutions of the shamans. ''The poor shamanists were everywhere hunted down. No forest, no mountain could hide them from the vengeance of the lamas, who scoured all of Transbaikalia and even the vicinity of Irkutsk in large bands.''[1]

Shamanism was also fought by the Orthodox church, which in the seventeenth and eighteenth centuries began actively introducing Christianity into the life of the native peoples of the Far North of Europe and Siberia. Only toward the end of the nineteenth century did a change of course take place in the missionary activity—it was recognized that the ''non-Russians'' must consciously adopt the Christian faith. But in the beginning they were not fastidious about methods. Forcible conversion, destruction of holy places, and direct persecution of those who kept their former religion (primarily shamans) occurred. One of the reasons for an uprising of Nenets and Khanty in 1841 was dissatisfaction with forcible Christianization.

The impact of the missionaries, as well as the destruction of the traditional lifestyle, inflicted a heavy blow on the ancient cult. Observers of the last century speak of a universal decline of shamanism. The native population itself was convinced that the power of the shamans was diminishing and that they could not perform what earlier shamans had done. Shamanism continued to survive, however, intimately connected with customary beliefs and the entire way of life. Shamans of the ''non-Russians'' sometimes enjoyed favor among the Russians themselves. There are known cases when even priests consulted shamans.

Yet shamanism was unable to escape the influence of the world religions. The more firmly the new religions entered the life of the people, the stronger was this influence.

In Central Asia and Kazakhstan, shamanism took on a Muslim cast. Conflicts between mullahs and shamans remained, but this was then a professional competition, not a collision of different ideologies. In their outlook, shamans did not differ from other orthodox Muslims. When beginning a ritual, shamans appealed first to Allah, then to the various Muslim saints, and only afterwards to their helping spirits, who were considered a kind of genie [*jinn*], so often mentioned in the holy book of Islam—the *Koran*.

Uzbek shamans began a seance by singing:

For this undertaking of mine—*bismilla.*
For all of my undertakings—*bismilla.*
I lie down, I get up—*bismilla,*
I set out on the journey—*bismilla.*

*Bismilla* is a shortened form of the Muslim formula *bismillakhi-r-rakhmani-r-rakhim,* "in the name of Allah, the merciful, the good." It was to be uttered before beginning any undertaking. The shamans of the other Central Asian peoples also began their ritual singing with similar phrases.

Islam abolished the shamanic ritual costume. The meaning of the seance also changed. The Muslim shaman does not journey to other worlds, but merely sends his spirits after the malignant demon causing a person sickness. The spirits wage battle with the demon, but often report to the shaman that a ransom, a sacrifice, is required—a ram of a certain color or, if nothing better, a hen. Many Uzbek and Tadzhik shamans deemed it necessary to obtain the blessing of a clergyman; this blessing was essentially an ordination to be a shaman. Some shamans and shamanesses renounced the traditional drum, replacing the musical instrument with rosary beads. The protector-spirits themselves were commonly portrayed as Muslim saints. One Samarkand shamaness (early twentieth century) refused to tell fortunes on bazaar days, claiming that her protector-spirit "grandpa-*ishan*" (*ishan* means clergyman) had gone shopping.

Shamanism, in turn, exerted influence on the activities of unofficial Muslim clergy. The residents of Bukhara, for example, thought that certain *ishans* possessed a special ability to cure ("berate") the sick, because they had a protector-spirit. In Turkmenia, certain people claiming to be the descendants of the prophet Muhammed claimed to possess a whole "host" of helping *jinn.* Assisted by the *jinn,* they prophesied and tried to cure the possessed. Their *jinn* were handed down as an inheritance.

Lamaism also had a deep impact on the shamanism of peoples adopting this form of Buddhism. Among the Buryat, former ideas regarding the soul, the other world, and the structure of the universe underwent change. The old tribal and clan shrines, or *obo*—a pile of stones heaped up in honor of the owner-spirits of the locality—received a Lamaist interpretation, and idol shrines [*kumirnia*] were erected in

Muslim prayer before the beginning of a seance by an Uzbek shamaness. Author's photograph (1979).

places. The lamas appropriated certain shamanic rituals. Deities with Buddhist names and titles took their place among the shamanic gods. Priests appeared who combined the functions of the shaman and the lama, having both shamanic attributes and implements of the Lamaist cult.

Tuvinian shamans also had objects of the Lamaist cult (such as carpets with images of the Buddha) among their sacred articles. Lamas who took ill thought it natural to consult a shaman. Indeed, a new type of half-shaman, half-lama, came into being at Tuva: the *burkhan-böö* (*burkhan* is the Lamaist word for deity, *böö* is the Buryat-Mongol word for shaman). These "godly shamans" were instructed at Lamaist monasteries. Their garments combined shamanic and Lamaist elements. A fringe of threads, covering the face, would be attached to the lama's headdress, like a shamanic cap. The *burkhan-böö* conducted their rituals with the implements and books of the Lamaist cult. But they also arranged nocturnal seances near graves and at so-called "shamanic trees." It was held that a "godly shaman" could cause harm to an evil shaman, recover a sick person's soul stolen by an evil spirit, and even destroy an evil spirit.

The influence of Christianity on shamanism was not the same among the different peoples. Where Christianization was superficial, shaman-ism incorporated only a few elements of the new faith. When the Orthodox religion was implanted more deeply, the population con-formed to the idea that shamanism was incompatible with the "faith of Christ." There are known cases of Yakut and Altaian shamans being converted and resolving to renounce the service of the spirits, but failing to overcome the beliefs of their ancestors: they imagined that the spirits were avenging the apostasy and tormenting them. The Khakass when shamanizing would cover icons or turn their face to the wall, and shamans would remove their crucifix. At the start of the twentieth century, the Khakass believed that, if a Christian prayer were said during a seance, the "evil one" would torment the shaman and disrupt the ritual. Therefore, Russians attending the seance were asked "not to say any prayers."[m]

But here and there, a fusion of shamanism and the Orthodox faith would occur. "The christened non-Russians have a dual faith (reports ethnographer V. I. Iokhel'son at the start of the twentieth century). The shaman of the Yukagir, the northern Yakut, or the Tungus, before beginning to summon the shamanic spirits, burns incense and says a prayer before the icons, asking their help in the battle against the evil spirits." Among the Even, starting in the eighteenth century, the Orthodox religion gained an equal footing with the former beliefs and cults. The Even properly performed the church rituals—matrimony, christening of children, the burial service, observance of fasts and Christian holidays. But shamanism also survived (clandestinely, so as not to offend the missionaries). And those abiding by Christianity with the most rectitude were the shamans themselves. Shamans of the Oro-chi were also the most exemplary of Christians. No one here paid attention to the icons hanging in every dwelling, but "the shaman considered it his duty to cross himself in front of the icon before beginning the seance."

The radical transformations in the existence of all the peoples of our country, occurring after the Great October Socialist Revolution, led to a sharp decrease in activity of the shamans. At first, a good many of the shamans opposed the Soviet state, and tried to entice some of their tribe to follow them. Shamanism itself, being an important component of the entire traditional structure, was an objective hindrance to the construc-tion of socialism. Therefore, Soviet organizations criticized the sha-mans and conducted an active information campaign to eradicate their influence on the life of the peoples of the North and Siberia. Judging from newspaper articles, many shamans gave up shamanizing in the 1930s. However, in order for shamanism to become extinct, people raised on belief in the gods and spirits required a radical transformation of their philosophy. And this was no easy matter. As long as the old beliefs survived, so too would shamanism. Apparently, it enjoyed a certain upsurge during the difficult war years, when concern for the fate of loved ones at the front brought some people to the shamans.

Even in the 1960s and 1970s, shamanism preserved its traditional forms here and there. For example, in the 1960s, A. V. Smoliak interviewed Nanai shamans, who assured her that their predecessors had been able to fly to the sun. In 1964, Shonchur, considered by S. I. Vainshtein the last "great" Tuvinian shaman, was still plying his drum. In the early 1970s, according to V. M. Kulemzin, there were those among the Khanty who performed certain functions of the shamans. In the 1970s, at the request of elders, the Nganasan Demnime Kosterkin, son of the renowned Diukhade, was still shamanizing. In 1974, Ch. M. Taksami witnessed a seance of the Nivkhi shamaness Kazyk. The old shamaness asked her spirits to see whether the road would be good for her guest, and then consented to shamanize over a sick member of the expedition. Kazyk declared that, on the days when she does not shamanize, she does not feel well and is sick. The helping spirits beset her and demand "activity."

Shamanism is alive today in vestigial forms. Certain peoples no longer have shamans, but beliefs until recently closely connected with shamanism survive. Thus, in a number of regions of Buryatia, according to the materials of N. L. Zhukovskaia, the cult of Daian Derkhe, the protector-spirit of shamans, is still found. Formerly, his shrine (in northern Mongolia) would be visited to receive the shamanic gift. A strong person would become a shaman, while a weak one would perish on the spot, beside the stone believed to embody Daian Derkhe. This spirit is now worshipped as the patron of childbirth. Some groups of Buryat also make offerings to him as a protector-ancestor. Sometimes they present him with a horse, its mane decorated with white ribbons, for the spirit to ride on.

Shamans may even be found in some localities. The photograph on page 31 (taken by S. I. Vainshtein in 1983) shows a Tuvinian shamaness holding to her lips the ancient instrument *vargan* [jew's harp], which emits a dismal, droning, "otherworldly" sound. Ribbons and trinkets are attached to the *vargan*, scaring away the evil spirits. The *vargan* replaces the drum in her seances. The *vargan* is no novelty

Balbike-baksy with a *kobyz*. Photograph by K. Baibosinov (1978).

to shamanism, having also been used in the past.[n] Thus, the traditions are still being observed here. But in the Altai, those who may be conditionally ranked as shamans usually perform their simple rituals with neither drum nor special costume.

Shamanism is most deeply entrenched among the peoples of Central Asia and Kazakhstan. This is strange only at first glance. Shamanism here had long become part of Islam, and this is one of the reasons for its longevity. Belief in spirits, in saints, or simply in certain supernatural forces continues to attract to shamans people, chiefly women, who are troubled with the illness of a child or their own ailments. Sometimes those whom modern medicine has not been able to help will go to shamans. They reason: Why not try my luck, just in case? And like hundreds of years ago, a homemade lantern for the spirits will be lit and the drum will sound.

Shamanic healing practices are still the same. In 1978, K. Baibosinov was a guest of an eighty-year-old Kazakh shamaness, Balbikebaksy (southern Kazakhstan). She told how she cures patients by playing on the *kobyz* and summoning the Muslim saints and spirits, the *peri* [*pari*]. At times, she puts aside the *kobyz* and takes up a knife. Recounting the names of the saints, she touches the patient's body with the knife. "The *jinn* run away, fearing the knife." There is also another way to remove malicious *jinn*: kill a live chicken next to the patient and immediately carry it away to a "holy" place. Blood is a delicacy to the spirits. They assemble about the bleeding chicken and are enticed away from the patient. Balbike also makes small puppets, which are placed around the patient's head, then wrapped in a piece of fabric and put in a "holy" place; the spirits causing the disease will remain with them. If the illness is grave, it is necessary to perform a *zikir*: those attending the ritual, along with the shamaness, shout the names of Allah or phrases such as "There is no god but Allah."

Traditions of shamanism are preserved among the Tadzhiks and Uzbeks. Their shamanism has long been distinguished by great diversity. Male and female shamans have different helping spirits, and differentiated healing and fortune-telling practices. Instead of the drum (or sometimes along with it), a lash, a sieve, a wooden serving spoon, a staff, a mirror, and a cup with water are used as ritual objects.

The characters of the various shamans and shamanesses are quite different. For example, the picturesque figure of the aged Tadzhik shamaness Ouliia-folbin is interesting; imperious, resolute, and self-confident, she inspires the faithful with fear and awe. Her ritual hymns have been recorded on tape by O. Murodov. She has a special waiting room for clientele, seldom admitting men. When summoning the *pari* spirits, the shamaness sits on a prayer rug, beating the drum. On the wall is a white cloth, where the spirits that appear will sit. The spirits prescribe the most diverse procedures for healing of sickness (set up a lantern in such and such place, throw two peas into such and such a brook, and so forth).

I was able to witness Uzbek shamans and shamanesses on many occasions. The last meetings were in 1983 in southern Uzbekistan. It was interesting that the shamanic spirits are not averse to modern trends. I found myself the guest of an elderly fortune-teller, along with the ethnographer K. Kubakov. She called her *pari* spirits by playing the drum, and then looked at the open pages of a book—the *Birth of Ker-ogla*, a folk epic [*dastan*]. The spirits also inspired her to sing. After we became better acquainted, she took up the drum and in a high strong voice sang a song praising the scientists of the Academy of Sciences. "You see, my *pari* send you greetings," she said. The spirits are also favorably disposed to modern fashion. I recall the village women talking about a twenty-year-old girl who had become a shamaness: "Her dress is short, and her shoes are high-heeled. And she wears lipstick!" There was no censure in these words: after all, the girl was dressing as the spirits commanded.

Shamanism is steadily declining, but continues to survive. How long will this go on? In 1892, V. M. Mikhailovskii wrote: "Shamanism among the Siberian peoples is dying out." As we see, this state has continued for nearly a century. And it should not be surprising if shamanism sprang up in new forms—based not on a common tradition, but on infatuation with mysticism. The motley mystical teachings that are proliferating in capitalist countries, especially the United States, eagerly use information about shamans to convince the average person of the existence of otherworldly forces. The ancient beliefs are clothed in a sophisticated "scientific" terminology. The shaman, it turns out, is in contact with a "divine consciousness that permeates the world," with the "spiritual energy of the universe." He has attained "special dimensions of the sacred." "Invisible psychic forces" are for him "a living component of reality." And ecstasy? This is a transposition from "conventional reality" to "nonconventional reality." The Western fashion may also prove attractive to some of our people.

Indeed, the extinction of religious vestiges is not a straightforward process. Under certain circumstances, they may revive, influencing some groups of people. But the general tendency of the development of society inevitably dooms them to gradual extinction. The crisis of religion is also exemplified by the disappearance of shamanism—an irrefutable fact, witnessed all around us.

### Editor's Notes

a. Sergei Shirokogorov (also spelled Shirokogoroff) was known as a foremost scholar of Siberia and of shamanism after his emigration from the Soviet Union. Shirokogorov's detailed monographs (hard to find in the Soviet Union) include: *Social Organization of the Manchus* (Shanghai: Royal Asiatic Society, 1924); *Social Organi-*

*zation of the Northern Tungus* (Shanghai, 1929); *Psychomental Complex of the Tungus* (London, 1935). The passage cited here, from a 1919 article in *Zapiski Vladivostokskogo Universiteta*, refers only to an initial stage of "illness"—later cured when Evenk (or Tungus in some historical literature) shamans accepted their perceived destiny.

b. *Mukhomor* is one of several Russian colloquial terms for the red-with-white-spots mushroom *amanita muscaria* (also called "death cap"). Its use in shamanic seances is well known, but the significance of that use is widely debated. For history and cross-cultural analysis, see R. G. Wasson, *Soma: The Divine Mushroom of Immortality* (New York: Harcourt Brace Jovanovich, 1960); M. Eliade, *Shamanism: Archaic Techniques of Ecstasy* (Princeton: Princeton University Press, 1972); P. Furst, ed., *Flesh of the Gods: The Ritual Use of Hallucinogens* (New York: Praeger, 1972); M. Harner, ed., *Hallucinogens and Shamanism* (London: Oxford Univ. Press, 1973). In most areas, alcohol was a relatively recent way of altering consciousness. Also debated is the degree to which drumming produces changed perceptions in shamans and their audiences. See A. Neher, "A Physiological Explanation of Unusual Behavior in Ceremonies Involving Drums," *Human Biology*, vol. 34 (1962), pp. 151–60; and G. Rouget, *La Musique et la trance* (Paris: Gallimard, 1980).

c. This data on the Ket of central Siberia is from E. A. Alekseenko (1981). See also Demitri Shimkin, "A Sketch of the Ket, or Yenisei Ostyak," *Ethnos*, vol. 4 (1939), pp. 147–76.

d. This material on the Nganasan of the Tamyr Peninsula is from A. A. Popov (1936, 1948), a talented Yakut ethnographer whose published work has been supplemented posthumously: *Nganasany: sotsial'noe ustroistvo i verovaniia* (Leningrad: Nauka, 1984); and "How Sereptie Djarouskin of the Nganasans (Tavgi Samoyeds) Became a Shaman," *Popular Beliefs and Folklore Tradition in Siberia*. Ural-Altaic Series 57 (Bloomington, 1968).

e. The quote is from A. A. Popov (1936), whose description of the Nganasan Diukhade's "shamanic calling" was featured earlier in the Basilov book from which this chapter is taken.

f. This unflattering view may come from the missionary Veniamin (Smirnov), "Samoedy mezenskie," *Vestnik Russkogo geograficheskogo obshchestva* (1855), ch. 14; or from the explorer I. Lepekhin, *Dnevnye zapiski puteshestviia po raznym provintsiiam Rossiiskogo gosudarstva*, ch. 4 (St. Petersburg, 1805) (Veniamin's mission among the Nenets began in 1825, and Lepekhin traveled earlier in the region.)

g. On Khanty (also called Ostyak) shamanism see V. M. Kulemzin (1976); M. M. Balzer, "Doctors or Deceivers?" in *The Anthropology of Medicine* (New York: Praeger, 1982); idem, "Behind Shamanism," *Social Science and Medicine*, 1987, vol. 24, no. 12, pp. 1085–93.

h. The preceding Nanai references are from P. P. Shimkevich (1896) and the Ul'chi ones from A. V. Smoliak (1966). On Amur River shamanism and folklore see also D. Nagishkin, *Folktales of the Amur* (New York, 1980); L. Black, "The Nivkh (Gilyak) of Sakhalin and the Lower Amur," *Arctic Anthropology*, 1973, vol. 10, no. 1, pp. 1–110; L. Shternberg, "Die Religion der Gilyaken," *Archiv für Religionswissenschaft*, 1905, vol. 8, pp. 244–73 (Leipzig).

i. A previous chapter in Basilov covered issues of the shaman's relationship to clans. Debates exist on Siberian clan and tribal organization, and totemism. See B. Chichlo, "K probleme kul'ta predkov i totemizma u narodov Sibiri," *Problemy arkheologii i etnografii*, 1977, vol. 1, pp. 130–40; "L'Ours-chamane," *Etudes Mongoles*, 1981, vol. 12, pp. 35–112.

j. Material on Guillaume Rubruc probably comes from Potanin (1881–83, 1888).

k. N. A. Alekseev's historical analysis (1969) of white or pure shamans is used cleverly here to refute M. Eliade (1972), whose book is helpful for its scope but

remarkably inaccurate on details about Siberian shamanism. See the excerpt of Alekseev (1984) in this issue.

l. For sources on Buryat shamanism and Lamaism, see Zhukovskaia (1969, 1977);
C. Humphrey *The Karl Marx Collective: Economy, Society and Religion in a Siberian
Collective Farm* (Cambridge: Cambridge University Press, 1983); idem, "Theories of
North Asian Shamanism," *Soviet and Western Anthropology*, pp. 243–54 (New York:
Columbia University Press, 1980); Roberte Hamayon, "Des chamanes au chama-
nisme," *Etnographie*, 1982, vol. 87–88, pp. 13–48.

m. See the following excerpt of Alekseev in this issue.

n. An entire journal, *VIM*, is devoted to this instrument, often called, for obscure
reasons, the jew's harp (among other names). See F. Crane, "Jew's (Jaw's? Jeu?
Jeugd? Gewgaw? Juice?) Harp," *VIM*, 1982, vol. 1, pp. 29–41. It is still widely
played in Siberia, usually outside of the shamanic context, though with awareness of its
shamanic roots. *Vargan* is the Russian word for it.

## Notes

1. S. A. Tokarev, *Rannie formy religii i ikh razvitie* (Moscow, 1964), p. 292.

2. S. M. Shirokogorov, "Opyt issledovaniia osnov shamanstva u tungusov,"
*Uchenye zapiski istoriko-filologicheskogo fakul'teta v g. Vladivostoke* (Vladivostok,
1919), vol. 1, p. 99.

3. E. D. Prokof'eva, "Materialy po shamanstva sel'kupov," *Problemy istorii obshchestvennogo soznaniia aborigenov Sibiri*, p. 67.

4. K. Marx and F. Engels, *Sochineniia*, vol. 21, p. 315.

Translated by Ronald Radzai

# Shamans and Their Religious Practices
## *from Shamanism Among the Turkic Peoples of Siberia*

Nikolai A. Alekseev

## The Shamanic Seance

Shamans of the Turkic peoples of Siberia performed rituals associated with many aspects of human life and activity. Analysis of the materials shows that the most important rituals were conducted in the form of seances [*kamlanie*], which usually followed a general pattern. Not too long ago, it was virtually impossible to transcribe the mysteries of the shamans. A. V. Anokhin, well-known for his studies of Altaic shamanism, once noted that "the texts of the seance can be recorded in their entirety only by means of a grammophone: not even a person in full command of the language can transcribe the dictation of the shaman, who utters only disconnected fragments of his invocations" [1924, p. 65]. Therefore, the author regarded his published materials on shamanism as detached, often incomplete, and hence incomprehensible portions of the shamanic invocations. As far as recording the shamanic mysteries with special equipment is concerned, this also involves great difficulties. First of all, when the ritual is performed in full garb, using the drum, the voice of the celebrant is muffled by the rattling and din. Frequently, in "conversing" with the spirits, the shaman changes to a whisper and talks in the shamanic "language," incomprehensible to the audience. If the ritual is recorded without the costume and drum, the ambience in which the "cure" or a different operation was performed is lost. This has an effect on the celebrant, and the texts of the incantations (always more or less improvised) are changed. Therefore, here the process of the shamanic seance is reconstructed by generalizing and contrasting the data recorded by different investigators.

Russian text © 1987 by "Nauka" Publishers. *Shamanizm tiurkoiazychnykh narodov Sibiri* (Novosibirsk: Nauka, 1987), chapter 4, pp. 179–214.

## The Yakuts

Among the Yakuts, an invitation to a shaman involved a series of rules and taboos. When a family member fell ill, a special runner was sent for the shaman. The shaman was met as an honored guest at the hitching post, his reins were taken, he was helped to dismount, and so forth. Preparations for the seance began even before his arrival. The hosts prepared various morsels as refreshment for the spirits, depending on the "whims" of the supernatural helpers of the particular shaman, as declared in advance. An experienced person, usually called *kuturuksut*, or guide, carefully dried the drum. His task was to assist the shaman during the seance. Among the Yakuts, there were people permanently employed in this function—for example, our informant I. Tumanov (a pensioner, Leninsk region of the Yakut ASSR, 1962) had often been a *kuturuksut*. Prior to the seance, the housewife swept the yurt so that evil spirits could not hide in the dirt [Vitashevskii, 1918, p. 177; AIV AN SSSR (LO), f. 22, op. 1, d. 21, ll. 1–3].[a]

Shamanic mysteries were usually held in the evening, after sunset. Any who desired could attend the seance. The spectators had to arrive early, since the door of the yurt was locked at the beginning of the ceremony and no one was admitted or allowed to leave [Vitashevskii, 1918, p. 165; AIV AN SSSR (LO), f. 22, op. 1, d. 7, l. 15; d. 21, l. 3; etc.].

Sometimes the shaman performed the *d'albyiyy* ritual at the start of the seance. A branch [*d'albyyr*] to the end of which were attached three, seven, or nine strands of horsehair was waved over the sick person. A weak shaman was entitled to attach three strands, an average shaman seven, and a strong shaman nine. The shaman pronounced an incantation while waving the *d'albyyr*. According to Yakut beliefs, shamans at this time either discovered the cause of illness or delivered the patient from the persecution of a lesser spirit [AIV AN SSSR (LO), f. 22, op. 1, d. 7, l. 15; Vitashevskii, 1918, p. 172; Ergis, 1945, p. 51].

Before the seance, the fire in the hearth was reduced until just smoldering; a horse-hide rug was spread on the floor before the fireplace [Seroshevskii, 1896, p. 640]. The shaman sat on it, asking for his ritual attire. A bystander helped him to dress. Among the northern Yakuts, the shaman feigned reluctance at this point. Contrary to the southern shamans, he would leave the yurt before the seance in order to embody the main spirit in himself [Ksenofontov, 1929a, p. 127].

In ritual attire, the shaman would pick up the drum, sit down, yawn loudly three times, and beat the drum vigorously three times. After this, nodding his head to the rhythm and singing, he addressed the inhabitants of the upper and lower world and the local spirits [*iuer*] that were "present" in the yurt, exhorting them to leave. An example of such exhortation is the following:

> Eight-legged tribe of evil spirits,
> Take your kinsmen unto yourselves.
> Eight-legged tribe of evil spirits, let the exorcism
> Proper to you be accomplished.
> Let the song devoted to you be complete.
> Be not angry with us.
> Thirty-nine tribes of evil spirits
> Of the upper world, suddenly awakening,
> Let the song devoted to you be complete.
> Let the exorcism proper to you be complete!

[AIV AN SSSR (LO), f. 22, op. 1, d. 21, l. 7 ob.]

Once the yurt had been purified of uninvited "guests," the shaman addressed the protector-spirits of the family (the spirit-owner of the hearth, the home, the territory, and so on). He explained the time had come to leave the native land and set out for the evil beings, and begged them to protect him [Ksenofontov, 1929a, p. 130].

Next, the helping-spirits were invoked. The shaman eloquently described the strength of his spirits:

> If I should fall face down,
> They have promised to support me.
> If I should fall backwards,
> They have promised to sustain me.
> Stammering,
> They have given me speech.
> Blind, they have given me sight.
> Deaf, they have given me hearing.
> Me that have no shaman-ancestors,
> They have made a shaman.

[AIV AN SSSR (LO), f. 22, op. 1, d. 21, ll. 9–10]

The shaman then asked them:

> Reveal unto me
> All easy pathways,
> Give me strength to sing
> The far-piercing song.
> Go before and be vigilant!
> Remove the obstacles from the path,
> Smooth the roughness of the road!
> And I beseech you, do no harm
> To the people of the middle earth.
> Create no obstacles (mistakes)
> For the cattle of my shining gods.

[AIV AN SSSR (LO), f. 22, op. 1, d. 21, l. 10]

Among the northern Yakuts, the shaman pretended that the helper-spirits, "responding" to a call, would "ask" (at times indignantly) the reason they were being disturbed. Those attending the seance would respond in chorus:

> For sake of the husband, the human!
> It is said—the day has come when the eight-legged evil power
> Is preparing to mount (us)—like a horse,
> For this reason it may be,
> It is expected (from you) helping power!
> The day is coming,
> When the entrance door in the hot house
> Faces from the western side,
> We pray that (you), by changing this,
> Would save and defend us!
> The time is coming when
> The entrance door in the spacious house
> Faces from the backward side,
> That is why we beg and pray!

In response to this, some spirits "sang," through the mouth of the shaman, that only they could protect [Ksenofontov, 1929a, p. 129].

The above examples are taken from descriptions of shamanic seances for the spirits of the lower world. The supernatural beings were addressed in a similar manner in the offering to the spirits [*abaasy*] of the upper world [*Sakha fol'klora*, 1947, pp. 58–61].

Thus, the summoning of the shaman's helpers was a compulsory feature of each seance. An incantation delivered at the "appearance" of the spirits, like other forms of ritual poetry, could be long and eloquent or brief, depending on the shaman's talent.

After summoning helpers, the shaman pretended he could not pry himself from the rug. One of those present—his guide [*kuturuksut*]—then struck sparks three times over him with a flint, i.e., performed the traditional magical "purification" by fire. After this, the shaman arose [AIV AN SSSR (LO), f. 22, op. 1, d. 9, l. 15 ob.; d. 7, l. 10 ob.].

In northern Yakutia, to get the shaman up from the rug, a helper broke three twigs on his knees. After this, the shaman "holding the drum, approaches the burning hearth and makes an incantation to his drum, calling it his mount":

> Oh, my faithful riding-reindeer
> (He sometimes calls it: my young colt)!
> Having gorged on the food from the sacred hearth,
> Prance with a rushing, rapid pace,
> And do not tire.
> Let your tiny delicate hoofs
> Not change
> Their wonted trot!

> [Ksenofontov, 1929a, p. 132]

This ritual was not performed in central Yakutia.

After getting to his feet, the shaman "purified" the place he sat. The Yakuts believed that, as a result of his summoning helpers, hostile entities could "arrive." Under their weight, the floor beneath the shaman's rug (made from the hide of wild animals, a horse, or an ox) *dzheleriuien khaalar* (sinks), and the shaman is embedded in the ground (the floor of the Yakut yurt was usually dirt), according to his "power": as far as the upper hips (a weak shaman), the armpits (a middling one), or the neck (a strong one). The shaman pronounced an incantation and "drove" all "impurity" collected at his seat into the lower world. He then asked the opening to close and grow over with green grass, i.e., be cleansed of the influence of the evil spirits. This ritual was accompanied by rattling the drum, while the celebrant turned three times against the path of the sun. Each time when his back was to the fire, he imitated the neighing of a horse and kicked backwards. In this way, the shaman seemed to be destroying various evil spirits in the form of earthworms and reptiles [AIVAN SSSR (LO), f. 22, op. 1, d. 21, ll. 11 ob.–12; d. 7, ll. 15 ob.–16].

Among the northern Yakuts, the shaman appealed to the spirit-owner of his seat to protect him and not harbor evil spirits. After pronouncing the incantation, he kicked at the rug, missing it twice, the third time turning it over [Ksenofontov, 1929a, p. 133; AIV AN SSSR (LO), f. 22, op. 2, d. 7, l. 16]. In this part of the seance, possible survivals of that time when Yakut shamans "turned into" horses during the course of their mysteries are preserved with particular clarity.

In the seances of southern Yakutia, after purifying his sitting place, the shaman "caught" the evil spirit(s) causing illness [*bokhsuruiuu*]. This ritual existed among northern Yakuts as well. In certain cases, the above-described magical elucidation of the cause of the illness [*dzhalbyiyy*] was performed before the *bokhsuruiuu*. N. A. Vitashevskii attests a case when these two rites were combined [1918, p. 177].

In order to catch the evil spirit, the shaman delivered a loud incantation, asking it to appear:

> Arise now, show yourself
> Even to your slender waist!
> Because I with the shaggy head
> The stallion-shaman
> Sing and perform the ritual,
> Do not dare to pluck away and carry in
> From the hallowed earth
> A piece the size
> Of a goodly island.[1]
> Relax, then, the burning bouts of pain,
> Turn away your jagged fangs.

[Ksenofontov, 1929a, p. 135]

After the incantation, the shaman threw himself on the patient, pretending to catch the evil spirit [*iuer*] hiding in or near him [Vitashevskii, 1918, p. 178].

Among the northern Yakuts, after cleansing his seat the shaman would ask to be fed before "setting out" on his voyage. He was given a pipe and a cup with reindeer blood. After this, the shaman "animated" his "material helpers—a fish, a bull, and a piece of bear skin" [Ksenofontov, 1929a, p. 134]. To accomplish this, he asked these objects to become living and capable of action, sprinkling them with blood. They would be "transformed" into the shaman's helper-spirits in the form of a fish, a bull, and a bear. The shaman sent them to the lower world, shrieking like a loon three times and prostrating himself on the floor, on a dark cloth, his head turned to the north. After "reaching" one *olokh*,[2] he left them and "ascended" to the middle world. Then followed the ritual of catching the evil spirit responsible for the illness—*bokhsuruiuu* [pp. 134–35]. During this ritual, the shaman enacted a conversation with the evil spirit. Speaking for the latter, he claimed that nothing would make him leave:

> Oh, people,
> I would not like to be caught,
> And you, shaman-fellow,
> Don't you know me,
> How can you not be destroyed!
> Go away, do not interfere!
> Behold: Why should I, a fine person, not eat?
> Am I not descended from a noble person?
> Am I not the child of an honored person?
> Behold my wonderful appearance,
> My beauty.
> Behold: I am she who is called the daughter of Lord *Ilbis*.
> I am here and I intend to stay.
> How can you not retreat?
> Go away, human!

As soon as the shaman is finished singing on behalf of the evil spirit, the shaman's helper exhorts the spirit to have pity:

> Oh for shame!
> Talk like a person,
> Speak like a Yakut,
> Sing like a person,
> My dear lady!
> Give token that you will leave,
> That you will give your word of honor!

[AIV AN SSSR (LO), f. 22, op. 1, d. 22, l. 11]

The above incantations were uttered while "catching" a spirit from the upper world. The dialogue with an inhabitant of the lower world, having sent an illness, was substantially the same:

Oh, oh, how painful!
Oh, my flabby body,
Oh, my aching body,
Was I not here, not wanting to be caught.
Why did you remove me, fellow,
Shaman-fellow,
You will surely be destroyed!

The shaman's helper responds:

Oh for shame,
Talk like a person,
Speak like a Yakut!
Why do you say such things?!

[AIV AN SSSR (LO), f. 22, op. 1, d. 21, ll. 16–16 ob.]

The spirit causing the illness at first cursed and would not leave, but then agreed to withdraw if a special offering was made. It tells about this through the mouth of the shaman:

The day after tomorrow,
On the second evening,
To the bright northern headland
Of this wide field,
At the instant of sunset I will come.
At that time, have ready
A four-year-old
Light-colored piebald horse.
Assisted by three young people,
Present the still living heart and liver
Stabbed with lances alone!

After long wrangling and bargaining, the spirits of the lower world also agreed to depart, but they asked for a cow as sacrifice [AIV AN SSSR (LO), f. 22, op. 1, d. 22, ll. 13–14; d. 21, l. 18].

Sometimes the *kuturuksut*, instructed in advance by the shaman, refused to pay the cow, and then the evil spirit would be "driven" or "led away" to its abode with a trifling gift. In those cases when it was deemed necessary to give what was demanded, the time for making the offering was "negotiated" with the spirit. If the spirit's request was already prepared, then according to some accounts the spirit was on the spot joined with the sacrificial cow, and sent away riding the animal; by other accounts, the spirit was sent on ahead, and the shaman would later bring the soul of the offered cow to the abode of the spirits [d. 21, ll. 18 ob., 19; d. 22, ll. 13–14; d. 7, l. 16].

On some occasions, the actual sacrifice was postponed and the shaman sent the spirit away to its abode [*iuëter*] with incantations.

Before setting off for the upper world, the shaman bade farewell to his native land [d. 7, l. 16]. He then acted out "riding" to the abode of the spirit that had sent the illness, hopping and beating the drum. The road to the upper world, according to the ideas of the Yakuts, was measured in levels [*olokhs*]. At each of these the shaman halted, asking permission of the owners "living" there to proceed further and sometimes making them an offering of a strand of horsehair, thrown onto the coals [Vitashevskii, 1918, p. 179].

Upon arriving at the destination of the seance, the shaman asked the captor to return the soul [*kut*] of the victim. If the spirits approved of the offerings, they would release it voluntarily. In some cases they would not hand over the soul, and the shaman would take it by force or by trickery. Having received or stolen the *kut* from the spirits, the shaman temporarily placed it in his ear and return home. This part of the ritual was a repetition of the upward journey, but in the other direction [AIV AN SSSR (LO), f. 22, op. 1, d. 7, l. 16; Ksenofontov, 1929a, pp. 60–61].

The shamanic seance to the lower world had much in common with the above description of an offering to the sky-dwelling *abaasy*. This ritual is described most fully for the northern Yakuts. Their shaman reached the underground world by "diving" into the ocean of death. The distance from the earth to the region of the lower world inhabited by the spirits of sickness was also measured in *olokhs*. Giving the cry of a loon, the shaman would descend to one *olokh* and then halt. At these stopping places, participants in the seance enacted a conversation with the captured spirit. In substance, these dialogues concur entirely with the above conversation between a shaman and a spirit of the upper world. The only difference is that the shaman and the spirit "conversed'' not in the middle world, but on the way to the habitation of the evil spirit. Curiously, the shaman ''descended'' into the ocean of death in the form of a loon, yet starting from the fourth *olokh* he began to beat the drum, when he was en route and thus ''riding'' it. ''Having arrived'' at the abode of the culprit, the shaman ''searched'' for and ''grabbed'' the *kut* of the patient, whereupon he ''set off'' for the middle world. He ''returned'' by riding: facing the south or the southeast, he acted out a fast ride and sang:

> My little lark,
> Flutter, fly up!
> My little bird,
> Chirp and twitter!

Thus, the *kut* of the victim is imagined to be a bird [Ksenofontov, 1931, pp. 135–40]. Everything the shaman sang on the homeward journey was repeated in chorus by all those present. The shamans of the central regions of Yakutia performed a seance to the spirits of the lower world in exactly the same manner [p. 142].

Upon return to the middle earth, the shaman ''shook'' the *kut* from his ear, with an appropriate incantation, and went to the patient's side to ''incorporate'' the soul in him [AIVAN SSSR (LO), f. 22, op. 1, d. 7, l. 17].

During a seance, the shaman demonstrated his ''strength.'' At times, this involved mere tricks, but along with them, Yakut shamans displayed ''miracles'' that may be explained as hypnotic suggestion. For example, it is reported that shamans '''uncovered' the ceiling of the yurt by waving a drum beater, so that snow began to fall'' [Arkhiv GO SSSR, r. 64, op. 1, d. 65, l. 294].[b] It is told how a shaman ''cut off'' his head and placed it at his side [Shchukin, 1833, p. 203]. According to the Yakuts, shamans sometimes embodied the *Keeleeni* spirit, of which several types were mentioned—for example, male and female *Keeleeni*. These were usually presented as limping and stuttering. Speaking for the *Keeleeni*, the shaman would ask various, sometimes indecent questions, which the bystanders were expected to answer in the negative. Basically, the *Keeleeni* was used as a character to divert the audience. But according to the documents of V. M. Ionov [1913], the *Keeleeni* ''rendered'' assistance to the shaman. They were summoned after the ritual of ''purification'' of the sitting place of the shaman, and not at the end of the seance. Shamans addressed them with the following prayer [*algys*]:

Quickly,
Here and there,
Let your smeared head be pointed,
Let your flaring tail be stretched out,
Catch the escaping one,
Hold the fleeing one.

In this connection, Ionov noted that the *Keeleeni* were sent to escort the spirits crossing over to the beyond, and would keep order, being in the ranks of the shaman's helpers [AIVAN SSSR (LO), f. 22, op. 1, d. 21, ll. 12–13].

At the end of the ritual, after the display of "miracles," shamans predicted the future [Ksenofontov, 1929a, p. 128].

The final event of the seance was the "seeing off" of the shaman's spirits. These were sent off like the other spirits, blowing them through the window, after first refreshing them (through the fire) with morsels of food, strands of horsehair, and sprinkled water [*Istoricheskie predaniia*, 1960, pp. 263–64]. The above seance description of a shamanic mystery for driving away sickness is only a general reconstruction of the rituals, demonstrating that the same canon was followed among the Yakuts.

The seance of the Yakut shaman was not only a frenzied dance, placing him in an ecstatic condition. It was essentially a multiact, dramatic, at times comedic event, not without its theatrical aspects, held in a definite sequence, and containing many incantations of "frightful" content, which were often delivered with eloquence. At times, these were poetic productions of high art.[3]

The influence of the ritual celebrant was also heightened by the setting in which the seance took place. Usually, it was held at night, with windows and doors shut, and barely flickering embers in the fireplace, i.e., in darkness. The rituals always took a long time. According to N. A. Vitashevskii, the preparatory part itself took up to two or three hours [1918, p. 167]. According to the testimony of many witnesses, shamanic mysteries lasted until morning or even two nights in a row.

The shaman's helper, and sometimes all those present, took part in the ritual. The impact of the actions of the celebrant was greatly augmented by the diversity of sounds produced from the drum and the jingling of iron pendants caused by unusual postures and movements.

As was discussed, those possessing the shamanic gift suffered from a neuropsychological illness.[c] The seance was for them a controlled neuropsychological seizure, during which they believed themselves to be confronting and struggling with fearful supernatural beings. Shamans, "fighting" with the spirit that was "possessing" the patient, went into trance, sometimes falling down and thrashing in convulsions, emitting shrieks, losing consciousness, and foaming at the mouth. This was considered to be the highest pitch of their ecstasy. Reviving, they told of their "visions." The grave nature of the seizure was a confirmation, in the eyes of believers, of the truth of their words, "evidence" of their encounter with invisible beings.

The actions of the shaman had such strong influence on the company that they sometimes induced a group neuropsychological attack. N. A. Vitashevskii has left a vivid description of such an event. He wrote that a shamanic seance on behalf of a sick infant, which he happened to attend, made a strong impression on many of the witnesses of the ritual. The attack first began in an old woman, then spread to several other women. Finally, the mother of the child joined in [1918, p. 200].

The validity of the interpretation of the shamanic mystery as a controlled mental seizure with strong action on the bystanders is also confirmed by descriptions of the shamanic seance by ordinary Russians (not scientists). According to one such report, during a "healing" ritual the patient trembled at each invocation of the celebrant, and then jumped up as though scalded, while the shaman fainted [Arkhiv GO SSSR, r. 64, op. 1, d. 65, ll. 303–6].

In their "healing" practice, some Yakut shamans resorted to hypnosis, bringing relief, naturally, only in certain nervous illnesses. In such cases, to be sure, autosuggestion in the patients, their belief in the "magical" gift of the healer able to expel supernatural beings making people suffer, also played a positive role.

The full seance was performed for serious illness. This would be done by the strongest of shamans. For trifling complaints, the rituals were simplified. For example, when treating a mild eye disorder, shamans confined themselves to summoning the spirits, and after a brief (about ten-minute) incantation, suddenly spit in the patient's eyes. The patient would start, causing the evil spirit to be frightened and leave him. As a result, the person would presumably be cured [Priklonskii, 1890, p. 42; Troshchanskii, 1904; Vitashevskii, 1918; Ksenofontov, 1931; and others].

## The Altaians

Materials published on Altaic shamanism unfortunately contain no complete record of the performance of the complex mysteries or any special investigation of this subject. The most interesting information was gathered by A. V. Anokhin. Thanks to him, as well as the data of other investigators, it is possible to describe in general outline the rituals of the Altaic shamans.

*The southern Altaians.* Examination of available materials reveals that the Altaic shamans dealt with the deities and spirits of the upper, lower, and middle worlds. The sacrifices to these beings had both common obligatory elements and others confined solely to this ethnic group. At the beginning of each religious ritual, the Altaians regaled the tutelary spirits of the given family and asked their blessing. The person celebrating the ritual sprinkled wine on the images of the spirits, which were present and worshipped in each community [*ail*], and pronounce the appropriate prayer. After this, a shaman or shamaness called upon their personal protector-spirits in turn. Most of the time, the shamans performed their actions "in dark of night, with the complete trappings of the shamanic ritual." During the encounter with the spirits, "that which they themselves or other spirits desire of the person" was revealed. In the conversation, the "protectors" gave "appropriate advice concerning further actions to conciliate the particular spirit." The shamans reported the results of the "negotiations" to the audience [Anokhin, 1924, pp. 28–29].

The cause of the illness or other misfortune discovered, the shaman told onlookers it was necessary to conciliate the spirit, to coax a return of the person's health. To achieve this goal, he set out for the abode of the spirit causing the harm. This could only be done with the help of protector-spirits. Therefore, the seance began by addressing them. In the invocations to the protector-spirits, shamans emphasized the magnificence of their supernatural allies in every detail. The shaman Polshtop, for example, addressed the spirits thus:

My moon and sun—*Shulmusy!*
The cloudy-eyed *Bura-Khan!*
*Bii-kizhi*, with the icy feet!
*Tai-Buura*, with the cloudy eyes!
The three pure and equal *dzhalbis!*
Never entering (the yurt), where in dying

You cut away my brightness (sky),
Three-stepped *Bai-Karshyt*!
My golden-edged *Ak D'aiyk*!
Three-horned *Kara Kaia* (black rock), My Altai!
*Ker Buura* of the milky lake!
The white stars in the whitening (sky)
Rain down from my White Father.
Let the piebald falcon screech before me.
Let the gray eagle give forth sound
Above my two shoulders.
*Chuiuk*, rushing with the *D'ezim* of the forest!

[Anokhin, 1924, p. 66]

Each spirit mentioned in the incantation had a definite purpose:
*Karshyt*, according to the Altaians, was the son of *Ul'gen*; *Ak D'aiyk*, a
celestial goddess, sent to earth by *Ul'gen* to protect mankind, and
therefore residing in each *ail*; *Kara Kaia*, the owner of the territory of
the clan *ochy*; *Chuiuk*, likened to a piebald falcon and a gray eagle, was
the protector of Polshtop, the chief of his long-dead shamanic ancestors
in the maternal line [Anokhin, 1924, pp. 65–66]. All of these assisted
Polshtop in his dealings "with the spirits of the sky and the underground world, the way to which is blocked by obstacles" [p. 29]. The
way to the upper world was accessible only to male shamans. But they
could reach only the fifth obstacle (*altyn kazyk*, or golden stake, as the
Altaians called the Pole Star). Here, the shaman and his helping beings
were met by *Utkuchi*, the messenger of *Ul'gen*. "He conveys the will
of *Ul'gen*, and then takes the sacrificed animal, which he leads through
the golden gates to the throne of *Ul'gen*. At the *altyn kazyk*, the shaman
receives geese [*kas*] from *Utkuchi*, on which he returns to earth with his
companions" [pp. 9, 14].

Actually, the role of the ancestral tutelary spirits and helpers was
more passive in the sacrifice to *Ul'gen* than in the dealings with the
spirits of sickness. This is related to the connection of the ritual with the
functions of priests of a tribal cult of tutelary deities. It seems these
were preserved, in part, among the Altaians, since Anokhin mentioned
"white" shamans [*ak kam*], not having a ritual costume and not making
supplications to *Erlik* [p. 33].

In event of sickness, epidemic, or other adversities, the faithful
would make an offering, through the shaman, to *Erlik*—the chief of the

evil spirits of the lower world. Anokhin reported that, in spite of their fear, the Altaians sacrificed "a lean and even sickly animal. The skin of the animal is not left on the pole, as is done for the other *tës* [spirits], but taken home. The poles, stakes, and wood used to construct the altar [*tailga*], on which portions of the sacrificed animal are hung, are chosen of poor quality, old and crooked. In order to reduce the appetite of *Erlik* in future, the *tailga* is sometimes set up around a dog-rose . . . , a hawthorn . . . , or a sea-buckthorn, which he fears, and is always arranged on the northern . . . less preferable side, at a distance from the community, beyond the fencing in a dark nook where the rubbish and carrion are discarded" [pp. 2–3].

A seance described by Anokhin began by treating the tutelary spirits of the family of the sick person. After this, the shaman addressed a prayer to *Erlik*:

> God created our shaggy heads,
> But *Erlik* took our skull . . .
> We make a sacrifice of this horse,
> These broad cloths of many colors, we bring them to you as ransom.
> We give you this excellent horse with a saddle-cushion.
> Let this our offering suffice.
> Let it be asked: will he (*Erlik*) make our heads healthy?
> For seven generations we have exalted (you)!
> Worshipped, prayed, beseeched you, our *tës* (*Erlik*),
> When *Erlik* is angered, our black heads also feel adversity.
> If this offering is sufficient,
> Let our heads be in peace.
> Oh magnificent *Erlik-bii*, you have your messengers—the *elchi baila*.

[Anokhin, 1924, pp. 84–85]

After this, the shaman summoned his personal protectors and "set out" for the lower world. On his journey, he was "helped" by his deceased shaman relatives, who have "turned" into spirits, the owner-spirits of the drum and the cap, *Diaiuchi* and *Suila*, as well as the sons of *Erlik*. The latter "acted" as intermediaries between the shaman and their father [pp. 7, 14, 28, and elsewhere].

On the way to *Erlik*, the shaman "overcame" seven obstacles, which he described very vividly. The first obstacle is:

A black stump—a fortune-telling place,
A large place, where one may learn of human life and death.
A black path, deep as the (saddle) poles,
A black path, along which the old ones gallop
A black game that the old ones play,

[Anokhin, 1924, p. 85]

The second obstacle was even more dismal:

A black playing field, quivering.
A square iron threshing floor;
A sacred four-faced anvil;
Black tongs, endlessly opening and closing;
A black ringing hammer,
Black moaning bellows—
The creation of my Father *Erlik*!
A place that takes the power from great shamans,
And the head from the poor shamans.
When he approves, at a favorable time,
Then we shall cross this open place,
This place where, at an inauspicious time,
One can lose one's head.

[Anokhin, 1924, pp. 85–86]

"Awaiting" the shaman and his supernatural helpers at the other obstacles were "black ravines, across which the voice could not carry," "swarms of black frogs," "swarms of black gluttons," "roaring black bears," "a boiling black lake, a boiling black hell," "a place where nine bulls fight against each other," and so forth [pp. 86–87]. At the last obstacle:

Pale gluttons,
With greenish legs.
The shore of a blue river,
The shore of *Toibodym*,
For worship . . . place of nine rivers.
*Umar-tymar* (is) the nine rivers worship place.
The river *Toibodym*

The mouth of nine rivers;
The shore of the mouth of the rivers
With a stone palace and the residence of the khan.
With a palace of black clay
Of *Kan Erlik*,
An iron hitching post, with pale head and chain.
Hook-wielding swimmers of *Erlik-bii* and goat-killing shooters,
Assembled at these doors.

[Anokhin, 1924, pp. 87–88]

Once arrived at *Erlik-khan*, the shaman negotiated with him:

Let this my sacrifice be handed to you,
Let my head be greeted!
Do not compel worship, looking behind you.
Always bestow your mercy.
I bow to my father *Erlik*
If I live three years in peace,
Another sacrifice will be sent (to you).
Even a good shaman is made powerless by you,
When your excellent mercy is sent,
Then we become gray, respected
(Elders, we live to old age).
Father *Erlik*, bestow your blessing!

[Anokhin, 1924, p. 88]

This concluded the "voyage" to the lower world.

Regrettably, Anokhin's record lacks a description of the return trip of the shaman to the middle world. There is an abrupt transition to an explanation of the actions of the shaman upon "arriving" at the *ail* where the ritual was held. The shaman accepted a pipe offered by the host and answered questions on the outcome of the seance. He then addressed the owner-spirit of the drum and the other personal protectors, thanking them, begging their favor, and dismissing them:

My bands created by god (protector-spirits)!
Disperse (as clouds disappear in the sky).
Shaggy band of my head,

Let the owner of the "bird cap" (also) go out.
With a hundred different kinds of braid,
Bands (protectors) of the clothing I wear,
Disperse,
Make your peace with the dreadful *tës*, my *Khan*.
The one called by my six forebears (*Abu-Khan*)!
Lean against *Abu-Khan*, the white dawn.
My fearsome shaman, *Kachy*-shaman!
You have given praise to the cruel, the exalted, the dreadful *Erlik*.
My (paternal) uncles: *Tiinesh*-shaman,
*Surdyk*-shaman, *Manysh*-shaman.
*Er-Saadak*-shaman, whose weapon is a bow:
*Këstëi*-shaman, with the drums and bells.
*Tosh*-shaman, with the sunshine
Against the cruel, the exalted and dreadful *Erlik*,
Until the dawn give praise!

[Anokhin, 1924, pp. 90–91]

While shamans protected people against the doings of *Erlik* by sacrifice, "ordinary" evil spirits were driven from the *ail* by means of the *aru kërmës*—the blood *kërmës*—spirits of dead relatives [pp. 26–27].

Altaic shamans performed rituals devoted to the spirits of the middle world, such as the owner of the Altai. This was done in the same way as the mysteries devoted to the sky-dwelling gods. First, the shaman addressed the fire-owner, *D'aiyk*, his ancestors, and so on. Next, he "set out" for the Altai. Once again, various obstacles along the way were overcome with the help of his own protectors [pp. 80–84].

The Altaians did not cut the animals intended for the spirits, but strangled them. If "an animal were killed in the ordinary manner, the *siur* would escape through its mouth and the sacrifice would not achieve its purpose" [Arkhiv AN SSSR, f. 202, op. 1, d. 20, l. 13].[d]

The materials of A. V. Anokhin on the rituals of Altaic shamanism are in many respects supplemented and corroborated by L. E. Karunovskaia's data. In her publications, she provided "a picture of the three parts of the universe: the sky, the earth, and the underground realm" and a detailed description of the itinerary of the shaman to the underground realm and *Temir-Khan*—one of the sons of *Erlik*; and in a second illustration, the route of the shaman to the region of *D'eri-Su* [Karunovskaia, 1935, pp. 160–83]. Commenting on the illustrations, she gives very interesting information on the types of offerings to the different spirits.

Thus, members of the *ëelip*, *modor*, *tandy*, *aara*, *mungol*, and *tërbët* clans would offer to *Bai-Ul'gen*, the son of *Kege Menke* (Eternal Blue Sky), "three buckets of fresh mare's milk or *chegen'*. On the next day, a light gray horse and white ram" (p. 175). To *D'eri-Su*—the chief deity of the middle world—they consecrated a chestnut horse, a white ram, *araka* [moonshine distilled from milk], milk, *chegen'*, and light-colored fabric [p. 164]. To *Erke Solton*, a son of *Erlik* inhabiting the ninth level of the underground realm, the faithful offered a black goat. The meat was consumed, while the bones were placed on a special altar made of pegs. The skin was used for various household purposes. These rituals were held in the winter [p. 178].

Concluding this description of the religious rituals of Altaian shamans, it should be mentioned that they were naturally of little effect. After these operations, recovery was rare. "The opposite can occur: the patient gets worse and worse. Yet he continues the treatment—shuttling from one sacrifice to another, from one *kërmës* to another. The praying is intensified and gradually the sacrifice increases in value. In such cases, a wealthy family will bring as many as seven cows in sacrifice, a poor one as many as five. But this norm, increased by need, sometimes leads the patient to total ruin" [Anokhin, 1924, p. 26].

The nocturnal mysteries of the shamans and shamanesses had much influence on the believers. "We chanced to observe a grim scene," writes Anokhin, "in the village of Saidys, when the shamaness Ëlëng-chi told the onlookers that the spirits are sending menace to her *ail* and intend death for one of the members of her family. Everyone was gripped with terror and broke into weeping" [p. 29].

## The Kumandin

According to the beliefs of the Kumandin, to prevent the evil supernatural beings from molesting people it was necessary to offer domestic animals in sacrifice. The same purpose was served by sprinkling with "beer [*braga*] made from barley or meal. The shaman 'treated' the impure spirits causing the illness to such beer, requiring them to return the soul [*iurgen-chula*] of the person. If the *kam* were shamanizing over a sick woman, he 'offered' seven cups of beer to the chief spirit of the underworld—*Erlik*, and if he were shamanizing over a man, nine cups of beer." The beer was offered as ransom for the victim's soul. Kumandin shamans appealed to *Ul'gen* and the clan tutelary spirits, soliciting success in the hunt, a good wheat harvest, health for the people, an increase in livestock, and so on. To these deities "they offered in sacrifice a horse of light bay, gray, light chestnut, or liver-chestnut coat" [pp. 160–61]. The ritual of the Kumandin "is little different from the sacrifices of the other Altaic tribes" and bears "a social clannish character. . . . A horse destined for sacrifice to the *aryg tës* (the good, pure gods) was held to be inviolate. It could not be used for working or riding; no woman could even touch it. With exogamous marriage, the woman was a stranger in the particular clan [*sëëk*]" [p. 161]. The Kumandin organized the performance of the ritual "in early spring, less often in the fall." Traces of a lingering cult of clan tutelary spirits are clearly evident here.

**The Khakass**

The most detailed record of the seance of Khakass shamans is that of N. F. Katanov in 1897. Curiously, the ritual was performed by the Koibal shaman Ulkan Aloktoev, and he was invited by the Sagai, Apchai Itpalin. Prior to the seance in the evening, a gelded white ram was slaughtered as directed by the shaman. The meat was cooked. Next, a high table was set up in the honored front corner of the yurt. The skin of the ram offered in sacrifice was spread on the table, and on top of this a white felt mat. The freshly cooked mutton was placed on this table in a wooden bowl, curds in another bowl, and *araka* in several vessels and bottles. The shaman ordered all bottles to be opened, explaining that the "vapor" from the food and drink would rise in offering to the spirits. In the southwestern portion of the yurt, a black felt mat was spread out for the shaman. On the south side of the yurt a rope was stretched, on which nine articles of clothing (shirts, shawls, belts) were hung. These also were an offering to the spirits. In the yard was tethered a consecrated horse [*yzykh*]—a steed offered while living as a sacrifice to the tutelary spirit of the clan and regarded as belonging to it. According to the custom, the horse was decorated with ribbons.

Prior to the seance, one of the participants dried the drum over the fire. At the start of the seance, the shaman Ulkan removed his shirt, and a shamanic fur coat was put on him. Ulkan put on the cap himself, and as of this moment (according to the Khakass) he was no longer an ordinary man, but became a person able to perform the offering to the spirits. The next operation in the ritual of the shaman Ulkan was the "treating" of the various spirits. For this, he was given a spoon and cup filled with "pure" *araka*, which none of the ordinary mortals had yet tasted. Taking the liquor, the shaman splashed some with a spoon, first into the fire (to the spirit-owner of the fire), then in the direction of the smoke hole of the yurt (to the spirit of the sky), and to the front corner (the spirit-owner of the yurt). After this, he moved in a circle, according to the path of the sun, and "treated" all the "owners" of the streams and mountains of the Sagai and Koibal steppes. After "feeding" the spirits, Ulkan performed a cup-prophesying ceremony. The point of this was that the soothsayer would throw the cup and depending on how it landed (bottom up or down) "determine" the outcome of the upcoming seance. Ulkan's cup landed with the bottom down, which was taken as a favorable forecast. The fortune-telling over, the shaman selected two from those present as his helpers. These were supposed to assist him where necessary during the seance. Next, Ulkan requested all those seated in the yurt not to sleep, for if they should fall asleep it would go hard with him in the course of the ceremony, especially when ascending mountain ranges. He then sat down on the black felt mat at the southwestern side of the yurt and, taking the drum in his left hand, the clapper in his right, began shamanizing. At first, he breathed in deeply and began to summon his helpers—the *testar*—for the "journey" through the mountains.

The entire ceremony lasted until 4:00 in the morning. The shaman spent very little time smoking tobacco and drinking water. There were five or six such intermissions in the course of the night, consuming eight to ten minutes. Mostly, the shaman sang verses addressed to the spirits—the mountain, the water, and the fire spirit. After each quatrain, he very skillfully caught his breath, in order to sing the next more easily. The faithful called such drawing in of air the "taking in of powers infused into the shaman by his helpers."

The incantations told about each spirit: where it lives and where it likes to relax, what horse it rides, what whip it uses to goad the horse, and which lake it uses to water the horse; what bedding it sleeps on and what blanket it covers itself with; what costume it wears and what hat; whom it protects and assists; what offerings are made to it and which horses, cows, and sheep are devoted to it; where it rides and where it feeds its horse. Should the shaman fail to accomplish this program, his efforts may not always succeed, as the spirit [*ezi*] would not be sufficiently persuaded and appeased.

During the seance, the shaman Ulkan appealed more often to the mountain spirit, since the ritual was dedicated to it. In the night, it was discovered that some of the women were asleep. The shaman woke them, striking each of them once with the drum beater.

The shaman took a drink of the liquor and thanked the host, proffering the traditional Khakass well-wishing: "'May you be long-lived and your clan prosper. Live (in happiness) until your black hairs become white! Let your home be filled with your descendants, and your yard filled with livestock! May your footsteps (on the path of life) be firm as the bark of trees, and the repulsing (of your enemies) as strong as iron.' In reply the host declared 'Choktanysh polzyn!'—let it be as you have said" [Katanov, 1897, p. 29].

Later, while delivering the third prayer to the mountain spirit, Ulkan requested everyone present to assist in the singing, and they all repeated after him in unison for nearly half an hour. They stopped singing when the shaman was "picking his way" up the last range, beyond which lived the spirit to whom the sacrifice was made. From this spirit, the shaman "learned" what must be done to protect the household and family of Apchai.

At the end of the seance, the shaman first divested himself of the cap, then put down the drum and beater, and finally took off his ritual costume. His regular coat [armyak] was put on him, and he told in verse of his return from the journey to the mountain-owner, loudly exhaling several times, by which he showed that he was "dismissing" his helper-spirits. The entire seance lasted five hours. In this time, Ulkan circled the yurt three times in the path of the sun. Katanov mentioned that, while invoking the fire-spirit, Ulkan "sat on the felt mat in front of the fire; addressing the mountain spirit, he walked around the fire, and addressing the water spirit, he stood in the yurt, facing south, since Abakan happened to be south of the yurt; he stood in front of the door of the yurt when it was necessary to call the mountain spirit and travel to it. In the latter case, the door was supposed to be open" [p. 30].

The faithful took an active part in performance of the ritual. Thus, when Ulkan reported that one person would soon die, they asked him whether it was possible to avert the misfortune. When Ulkan predicted something pleasant, the faithful would express their satisfaction [pp. 22–30].

Katanov observed another household sacrifice on July 10, 1896, in the yurt of the Sagai, Aleksandr Chertykov, living not far from the aforesaid Apchai Itpalin. The ceremony was conducted by the shamaness Sotkang, also a Koibal by descent. She was invited in connection with the sickness of an infant. The preparation for the ritual was basically the same as the seance of Ulkan. However, the amount of clothing suspended from the rope as a sacrifice was increased—not nine, but nine and seven. Furthermore, a special offering was prepared for the spirit-owner of the fire, to whom the horse was dedicated: seven small birch twigs, to each of which was attached a piece of lard and a strip of red and white fabric. Prior to the seance, the host fumigated the yurt with wild thyme. The staging of the ritual was nearly identical with the above. Katanov thought it necessary to mention that the shamaness was very decrepit—around seventy years old, leaning on a pole to walk, yet she shamanized from 10:30 at night until 3:15 in the morning. During the entire time, she drank water and liquor only once each and smoked three times. For performing the ritual, the shamaness was given the skin of the ram and the hind portion of its body [pp. 35–37].

## The Kachin

The operations and prayers of the Kachin shamans largely coincided with those of the Koibal. The ritual was also celebrated in the *ail* at night. The shaman sat down on a white felt mat, placed in the men's half of the *ail*. He fumigated his drum with wild thyme and dried it. Next, he summoned his personal helping spirits and "journeyed" to the beings who have brought harm on the family. During the seance, the shaman asked the "fire spirit" to be well disposed to him and praised the remarkable qualities of his helpers, which he regales with *araka*. In conclusion, he performs the cup soothsaying ceremony [Ostrovskikh, 1895, pp. 337, 342–47].

For deliverance from disease, Kachin shamans consecrated various animals to the spirits and made many sacred images. For example, a chestnut mare was devoted to the fire spirit. No one used the animal for riding [Katanov, 1907, pp. 547, 575]. The horse cult is perhaps a ceremony from the cult of clan protective spirits, transformed by shamanism. While previously the Kachin consecrated animals only to the protective deities of the clan and tribe, in the period of breakdown of clan relations they began to "bestow" a horse on any being "causing" a serious disease.

For minor ailments, the Kachin shamans would construct various sacred images [*tëstar*], in which were embodied the spirits believed to protect against the attack of various hostile beings (see photo). Of

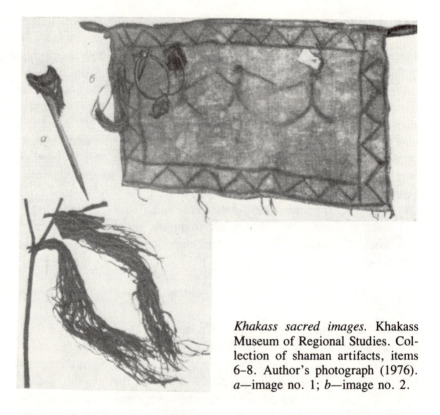

*Khakass sacred images.* Khakass Museum of Regional Studies. Collection of shaman artifacts, items 6-8. Author's photograph (1976). *a*—image no. 1; *b*—image no. 2.

these, there were "no less than twenty, and perhaps even more designations" [Ostrovskikh, 1895, p. 348].

## The Sagai

The shamans of the Sagai performed rituals the same as the other ethnic groups of the Khakass. Like the Kachin, they made use of images of the tutelary deities as a kind of icon [Katanov, 1907, pp. 594–96] (see photo).

## The Shor

According to S. E. Malov, the shamanizing of the Shor was incomprehensible: their singing, drowned out by the noise of the drum, in most cases could not be understood by those attending their mysteries. In cases of disease, the shamans conciliated the spirits by feeding a gruel to the "sacred puppets" [*kyzrak*], made from the skins of the squirrel, the weasel, and several kinds of bird. These images "were kept in barns and brought to the house only on the day of the shamanic seance. When rituals were performed with them, the Christian icons were turned against the wall or covered with a shawl" [Malov, 1909a, pp. 40–41].

## The Tuvinians

The Tuvinian shamanic cult was characterized by "various sacrifices conciliating the spirits and soliciting prosperity and success, extensive healing practices, prophesy, and soothsaying." The duties of the shaman included "establishing" a diagnosis, which was done during the seance, when thanks to his supernatural abilities he would "identify" the cause of the disease and attempt to cure the patient. During the cure, the shaman would either hunt for and return a soul that had "gone out from" the person, or he would drive an evil spirit from him [Potapov, 1969a, pp. 348–49]. This brief outline of the Tuvinian shamanic seance, provided by L. P. Potapov, coincides with the previous descriptions of shamanic rituals among other Turkic ethnic groups.

There is little specific information about the mysteries of the Tuvinian shamans. But what is available likewise testifies that the Tuvinians preserved a number of rituals common to the Turkic peoples. Thus, animals sacrificed to the spirits had to be killed by strangulation [Kon, 1904, pp. 22–25, 30]. Their shamans "embodied" their helping spirits in pendants on their costume and "animated" primary seance personages. For example:

> I, shaman, have summoned *Khoor-Albys*
>     (i.e., the spirit of the Khoor-Taiga mountain).
> Come down from the sky,
> Jump onto my head,
> Gather from every quarter (or from the entire universe).
> Play on my back,
> Come to the flint and the knife,
> Gaze through the universe,
> Watch from every part of the world,
> My (shamanic) cap of bird feathers.
> Let my colorful (with *ereni*) shamanic cape I have put on
> Suffice in the sky of *Kurbustan*.
> I have caught a chestnut horse (untamed?).
> Whirl like a mill wheel,
> Like a mirage, stretch forth far.

Light the red fire,
Strike out the fire-flame (with flint),
Stretch, my long body.
Let us strive in the race and the struggle.
Blow from every quarter (or here and there),
Soar with the whirlwind,
Riding on my shoulders,
Ring, o black bells!
Riding on my shoulder blades,
My bells forged of iron.

[Potapov, 1966, p. 53]

The "flint" and "knife" mentioned in this incantation were hung from the shamanic costume, and the "chestnut horse" is the drum. The Tuvinian shamans in their incantations also emphasized the power of their spirits in every way:

My spirits move with a rush,
They whisper (my spirits).
My *aza* (i.e., demon) with forked tongue,
None can outtalk his tongue.
Without disturbing the peaceful sleep of little children,
Do not frighten the livestock.

Or:

Soaring headlong,
With writing in the wing,
With a cipher in the feathers,
Having sat in the red blood,
Having flown in the sky,
My lean black raven,
Soaring, turning (in the air),
My hungry black raven,
Emissary (messenger) of the white and black (drums). . . .

[Potapov, 1960, p. 323]

At the turn of the century, the Tuvinian shamans took part in religious holidays consecrating livestock to spirits of the sacred clan games. These rituals belonged to an ancient preshamanic cult, which "among the Sayan-Altai peoples represented the clan ownership of the various lands (hunting territory, nomadic ranges, and pastures), existing in the past and preserved in places up to the beginning of our century" [Potapov, 1969a, p. 358].

## The Todzhin-Tuvinians

The operations of the Todzhin shaman in curing the sick are described by S. I. Vainshtein: "During the seance, which was held at the onset of darkness, the shaman placed himself in a condition of intense ecstasy. Supposedly, he consorted with the good spirits, relying on their help, overcame considerable difficulties, and eventually conquered the evil spirits. He reported every vicissitude of his struggle to the onlookers in his songs, which were accompanied by movements portraying scenes of battle" [1961, p. 189].

At the beginning of the mystery, the shaman said that the patient was possessed of an evil spirit in the form of a wolverine. He then startled him. The spirit fled, becoming a fish, and dived into the water. With the assistance of his helping spirits, the shaman pursued it, catching and eating it [p. 189].

In "struggling" with evil spirits, the shaman endeavored to convince onlookers that he was on excellent terms with the grim owners of the forest and the protector-spirits of the shaman:

> *Chavag-Bazhy*, greetings;
> *Sharash-Taiga*, greetings!
> Twin-headed with many [snow—S.V.] caps,
> Mighty gray *Sharash-Taiga*!
> Asking help and protection from my owners, from you,
> I call upon you all, all of you.
> White lakes, greetings!
> Eternal snows, greetings!
> Owners of my mountains and soul
> At the mouth of *Kadyr-Os*
> Wide-mouthed *taimens*,
> From you, my masters,
> I seek help.
>
> [Vainshtein, 1961, p. 190]

Sometimes the Tuvinian shamans fainted during the seance. At the conclusion of the ritual, the shaman told of his return from the "voyage" and performed divination with the drum beater or cup. The former was supposed to land with the concave part up, the latter on its bottom. In this case, the believers "would exclaim: '*tëërek*!!,' which signified a favorable outcome of the sickness" [pp. 190–91].

During the seance of the Todzhin shaman, the faithful were allowed to enter or leave the yurt [Raikov, 1898, p. 449].

## The Tofalars

There is almost no information on the seance of Tofalar shamans. N. F. Katanov mentions only that, in order to extricate a patient, they presented the owner-spirit of the mountains and waters with a reindeer or horse, which were also termed *ydyk*. "First the shaman shamanizes and says that such and such a horse or reindeer must be sacrificed, and then on the second evening, after the horse is sacrificed, he shamanizes again" [Katanov, 1907, p. 18].

*      *      *

Analysis of the data regarding the major elements of the shamanic seance of the Turkic peoples of Siberia at the turn of the century reveals that they performed the initial portion of the ritual alike. The shaman's helpers prepared everything necessary to the seance in advance—the offerings to the spirits, the drum, and the sitting mat. The shamans asked for help and blessing from the local spirit-owners: the fire spirit, the spirit-owner of the area, the tutelary spirits of the family. Then, they "explained" the cause of the illness. The complexity of the healing ritual depended on the "power" of the spirit that had "entered" the body of the patient or "captured" his soul. In the case of a minor ailment, caused by a "lesser" evil spirit, the shamans made do with a recitation of incantations and trifling presents and refreshment. When the illness was severe, the full seance was performed, lasting the entire night. This was a complicated many-act mystery, in which the shaman with the "help" of protector-spirits "caught" an evil spirit, performed a "journey" to the realms where supernatural beings "resided," and paid for the "return" of health and well-being. In making sacrifice, Siberian Turkic people killed the animal "without allowing" the soul to leave it, since it was necessary to catch it and take it to the country from which the spirit responsible for the misfortune had come. The mysteries of the shamans concluded with a "dismissal" of the helping spirits and a divination as to the result of the ritual. It should be noted that the shamans, in colorful incantations that sometimes achieve the level of superb works of poetry, would emphasize the power of their protector-spirits and describe the difficulty of the "obstacles" on the way to the spirits and their titanic struggle for the sake of rescuing and protecting people. The shamans were themselves believers in the existence of the various deities and spirits. During the seance, they seemingly did consort with invisible beings and visit the places of their "habitation." In performing the ritual, the shamans often went into a trance or an ecstatic state, losing consciousness. For them, the seance was often a controlled neuropsychological seizure. Consorting with the spirits during the rituals "was for the shaman himself a psychoneurotic discharge, allowing him to alleviate his illness" [Gurvich and Belenkin, 1978, p. 120].

Shamanic seances, held at night, did much harm to the health of the believers, already tired from strenuous labor, and kept them in fear of the powerful spirits. Indeed, fear and lack of knowledge of the actual causes of many diseases have always been the foundation of religious ideas and have intensified the religiosity of the masses. Analyzing the nature of war, Lenin wrote that tumultuous human feelings disrupt "the ordinary condition of the sleepy mind. . . . Horror and desperation. And therefore—intensification of religion. 'The churches are again full,' the reactionaries rejoice. 'Where there is suffering, there is also religion,' says the arch-reactionary Barres. And he is right" [vol. 26, pp. 290–91].

Efforts to systematize religious theories of a given ethnos were undertaken at a relatively early stage in the history of human society. This led to the separation of the officiants of the ceremonies into a special social group. Thus, among southern Siberian peoples, shamans may have appeared in the middle of the first millenium of our era [Vainshtein, 1961, p. 176]. From these, Turkic-speaking ethnic communities evidently inherited most of the shamanic rituals and beliefs. Alongside identical elements in the shamanic seances of Siberian Turkic peoples are features peculiar to individual ethnic communities. Among the Yakuts, examples include the ritual of "purification" of the sitting place of the shaman, and the depiction of the "voyage" to the lower world as a "diving into the ocean of death." Southern Altaians had a specific belief that the shaman could not reach the abode of *Ul'-gen*, situated on high, but only "ascended" to the fifth "obstacle" on the way thereto. According to the Altaians, the shaman was helped by celestial spirits, in addition to his deceased ancestors. The Todzhin shamans, after "catching" the evil spirit, "ate" him. Such specific elements might have arisen by evolution of the ancient rituals or been borrowed from a particular people, especially after the termination of cultural contacts with ethnic communities having common ancestors. The genesis of the ideas and rituals under diachronous scrutiny requires a comparative study of the religion of all peoples of Siberia.

# The Role of the Shaman
# in the Life of the
# Turkic-speaking Peoples of Siberia

According to the beliefs of Siberian Turkic people, supernatural beings could exist among people, although most people are not aware of their presence—this was possible only for those endowed with the ability to "see" and "hear" them. Such people were known as clairvoyants—*kerëëchchiu* (Yak.), *këspëkchiu* (Alt.). The shamans could also perceive the spirits. Unlike clairvoyants, they not only "discovered" unseen presences, but could also "enter into" contact with them—talk to them, drive them away, and so on. Accordingly, the shamans were quite important in the daily life of Siberian Turkic people.

## The Yakuts

In the seventeenth century, one of the distinct social strata of Yakut society consisted of officiants of religious ceremonies—shamans, known as *oiuun*, and shamanesses, *udagan*. The latter term, with similar meaning, existed among the Buryats and Mongols [Pekarskii, 1959, p. 2975]. According to the calculations of S. A. Tokarev, shamans made up three percent of the total number paying tribute [*yasak*] [1939, pp. 90–94], i.e., the adult males [1940, p. 65]. The number of Yakut shamanesses, according to V. L. Priklonskii, even exceeded the number of shamans [1886, p. 107].

Scattered reports indicate that Yakut shamans still took an active part in the social life of the seventeenth century. For example, they were among the initiators and leaders of the Yakut uprising of 1642 [Tokarev, 1939, p. 93].

By the end of the seventeenth century, shamans came under persecution by the tsarist authorities. In 1696, Yakuts were forbidden to hold seances in the city of Yakutsk itself or its environs, and Russians were forbidden to attend them [Popov, 1924, p. 114]. The ban on shamanism was apparently connected with the beginning of mass conversion of the Yakuts to Christianity. Despite the restrictions and persecutions, shamanism not only survived, but even strengthened its position. In an account of the Yakuts of the Yakut province "Concerning Their Laws and Customs," written for the "Regulations Concerning Non-Russian Nationalities (1822)," it was noted that "shamanism is still used by the greater portion of the Yakuts, although surreptitiously'' [Pekarskii, 1925, p. 677].*

The strength of Yakut shamanic influence is also witnessed by the fact that not only Yakuts, but even Russians believed in their ability to deal with supernatural powers. And not only the lower levels of the service class, but also officials of the tsarist administration had resort to shamans. In 1679, the military governor [*voevode*] Andrei Barnashev, learning of his imminent transfer, appealed to a shaman for help [Tokarev, 1939, p. 102]. V. L. Seroshevskii personally verified a report that the assistant district constable of Kolyma region was regularly seeing a shaman. He established that this was a locally born person, suffering from some kind of nervous attack, who traveled to Nizhne-Kolymsk ''at regular intervals and took a cure from the shamans there. The illness is not going away, but after each trip it is lessened'' [Arkhiv GO SSSR, f. 64, op. 1, d. 65, l. 294]. Cases are known of priests calling upon shamans in the event of illness. The custom of making an offering to local spirits when traveling was also widespread among the Russian service class and merchants [Priklonskii, 1886, pp. 91–92]. A very interesting fact is that Russian long-term residents still had their own shamans in the eighteenth century [Seroshevskii, 1896, p. 628].

No exact information exists on the total number of shamans active in Yakutia in the seventeenth to nineteenth centuries. We do have a report by N. P. Pripuzov: ''In the entire Western Kangalass *ulus*, a territory of 400 square *versts* and 20,000 inhabitants, there are no more than 10 shamans and shamanesses, and only one of them is thirty-five years old, all the others being elders'' [1884, p. 66]. It may be supposed that there were 100–120 shamans and shamanesses living in Yakutia at that time. However, Pripuzov could hardly have counted all the shamans and shamanesses of the Western Kangalass *ulus*. Surely, in the *uluses* far from Yakutsk, where qualified physicians were almost nonexistent, the sick were actively ministered to by their own healers, most of them shamans. The number of shamans was much larger than was entered on official documents.

According to the available information, social differences also existed among Yakut shamans: there were both rich and poor. All of these led the same lifestyle as other members of Yakut clans—raising livestock, hunting, and fishing. But shamans had an additional income—they were paid to perform the rituals, an additional share was allotted them in the collective fish catch, and so on. As S. A. Tokarev properly points out, the shamans had an unearned income, i.e., "in their class interests, they bordered on the exploitative *toion* class" [1939, p. 66].

In the past, each shaman ministered to immediate clan members, as well as all neighbors. The area of activity of the shaman was directly related to success. People traveled from very distant villages to see "famous" shamans. Their main function was "healing" people and livestock by performing ritual operations aimed at "expelling" or "conciliating" spirits causing illness. The shamans also performed rituals previously belonging to a hunting cult, cults of clan and tribe tutelary deities, and so on. These were carried out in the form of a customary shamanic seance with such aspects as "embodiment" of spirits, but many archaic elements characteristic of these cults were retained in these traditional religious performances. Thus, the ritual of "cutting the cord" had very ancient roots, belonging in the past to the duties of "white" shamans [Alekseev, 1969]. It was used by the faithful in cases when many children had died. Essentially, it involved tracing a triple circle on the floor of the yurt with the stick used to stir the fire in the hearth. The woman whose children were dying was girdled in three places with hides—around the waist, the hips, and the lower legs. She was then placed in the middle of the circle. The person performing this ritual dropped to his hands and knees and had the woman sit astride him, exclaiming "*Khalakhyia!*" After this, each girdle was cut in three places. These segments and the knife that was used were hidden in a secluded area of the forest [AIV AN SSSR (LO), f. 22, op. 1, d. 1, l. 135]. The shamans entirely adhered to an age-old procedure in this purely magical operation to simulate removal of supernatural obstructions preventing a woman from giving birth to healthy children. Only at the beginning of the ritual did the shamans summon their supernatural helpers.

As is well known, the shamans occupied the supreme position in the rituals of burial and the memorial cycle [Alekseev, 1975, p. 175].

The shamans ascribed to themselves the ability to "blight" people and livestock, i.e., send sickness and kill them. Information on this aspect of their activity, as Tokarev has established, is contained in seventeenth-century archival materials. One document mentions the shaman Deki, who was believed to have turned into a bear and killed Bulgui. Tokarev considered this episode to be based on "the actual fact of a bear attacking a man," which for some reason was imputed to the shaman [1939, p. 98]. Most of the frightening stories of people being "blighted" are probably based on threats by shamans and interpretation of individual accidents by the believers as the handiwork of malicious persons who had the ability to "eat" a human soul, *kut*.

According to V. M. Ionov, shamans could "help" rid someone of an unwelcome wife. Thus, the shaman Doiompo shamanized at the request of a certain person and dispatched the soul of his spouse to one of the roots of disease. Subsequently, she died of consumption [AIV AN SSSR (LO), f. 22, op. 1, d. 1, l. 121].

Those who suddenly fell ill or died shortly after a shaman's visit were usually counted as "victims" of the shaman. For example, two days after shamanizing over Feodos'ia, who had an eye disease, a two-year-old girl, never before sick, suddenly died with no apparent cause. It was decided that she had been "eaten" by the shaman performing the seance, who was somehow dissatisfied [AIV AN SSSR (LO), f. 22, op. 1, d. 19, l. 3].

All the shaman's tricks and "strategems" were believed to be done with the involvement of his helping spirits. The Yakuts had many myths concerning the power of those possessing the ability to "eat" people [Arkhiv GO SSSR, r. 64, op. 1, d. 65, l. 299; Ksenofontov, 1929a, p. 44; *Istoricheskie predaniia*, 1960, pp. 259–62; etc.]. Certain shamans were reputed to be able to inflict harm on women, others on children. Thus, it was said of the shaman Khosogoi that he liked to "eat" children. One of the legends about him relates: "Once, a woman nursing a child spent the night in his household. The hosts also had a child at the time. In the evening, at bedtime, the guest switched children, placing her daughter in the cradle of the hosts and their child in her own cradle. In the night, as though dreaming, the guest saw Khosogoi wave his drum beater three times in the direction of the cradle and bring it to his lips, whereupon something resembling sour cream flowed into his mouth. After this, the woman again switched children. Early next morning, the household was awakened by a heart-rending howl from the hosts' child. The child cried for a while and soon died. Khosogoi tried to vomit what he had swallowed in the night, but nothing came out. He then said: 'What has been eaten can never return. And my spirits have left me forever, being angry that I fed them my own child'" (as reported by the Yakut Nikolai Dmitrievich Ignat'ev, born 1932, village of 1-Zhemkon, Ordzhonikidze region, Yakut ASSR, 1982).

The efficacy of the shamanic imprecations is evidently explained by the differing physiological reaction of people in stress situations. According to observations of medical pathophysiologists, during stress "hormones necessary to and positively influencing the metabolism and the condition of the cardiovascular system enter the bloodstream in sufficient quantity for a person with an active, optimistic temperament. But all these processes react to the detriment of a person seized with panic, despair, and hesitation in such situations." The actions of the shaman in "blighting" people are an "antipsychotherapy—using mental processes to disorient, oppress, and render a person powerless." The application of antipsychotherapy resulted in psychological isolation of the subject of the attack. He felt himself "given over entirely to the power of the spirits summoned by the shaman to punish him. Suggestion would become autosuggestion. The feeling of fear and doom induced an unfavorable metabolism, paralyzing the will and reason to live, and all of this ultimately disrupted the course of the physiological processes in the organism. A blind and absolute trust in the fulfillment of every possible prediction and prophecy fettered the person's willpower, forcing him to behave in an uncharacteristic manner and make serious mistakes, possibly leading to a tragic outcome. And the victim would inescapably perish" [Sofronov, 1972, p. 119]. This last conclusion of the Yakut physician and psychiatrist D. D. Sofronov is perhaps overly categorical. According to Yakut beliefs, people were divided into those susceptible to the influence of spirits and shamans and those resistant to them. The former were known as persons with an "open body" [asagas etteekh], the latter with a "closed body." The people with an "open body" were easily susceptible to suggestion and might take ill from a shaman's imprecation or any other "dangerous" omen. Furthermore, certain people were said to have strong personal protector-spirits, which defended them against the wiles of the shamans and the spirits. This may be explained by the experience, handed down from generation to generation, of autogenic defense, when a person by autosuggestion mobilized latent body resources. The believer appealed to his protector-spirit, and the level of his conviction determined the strength of the self-defense against the influence of another's will (according to the author's field observations among a group of Viliuisk regions of the Yakut ASSR).

Predicting the future also came within the purview of the shaman.

This might not always have been charlatanism. Modern medicine "admits that precognition and prediction are entirely possible." They are based on utilizing the considerable amount of information a person unconsciously stores in latent memory. "Using means and methods known to them, shamans would place themselves in a state where the forgotten was remembered by the 'spirits.' Evidently, this was a state of self-hypnosis, while communication received from 'spirits' was the shaman's own experience of previously unnoticed or forgotten life situations and their relationships, floating to the surface in this state and providing the clue to solve a particular problem" [Sofronov, 1972, p. 120]. According to accounts of our informants, shamans were able to "find out" about the future or events that had occurred during a dream. Therefore, they were often requested to dream a magical dream. Such technique was effective not only in predicting the future, but also in reconstructing the course of past events: finding stolen objects, a drowned person, and so on. If the shaman's prediction came true, his prestige was enhanced. But it should not be forgotten that shamans were skillful in deflecting blame from themselves for an incorrect surmise, since each of their solutions was hedged with conditions that the clients had to fulfill. The chief of these was to keep the shaman's prediction a secret. After the Great Patriotic War [World War II], several of those returning from the front in the Upper Viliuisk region of Yakutia attributed their return to "visions" of the shaman Badyl, who was practicing in secret. Of course, no one can say how many of those called up to serve did not return, having been promised a lucky fate by him (according to the author's field observations in 1962).

In the past, Yakut shamanism embraced most of the vitally important aspects of their existence. The shamans had an extremely extensive practice. They confirmed a religious view of the surrounding world in every way and justified social oppression as the will of supernatural beings.

## The Altaians

Altaian shamans were invited to perform most of the vitally important religious ceremonies. There is no information on their numbers in the literature. It is known, however, that each *sëëk* [clan] had to have a shaman. Believers appealed to him "for help" in case of sickness, animal epidemics, and so on. Some of the social holidays previously belonging to a cult of clan tutelary spirits and a hunting cult often came to be performed under the guidance of shamans at the turn of the century. The shamans were also entrusted with sacrificing to the spirits when leaving the community [*ail*] on a hunting trip, when tracking or returning from a hunt in the forest, during the gathering of nuts, and so on [Anokhin, 1924, p. 28]. In addition, shamans engaged in prophesying, divination, and so on. They then employed means and methods characteristic of those whose profession was divination. The Altaians had the following groups of diviners: "*iarynchi* (divining from the burnt shoulderblade of a ram); *tël'gëchi* (divining by means of a small bow); *kol-kërëchi* (divining from the lines of the palm); *arbyshchi* (casting spells); *iadachi* (influencing the weather), and others" [Chanchibaeva, 1978, p. 96]. The faithful resorted to diviners in cases of minor importance, or as a temporary substitute for the shamans in their absence.

The profession of shamanism among the Altaians was combined with livestock raising. It never served as a primary livelihood. General Altaian conceptions of shamans were similar to those of the Yakuts, but each group had its own peculiarities.

*The Altai Kizhi.* During an expedition to the Altai in 1981, special attention was given to the problem of ascertaining the number of shamans practicing on territory being used by members of a single clan. Of course, members of other clans also resided in this region, although they were the minority. My primary assumption was that the average number of shamans ministering to the religious needs of the faithful should be identical in each region with an approximately equal number of inhabitants. Knowing the number of shamans in one clan, tribe, or community of neighbors, it should be possible to approximate the number of all Altaian shamans. For this it was necessary to collect data in the different regions of the Altai, selecting the most typical areas of settlement for each Altaian ethnic group. Of the villages where the Altaians (Altai Kizhi) live today, Beshpel'tir of the Shebalinsk region of the Gorno-Altai AO [Autonomous District] was chosen as a place where ethnic and cultural originality is basically preserved. The oldest native inhabitants remembered more than ten local shamans and shamanesses practicing in this region in 1900–30. Furthermore, myths regarding the powerful Telengit shamaness Kanaga, who "flew here" from Ulagan, and legends regarding the shaman Sarmas of Ongudai, about whom we received information during the expedition of 1979, were written down at Beshpel'tir. Of the local shamans and shaman-esses, four belonged to the *tongzhoan* clan, and three to the *mundus* clan. There was one shaman apiece in the *iuliup*, *chapty*, *kirgil*, and *ochy* clans. Of eleven persons engaged in shamanism, two were sha-manesses. In the words of the informants, the faithful at the turn of the century would invite any given shaman to perform the rituals, accord-ing to the ''abilities'' of each shaman.*f*

Many traditions, legends, and myths ''affirming'' the supernatural abilities and activities of shamans were current among the Altai Kizhi. Most common are tales about the combat between shamans and their ''blighting'' of people, their ''vengeance'' for insult done to them. In addition, the more informed told of legends about the death of shamans who violated ''established'' shamanic canons. In one case, a shaman was said to have died from shamanizing while wearing the ritual dress of a stronger shaman; in another case, from careless performance of a ritual. Our informants also told of the superstitious nature of the sha-mans themselves, their rivalries, greed, and so on (according to infor-mants K. T. Manyshev, N. A. Diadeev, M. S. Agyldaev and others).

**The Teleuts**

An effort was also made among the Teleuts living in Belov region of Kemerovo province to establish the number of active shamans in this locality at the turn of the century. At the village of Bekovo (on the Bochat river—the Bochat Teleuts according to Anokhin), we were told of a shaman and a shamaness from the *iuty* clan and two shamanesses from the *kraachy* clan. In the village of Shanda, there were two sha-mans practicing at the beginning of the century (the informants did not remember their clan affiliation). This means that six persons were engaged in shamanism in two villages separated by approximately 10 km. According to accounts of those familiar with olden times, these shamans held seances for the sick and took an active part in many community, clan, and family rituals: solicitation of prosperity, perfor-mance of the main religious rites involving cattle-raising and hunting, funerals (according to the Teleuts V. S. Khlopotina, P. U. Todyshev, K. A. Boksarin, and others).

Like the Yakuts, the Teleuts equated those ''possessing'' the gift of shamanism with evil spirits. These, also, were able to capture the *kut* (life force) of a person. If a person died after insulting a shaman, it was believed that the latter had killed him. According to the beliefs of the Teleuts, "a shaman [*kam*] could also devour a *kam* entirely, or only take away his ability to shamanize. For this, the stronger *kam* would capture and bind the double [*tyn bura*] of the other *kam* with the help of his spirits [*baina*]. The defeated *kam* would take ill and possibly die, unless he rejoined his double soon. This was a sort of competition between *kams*, about which there are many near-legendary tales" [Arkhiv AN SSSR (LO), f. 202, op. 1, d. 20, l. 10].

## The Kumandin

According to F. A. Satlaev, shamanism among the Kumandin at the beginning of the twentieth century bore a "clearly professional aspect." For their services, the shamans often received money or livestock. At their insistence, the best horses, cows, or sheep were slaughtered in sacrifice to the spirits. They would receive the best pieces of meat, as well as the skin of the sacrificed animal. "The annual quantity of livestock given in sacrifice to the spirits was many hundred head, thus inflicting a major loss on the Kumandin economy" [Satlaev, 1974, p. 158]. During the seance, the shamans intimidated the faithful with threats represented as coming from the spirits. Here is a specimen of such incantation:

> Your extinguished wood I will turn into coal,
> I will destroy everyone, the flint will strike fire somewhere!
> Do you think that the coat once worn can never be taken off?
> The horse once saddled never be unsaddled?
> Do you pay homage to *Erlik-bii*, who lives in the three pits?
> Or do you worship the brown-haired one (i.e., the Russian god)?
> Against (your) door the vengeful-headed
> *Kuug-Chadyg* will place his chin,
> Against (your) door I will drive the red fog (typhus)!

[Satlaev, 1974, p. 159]

According to Kumandin beliefs, shamans were able to capture a person's *kut* with the assistance of their helping spirits. Toward this end, they would place supernatural traps along the path to be traveled by the intended person. The shamans would resort to "abducting" another's *kut* in order to exchange it for the *kut* of their patient [AGAI, f. AM, d. 216, pp. 143–145, 259].[8]

The Kumandin believed that a shaman could also "destroy" another, weaker, shaman. Rather detailed information on the "battle" between Kumandin shamans has been recorded by V. Diosegi and F. A. Satlaev. Without dwelling on common Turkic aspects, I shall mention only the specific features of the myths and legends of shamanic rivalry attested by them. Apart from ordinary human motives for enmity between shamans (insult or humiliation of one by another), the Kumandin declared that a shaman could be urged to battle by protector-spirits if one of his ancestors had suffered "defeat" in the past by an ancestor of his rival. Curiously, according to Kumandin beliefs, a shaman could call upon the protector-spirits of persons in his presence for help in the duel. This occurred if a rival "attacked" the shaman during the course of a seance. Diosegi's and Satlaev's materials contain reports on the ability of shamans to "arrive" with malicious intent, through the water, under the ground, in the form of the moon, and so on. A number of myths and legends tell of a long-lasting feud between shamans, during which first one and then the other antagonist would gain the upper hand. This is evidently a reflection of the actual rivalry between two shamans who constantly plotted against each other. In such cases, the death of one of them would be interpreted as a victory of the other still living. Thus, the battle between Arklei and Sachin allegedly lasted five years, and only after this time did Arklei die [AGAI, f. AM, d. 216, ll. 117–18, 129–30, 257, etc.]. Basically, the legends about shamanic combats reflected a continual testing of the "powers" of the shamans by the faithful. V. N. Basilov is surely correct in considering that the shamans were expected constantly to prove their supernatural abilities (as communicated at a seminar of the Institute of Ethnography in April 1983). The many myths and legends created an aura about the shamans, emphasizing their possession of supernatural qualities and strengthening their influence on the life of the community.

## The Chelkan

The number of Chelkan shamans may have been considerable. Informant B. I. Pustogachev counted fourteen shamans and one shamaness whose seances he had witnessed. The range of functions of the Chelkan shamans was the same as that of the southern Altaians. For celebration of the rituals, the shamans received pieces of fabric, money, and furs. Besides refreshments, a portion of meat from livestock sacrificed to the spirits was allotted to the shaman. By custom, the shaman was given the chest and the meat from the back [ud'zha], around 10 kg, as well as liquor [araka].

Along with general Turkic details as to the performance of the rituals by the Chelkan shamans, reports that some of them were engaged in fraud were collected during an expedition. For example, the shaman Mamet during a seance ran outside into the yard, supposedly fighting with another hostile shaman. He returned covered in blood. But after the ritual, freshly tied intestines of a farm animal were found at the scene of the "combat" (all nomads made sausage of fresh blood, poured into intestines).

Myths and legends of the combat of shamans and instances of their doing harm to people by sorcery are also described among the Chelkan (reported by the Chelkans B. I. Pustogachev, S. P. Pustogachev, M. A. Kandarakova, D. S. Kuruskanova, and others).

## The Khakass

According to the traditional beliefs of the Khakass, it was held that "only the shamans could conciliate the spirits and ward off their spite by means of sacrifices and various ceremonies" [Ostrovskikh, 1895, p. 336]. At the end of the last century, the majority of the Khakass of Abakan, Askiz, and Melets districts, despite the spread of Christianity, remained faithful to older religious customs. Thus, "of 124 heads of families providing the investigators information on their annual household budget, 23 indicated an expenditure on the performance of shamanic rituals, alongside expenditures on Ortho- dox rites. This figure is, of course, much reduced, since few of the non-Russians, aware of the recent cases of persecution of shamans and of shamanism, would have provided the investigators with cor- rect information on this score" [Kuznetsov, Kulakov, 1898, p. 55]. At the time, efforts continued to ban the performance of clan prayers with cattle sacrifice to the spirits, but the shamans, despite the ban by missionaries, conducted religious festivals of the whole tribe "each year in June and July (until July 20th), and what is more, in full costume, in almost every administrative area [*ulus*] and even near the villages. They shamanize during these two months because, first, the nights are warm for holding a seance; second, the young rams essential for the household and mountain sacrifices are coming of age at this time; and third, from June through the 20th of July work on the fields has not yet begun'' [Katanov, 1897, p. 220]. By established custom, the shamans themselves asked no payment for officiating at the religious rituals [Potapov, 1981, p. 133]. But they were always given something, of course, since an offended shaman might later ''wreak'' harm. Among the Khakass, unwritten payment rules existed for shamanic services, handed down from one generation to another. Thus, for performance of a ritual sacrifice to the clan tutelary spirits, an officiant necessarily received the skins of all the sacrificed lambs, which would be as many as ten for a single prayer [Katanov, 1907, p. 593]. The faithful also showed their gratitude for a cure with money and bread [p. 586]. Despite the additional unearned income, not all shamans of the Khakass were wealthy. As noted by Ostrovskikh, they ''differ in no way from the ordinary faithful in their daily life . . . they do not live affluently, but in small and wretched yurts . . . and they are just as superstitious and ignorant as the others'' [1895, pp. 344–45]. But this did not prevent their being called in at various junctures. In the late nineteenth century, the range of functions of the Khakass shamans included ''healing'' the sick and performance of rituals involving worship of clan tutelary spirits.

## The Kachin

According to available data, the services of the shamans were employed in many situations. When changing residence because of frequent stillbirths, a seance was arranged to prevent evil spirits from moving with the owners of a yurt to the new abode (as reported by the Kachin Semen Fedorovich Kangashov, *ak-sokhy* clan, a teacher of history, born 1927, Arshanovo village, Altai region of the Khakass AO [Autonomous District], 1977). This custom was surely based on people's age-old experience. A change of residence often eliminates conditions responsible for disease—bad water, the direction and time of the prevailing winds, and so on, i.e., it would improve the microclimate, bringing about a normalization of living conditions.

These objective results received a religious interpretation: the people believed that the spirits remained at the old campsite.

It must be remarked that Kachin shamans were not entitled to conduct all the major religious rituals of the society. For example, up until the end of the nineteenth century the Kachin did not admit shamans "connected" with the spirits of the lower world to the festival of the "great offering to the sky," which only the men of a clan or tribe were allowed to attend [Ostrovskikh, 1895, p. 336].

The Khakass believed in the ability of those in control of the spirits to cause a person harm. Supposedly, they could "propose" to the evil spirit taking the soul of their enemy, instead of the soul of the person being shamanized over [p. 342]. Stories of this type were evidently concocted by the shamans themselves. Thus, the Kachin M. Inkezhekov, from an *ulus* on the river Bar, told P. Ostrovskikh of his dispute with a shaman over a woman. The aggrieved Inkezhekov, stealing into the shaman's yurt, slashed the skin of his drum. This was done on the basis of the common Turkic belief that the spirits would punish the owner for the spoiling of the drum. The shaman, learning of Inkezhekov's action, allegedly tried to "send" a sickness to him, "but two years have already passed without event" [p. 344]. Along with legends of shamans "blighting" ordinary people, traditions of the combat of shamans with each other were widespread among the Kachin. According to their ideas, the shaman was most vulnerable during sleep, since his *chula* sometimes left the body and might be caught by his rival [Potapov, 1981, p. 131].

**The Kyzyl**

For information on the role of the shaman in Kyzyl life, we present only that which is attested in greatest detail or is characteristic of that ethnic group. The Kyzyl, like the other Turkic groups of Siberia, believed in clairvoyants—*keriugzhi*. Such persons were able to see and know everything occurring "in a radius of fifty versts." Hence, they were called at the death of someone [AGME, f. 1, op. 2, d. 4, l. 152]. This was to "track" the wandering soul of the deceased through the middle world, until it departed for the land of the dead [Alekseev, 1980b, p. 221].

A cult of family-clan protectors is known to have been maintained somewhat independently among the Kyzyl. But shamanism had infiltrated it, and shamans were said to best perform the complicated rituals. Only they could "handle" *Tongazy-tës*—a spirit able to send "all kinds of disease to a person. It is hard to deal with him, and therefore essential to summon a *kam* . . ." [AGME, f. 1, op. 1, d. 4, l. 150]. One of the *tës* formed under the influence of shamanism was *Kara-chaga*. Its image, in the form of a shirt, was made by the shaman himself in event of serious illness of one of the members of the patient's family [AGME, f. 1, op. 2, d. 4, l. 151].[h]

**The Sagai**

The shamans of this ethnic group were also called upon to perform difficult religious rituals, to "heal" the sick, and so forth. They enjoyed prestige in the community, while also inducing a feeling of fear and concealed hatred. Like the spirits, the shamans could wreak harm on people, and many misfortunes were attributed to their wiles. Interestingly, the Sagai believed it was possible to intercept such "activity" of the shamans. Toward this end, the Sagai invited a different shaman and asked him to "go" to the protector-spirit of shamans to complain about the "antics of the evil shaman." After holding a seance, the shamanic protector-spirits could "censure" the guilty one, as the Sagai believed. While the case was "pending," the evil shaman might fall into a sleep lasting seven or nine days. The Sagai believed that only shamans who had received their gift from the chief of the shamanic protector-spirit could be subjected to "trial." Shamans called by mountain protector-spirits were not subject to such a "proceeding" [AIE AN SSSR (LO), f. K-V, op. 1, d. 475, l. 5].[i] Perhaps it was believed that the clan shamans would not engage in unmerited "blighting" of people. The appearance of a belief in the punishment of evil shamans doubtlessly reflects a formation process of a common ethnic Sagai shamanism, the development of a rather orderly hierarchy of shamanic spirits, and establishment of rules of conduct among the shamans.

Myths and legends of combat between shamans were very common among the Sagai. It was said that "they may fight in the form of a stallion, a bear, or the spirit '*punchakh*' (the owner of a noose that chokes people)" [AIE AN SSSR (LO), f. K-V, op. 1, d. 475, l. 12]. These legends, beyond question, played an important part in strengthening the prestige of the shamans.

Concluding the description of the role of the shamans in the life of the Khakass ethnic groups, we note that the faithful considered it possible to invite any shaman at all: the Sagai could resort to a Koibal shaman, and *vice versa* [Katanov, 1897, pp. 22, 37]. Khakass shaman-ism at the turn of the century was basically intertribal.

**The Shor**

Each clan of the Shor had its own officiants of the traditional rituals, and shamanism retained its stature, despite the Christianization of the population. According to S. E. Malov, a considerable number of peo-ple possessed the gift of consorting with supernatural beings. By his observations, "almost every settlement has its shaman or shamaness, to whom the native may quickly, easily, and conveniently appeal for help with life's various adversities" [Malov, 1909, p. 38]. Certain of these were famed "for their skill over entire territories." Malov gave the names of two shamanesses and four shamans enjoying celebrity among the faithful. These observations are supported by N. P. Dyren-kova's materials. Dyrenkova emphasizes that a seance is held on each of life's occasions: difficult birth, conducting the deceased to the other world, and so on. Rituals were performed in event of success and misfortune. The Shor marked a successful hunt and a good harvest with a shamanic seance. The shaman was also called when the autumn wind knocked down the paling on which sheaves were hung for drying, or other accidents. But the principal duty of the shaman was the "healing" of the sick [AIE AN SSSR (LO), f. 3, op. 2, d. 61, ll. 17–18]. At each shamanic seance, an offering was made to the spirits and refreshment was given to the shaman. In addition, he was paid for performance of the rituals. Thus, A. V. Anokhin writes that, in the morning of the day after a seance, prior to a shaman's departure, the hosts "slaughter a horse and cook the meat, but not all: the heart, lungs, liver, three largest ribs, head, and tongue. The remainder of the meat is divided between the *kam* and the host. The *kam* is given the soft meat and the intestines, filled with blood" [AIE AN SSSR (LO), f. 11, op. 1, d. 101, ll. 27–27 ob.].

The people believed that shamans, if they so desired, caused harm to those not offering them refreshment, and that they were in constant rivalry with each other [ll. 12, 41–42; f. 3, op. 2, d. 61, ll. 1–3]. Stories about the wiles of the Shor shamans are similar to common Turkic legends and myths. For example, the legend of the shaman Apys tells how his wife was jealous of his mythical wife, the drum's spirit-owner. Apys revealed her to his "untrusting" spouse, whereupon the latter died, and he "left" the living for the upper world [AIE AN SSSR, f. 3, op. 2, d. 61, ll. 1–3].

On the whole, the shamans occupied a privileged position among the

Shor, ordinary believers holding them in awe. It should be noted that the Shor believed it possible to appeal to the shaman of a different ethnos for assistance. Thus, in one of the myths, a hunter who has fallen sick is helped by a Sagai shamaness, who happened to be flying by (as reported by the Shor E. N. Apanasova).

## The Tuvinians

Lamaism was planted in Tuva in the seventeenth century. It did not become the major religion of the Tuvinians, since shamanism was widespread among them. Lamaist deities did not replace the age-old gods and spirits of the Tuvinians, but "took their place alongside them, increasing the pantheon, while the *soiot* continues to feel himself in the power of the same spirits that his ancestors believed populated the universe" [Grumm-Grzhimailo, 1926, p. 133]. The apostles of Buddhism attempted to extirpate the traditional Tuvinian religious rituals, but did not succeed. In the late nineteenth century, the Tuvinian beliefs presented a "strange mixture of Lamaism and shamanism" [Kon, 1903, pp. 22–23]. Nor was it uncommon for a shaman to be a lama [AGME, f. 1, op. 2, d. 341, l. 3]. N. L. Zhukovskaia has conducted careful research in this field [1977, pp. 90–174].

The number of shamans in Tuva was considerable. According to V. P. D'iakonova, there were more of these than lamas in certain *khoshuns*. For example, at the *khoshun* Sëë Khemsik in 1934, 139 lamas and 163 shamans were counted; at Rach'"p, 92 and 112, respectively [D'iakonova, 1981b, pp. 129–30].

According to L. P. Potapov, "shamanism was dominant in the complex of religious beliefs, especially among average Tuvinians, having absorbed the most ancient magico-religious ideas" [1969a, p. 346]. By the early twentieth century, shamanism had become a professional occupation. It was characterized by "various sacrifices to propitiate the spirits and solicit prosperity and success, extensive curative practice, prophesy, and divination" [p. 348]. Shamans also conducted prayers at the sacred places [*obons*] [Katanov, 1907, p. 81]. Their "duties" included "conducting" the dead to the afterlife and "guarding" "relatives from various distress the deceased might cause them before going to the beyond" [D'iakonova, 1975, p. 42].

According to Tuvinian beliefs, those endowed with the gift of dealing with the supernatural could send a spirit [*puk*] against a person, producing disease. F. Ia. Kon records an account of the powerful shaman Shagdyr. Should he say that he would release his spirits against someone, even another shaman, "they would not have a minute of rest. The apparition sent by him would shamanize in the opponent's yurt, at times moving objects in the yurt around (this *puk* seems to exist outside the person possessed by it)" [Kon, 1904, p. 25]. The Tuvinians, like the Yakuts, believed that even a long-dead shaman could cause a person harm. This may account for the following, recorded by Kon: "A shaman, holding a seance over a wealthy *soiot* (Tuvinian) official who was sick, ordered that the bones of the deceased relatives of the sick man and those of the shaman whom they had consulted when living should be burned, and this instruction was carried out" [AGME, f. 1, op. 2, d. 341, l. 11 ob.].

## The Todzhin-Tuvinians

According to S. A. Vainshtein, shamanism was completely preserved among this ethnic group at the start of the twentieth century. "The functions of the shamans included primarily 'healing' the sick, finding lost objects and domestic animals, predicting the future, consecrating and 'healing' domestic animals" [Vainshtein, 1961, p. 186]. They held seances in the event of an unsuccessful hunt and performed the rituals of the burial cult (according to reports of the Todzhin-Tuvinians Kaastai Khurtuzhekovich Ak, *dag tozhuzu* clan, born 1903; Monkurg Chachakovich Ak, *ulug-dag* clan, born 1906, First of May *sovkhoz*; and Saiytgyk Erelchinovna Kol, *khem sumon* clan, born 1900, Adyr-Kezhig village, Todzhin region of the Tuvinian ASSR, 1977). As Vainshtein noted, shamans received pay for their "work." Thus, during a memorial banquet, only the breast from the sacrificed animal's carcass was "given" to supernatural beings. The remainder of the meat was taken by the officiant of the ritual for "escorting" the deceased, "purifying" the residence, and so on. It was often necessary to sacrifice domesticated reindeer to the spirits when "healing" the sick. For example, the shaman would say to the relatives of the sick person: "The sickness is deep. Bring a white reindeer with a black spot. Slaughter it, cut out the place with the dark spot and throw this meat into the fire, so that the *aza* will leave the patient and go into the meat." Thus, Mungu Saryg, a poor reindeer-breeder, shortly before the death of his wife in 1914, was forced to give one reindeer to the shaman in payment for a seance to heal her, and slaughter another in sacrifice to the spirits on the shaman's advice. The consecration of animals—reindeer and horses—which could not then be used for work or slaughtered for meat, undermined the economic position of the impoverished households [Vainshtein, 1961, pp. 191–92].

## The Tofalars

Shamanism was also a professional occupation among the Tofalars. Those who controlled "supernatural beings would 'heal' the sick and perform offerings to honor the owners of the mountains" [Katanov, 1891, p. 3]. These involved onerous expenses. In consecrating a horse to the mountain spirit, for example, the householder making the offering was obliged to find a horse of the color "demanded" by the spirit-owner of the mountain through the person of the shaman. The horse would be sought among the Tofalars, the Buryats, and the Russians: "The owner of the horse, guessing the bonds that tied his merchandise to the buyer, would ask an outrageous price. But even if you overpay, you must buy it where you find it" [Petri, 1928, p. 38].

*    *    *

Thus, shamans at the turn of the century held an important place in the life of all the Turkic peoples. They "healed" the sick and performed the main rituals of the formerly independent cults of clan tutelary spirits, the hunt, and burial. Turkic peoples of Siberia believed that these persons, supposedly endowed with supernatural abilities, could send sickness or even death to their enemies.

Analysis of documents on shamanism among the Turkic peoples of Siberia reveals that it had become their primary form of religion and had assumed an intertribal nature. Shamans received payment for performance of rituals and inflicted a substantial material loss on the poorer classes, compelling them to sacrifice livestock to the spirits. It is hard to assess how much moral decline of the Turkic peoples of Siberia was caused by the shamans, who were part of the exploitative stratum of their society.

But the shamans did not enjoy the full right to lead all the traditional religious rituals of the Turkic peoples of Siberia. Thus, even up until the twentieth century, shamans of Khakhass ethnic groups were not permitted to take part in the principal ritual of the tribal protectors' cult—the "great sacrifice to the sky." It is interesting that Yakut shamans, while officiating at sacrifices to disease spirits, formerly were not admitted to the ritual segment of the *ysyakh* festival, which was devoted to the common deities of the tribe, the *aiyy* [Arkhiv GO SSSR, r. 64, op. 1, d. 65, l. 318].[j]

# Conclusion

Generalizing from available information on the animism of the Turkic-speaking peoples of Siberia, their concepts of the upper realm appear to be based on ancient Turkic ancestral views. Ancient, because "religion always preserves a certain stock of ideas inherited from former times, since tradition is a great conservative force in all areas of ideology" [Marx, Engels, vol. 21, p. 315]. And religion, of all the numerous and diverse "nonlanguage" complexes of culture, generally exhibits "the greatest degree of 'rigidity' in the relationship of its individual components" [Bromlei, 1973, p. 59]. That is why archaic cosmogonic myths in the religious creeds of Siberian Turkic peoples, possibly going back to beliefs of a substratum population of Siberia, became interwoven with more recent beliefs regarding the creator-deities. Thus, all Siberian Turkic peoples have preserved elements of the worship of the sky, sun, moon, stars, the Great Bear, Venus, and so on. Alongside these existed a perception of the sky as a world inhabited by supernatural beings, comprising (like humans) individual tribes engaged in raising of livestock and the like. The dwellers of the upper world were regarded as the owners of the soul [*kut*] of humans and animals. They were viewed as deities capable of providing humans with happiness and prosperity and of defense from sickness and misfortune, if they so desired. Siberian Turkic ancestors evidently called these deities the "creators." The original variant of the term "deities"—creators—is apparently preserved among the Yakuts and the Khakass: *aiyylar* (Yak.) and *d'aiaglar* (Khak.). This same term is the derivation of the name of the Altaic deity: *D'aiyk*—the creating one. Analysis of materials concerning worship of the deities of the upper world reveals that they were not merely good, as is often affirmed by students of the religion of Siberian peoples. The deities of the upper world were able to provide humans with a prosperous life, but it also lay within their power to deny everything, thereby dooming people to poverty and disease. In the early stage of worship of the sky-dwelling deities, they were regarded as beings antagonistic to the spirits of the lower world, and when the latter appeared in the middle world the celestial beings would pursue them with thunderbolts. At the same time, in Siberian Turkic beliefs, the inhabitants of the upper world themselves became the cause of sickness and misfortune to humans when visiting the middle world, i.e., they became evil spirits.

General ancient Siberian Turkic ideas regarding the upper world underwent significant change during the evolution of their religious beliefs. At the turn of the last century, many peculiar features belonging to particular nationalities and ethnic groups existed in the ideas of Siberian Turkic peoples regarding the celestial deities. Thus, among the Yakuts alone, they were divided into two ranks of being—the *aiyy* and the *abaasy*. Originally, these two groups of deities were primarily the protectors of individual clans or tribes. In this period, the ideas concerning the chief of the *aiyy* deities began to merge with the Christian understanding of god. Folklore indicates that rituals in honor of the *aiyy* were in ancient times celebrated by the priests of a clan cult and had the nature of a propitiatory offering. Shamans dealing with the spirits of the lower world were not even allowed to attend clan rituals devoted to *aiyy* deities.

Alongside the *aiyy* (according to the Yakuts), in the upper world lived the numerous tribes of the *abaasy*, led by *Uluu toion*—formerly the spirit-owner of the Lena painted rocks. He and his sons were worshipped as protector-deities of some of the Yakut clans. Possibly *Azhirai uluu toion* was the chief of the pantheon of gods of the *Kurykan* tribe, who prior to moving to the present territory of Central Yakutia dwelt around the Lena painted rocks. The Yakuts offered sacrifice to this deity in the form of a shamanic seance. "Great" Yakut shamans were said to receive their gift from *Uluu toion*.

The Buryat component in Yakut ancestry is evidently the reason for ranking *Khoro tanar*—the protector of the Khora-Yakuts—with the deities of the upper world. He is sometimes represented as an eagle, i.e., the totem of the Khora clans was an eagle. Curiously, there was also an eagle among the *aiyy* gods—*Khotoi aiyy*. This apparently comes from the widespread worship of the eagle as the totem of various Siberian peoples.

Generalizing from available data regarding the Southern Altaic conceptions of the supernatural beings inhabiting the upper world, they appear to combine elements deriving from their ancient ancestors with beliefs belonging to a more recent stage in the genesis of animistic ideas. Thus, the worship of *Ul'gen* as the creator of the earth is similar to the Yakut conceptions of *Iuriung aiyy toion*. In the past, evidently, clan chiefs or venerable elders celebrated common tribal and clan offerings to *Ul'gen*. Southern Altaic shamans were more active than Yakut shamans in "asserting themselves" into the commonly held cult of the creator-deities—the *aiyy* (Yak.) and the *d'aiychu* (Alt.). In the first place, at the turn of this century they performed the rituals of this cult with the ''help'' of special mediator-spirits: *D'aiyk*, *Suila*, and *Utkuchi*. The first of these is genetically descended from the worship of the common Turkic protector-goddess, who gives children their *kut*. She is mentioned in the Yenisei-Orkhon inscriptions of the sixth to eighth centuries [Alekseev, 1980b, p. 307]. In shamanism, the functions of *D'aiyk* were significantly altered. She was ascribed the ability to assist shamans in appealing to the inhabitants of the upper world. Concepts of *Suila* and *Utkuchi* were evidently formed among the Southern Altaians at a later time than the belief in *D'aiyk*, since no such beliefs are found among the Yakuts. In the second place, the sons of *Ul'gen* were regarded as clan protectors, whom shamans summoned for assistance during the seance. The addition of these spirits to the sons of *Ul'gen* is the result of creative mythologizing by shamans, who arbitrarily affiliated spirits worshipped by different ethnic groups. The shamans assigned a less active role to the daughters of *Ul'gen*, and did not include them among their helping spirits. According to the data of A. V. Anokhin collected among the Teleuts, the daughters of *Ul'gen* themselves protected people against danger. Of the celestial deities, only their head—*Ul'gen*—was worshipped by all clans of the Altaians. Originally, he was also a deity exclusive to the Turkic clans living in the Altai in pre-Mongolian time [Tokarev, 1947, p. 145].

Teleut beliefs preserve a worship of the god *Tatai*, who was the owner of hail, thunder, and rain. Evidently, *Tatai* was an ancient Kirghiz and Buryat god. They still have the exclamation "*O tatai!*," which S. M. Abramzon (on Kirghiz) and T. M. Mikhailov (on Buryats) associate with the ancient, forgotten deity *Tatai* [Abramzon, 1971, p. 298; Mikhailov, 1980, p. 173]. On this basis, Mikhailov concludes that *Tatai* was worshipped by common Turkic and Mongol ancestors. It should be added that the exclamation "*At tatai*" in the same capacity as an expression of wonder, alarm, or indignation, also exists among the Yakuts [Pekarskii, 1959, vol. 1, pp. 310–11; vol. 3, pp. 260–62]. Perhaps among Yakut ancestors were also tribes worshipping *Tatai*, who may be assigned to the ancient common Turkic pantheon formed prior to the tenth century—the time when the Kirghiz and Yakuts departed from the main mass of Turkic peoples of Southern Siberia. Thus traces of *Tatai* worship among Buryats may be attributed to the Turkic component of their ancestry. Only if elements of *Tatai* worship were found among other Mongolian-speaking nations could the latter be regarded as a deity of the common ancestors of the Turkic peoples and Mongols, as surmised by Mikhailov [1980, p. 173].

The Kumandin, like the Southern Altaians, acknowledged *Ul'gen* as the chief of the celestial gods, but considered him the protector for clans of Southern Altaic (Teleut) origin. Some of the Kumandin deities also derive from the pantheons of celestial beings of the Tubalar, Chelkan, and Shor. Only the Kumandin have an attested myth of the marriage of an earthly shaman with a daughter of *Ul'gen* and the ensuing birth of the spirits *Kocho*, *Kurultai*, and *Kelei*. The ideas of the Tubalar and Chelkan about the upper world are evidently similar to the Kumandin.

Among the Khakass, like the Altaians, shamans were granted the ability to visit the upper world by means of helping spirits. But the genesis of ideas concerning these spirits was evidently different from that in Altaic shamanism. The Khakass shamans were able to "rise" into the upper realm if their helping spirits included a cuckoo, which enhanced the "magical" gift of the shaman. Other secondary spirits also helped the shaman into the upper realm during the seance.

The ideas of the Shor regarding the upper realm were more similar to the Altaians than the Khakass. Thus, in the opinion of I. A. Khlopina, the Shor borrowed the ritual of sacrificing to *Ul'gen* from their neighbors, the Altaians. Analysis of the available data reveals that the Shor transformed the ancient image of the common Turkic creator-god to suit themselves. They assigned him the recruitment of shamanic candidates: *Ul'gen* himself indicates future shamans by placing a mark on them in the form of a supernumerary bone, and only with his permission are the shamans able to construct their drums; *Ul'gen* "provides" the shamans with mythical horses for "journeying" to the upper world. The shamans appealed to *Ul'gen* through their clan protector-spirits. Curiously, *Sary Chalyg*, *Dzhangyraktu d'azhyzy kan*, and *Kanym* were ranked among the deities of the upper world by the Shor. These were also worshipped by the Kumandin. *Chalyg* (*Shalyg*) was the protector-spirit of the hunt, *Kanym* the owner-spirit of the forest. Possibly these deities were worshipped by common Shor and Kumandin local ancestors, given that ethnogenetic contacts between them were asserted more than once by L. P. Potapov.

Tuvinian shamanistic beliefs reveal elements common to the Altaians: the persecution of evil spirits with thunderbolts, the worship of *D'aiyk* as the chief helping spirit of the shamans, and so on. Alongside these, the Tuvinians had beliefs concerning the upper world exclusive to themselves. Thus, they and no other nationality believed that the gift of shamanism could be obtained from the sky through the spirit-owners of the rainbow. The beliefs of the Tofalars as to the upper world are virtually unstudied.

On the whole, the complex of ideas of the Turkic-speaking peoples of Siberia, although having a common ancient basis, was extremely complicated and had very specific elements, peculiar to the particular ethnic and local groups. In all likelihood, these were formed in more recent stages of the history of Siberian peoples.

Comparative study of the beliefs of Turkic-speaking Siberians regarding the lower world reveals, again, the presence of similar concepts, possibly inherited from common ancestors. Thus, all ethnic groups of Turkic Siberians viewed the lower world as largely identical to the middle world. It had its own mountains and rivers, the inhabitants of that country had yurts [*ails*], were engaged in livestock raising, experienced sickness and happiness, and so forth. But their world was less well organized, and gloomy and strange to the average person. In ancient times, it was considered the place where people went after death. The spirits of the lower world, according to the beliefs of Turkic Siberians, might appear in the middle world in the form of invisible spirits and occasionally harm people. But persons accidentally entering the lower world while living would also become evil spirits to its inhabitants. However, significant differences existed in the complex of beliefs as to the lower world among Turkic-speaking Siberians. The Yakut did not know of *Erlik*, worshipped by all the Altai-Sayan Turkic-speaking ethnic groups and the Mongolian-speaking nationalities as the sovereign of the underground kingdom [Mikhailov, 1980, p. 170]. Incidentally, his penetration into the religion of the aborigines of Southern Siberia occurred rather early, since mention of him has been found in the ancient Turkic runic inscriptions (Kliashtornyi, 1976, p. 266]. The lack of worship of *Erlik* among the Yakuts is possibly related to their early breakaway from the main mass of Southern Siberian Turkic peoples. Such an hypothesis has been advanced by Turkologist-linguists. In the opinion of N. A. Baskakov, the Yakut language separated from the Uigur-Oghuz group of languages in the fifth century A.D., thereafter developing on its own [1962, p. 53]. A. M. Shcherbak conjectured that the Yakuts became isolated from similar-speaking peoples prior to the seventh century A.D. [1962, p. 11].[4] Evidently, the borrowing by the Turkic Siberians of *Erlik-khan*, whose image was formed among the ancient Mongolian population of Central Asia (Purevzhav, 1975, cited in [Mikhailov, 1980,

p. 170]), took place after the seventh century A.D., when the Turkic-speaking ancestors of the Yakuts lost their ethnic and cultural contacts with similar-speaking peoples. At this time, it is plausible that the penetration of Buddhism to ancient Turkic peoples began. This is indicated by such facts as the following: in the Uigur Buddhistic cultural remains, *Yama*—the judge and ruler of the other world—is called *Erlen-khan (Erlik)* [ibid., p. 168].

Examination of the beliefs regarding *Erlik*'s children and the children of *Arsan Duolai*—the chief of the seven clans of evil spirits, residing (according to the Yakut) in the lower world—reveals them to be dissimilar in many respects. According to Yakut mythology, the inhabitants of the lower world are singularly hostile to normal people and, if appearing in the middle world, become invisible to them and cause them misfortune, sickness, and death. The spirits of the lower world obeyed only shamans, "trained" in their world. Among Southern Altaians, *Erlik*'s servants could also steal a person's *kut*, but at the same time the sons of *Erlik* patronized certain clans and protected them against attack by hostile spirits. In the beliefs of the Khakass and the Shor, *Erlik* gave their shamans helping spirits, which assisted them in the struggle with the supernatural beings sending sickness to a patient, regardless of the origin of the spirits responsible for the harm. Perhaps these specific features in ideas about lower world spirits resulted from late ethnocultural contacts of Turkic-speaking peoples of Siberia who had common ancestors.

Scrutiny of the details in conceptions of the lower world characteristic of particular ethnic and local groups makes it possible to discern how the belief in its existence came about. Careful study of groups of spirits of different Turkic peoples reveals that the identical spirit might be assigned to different worlds. Thus, the Southern Altaians regarded *Kara-Kusha* as the son of *Ul'gen*, living in the upper world. He was regarded as the protector-deity of several Southern Altaic clans. The Kumandin ranked the spirit *Kyrgys-khan* among the sons of *Ul'gen*. But the Shor regarded *Kara-Kusha* and *Kyrgys-khan* as the sons of *Erlik*. This contradiction may be explained, given that protector-deities of alien clans were ranked with hostile spirits, who were regarded as beings of the lower world.

According to the beliefs of Turkic Siberians, the earth—the middle world—was populated not just by people, animals, birds, i.e., real creatures. In addition, numerous spirit-owners of lakes, rivers, mountains, localities, individual objects, and natural phenomena "resided" here. The genesis of these supernatural personages is connected with the formation of early forms of religion—totemism, the deification of the surrounding world, with the hunting cult and cults of preclass society. These continued to be worshipped right up to the beginning of the twentieth century [Alekseev, 1980b]. Shamans automatically included them in the range of their activity, "enlisting" the local spirits as auxiliary helpers. All Turkic Siberians professed a belief in the might of the shamans, who could "influence" spirits of the middle world better than ordinary people. The shamanic sphere of activity included "wrestling" with the inhabitants of the other worlds, who were granted the ability to exist on earth and cause people various trouble. Only the shamans could prevail against them, thanks to the assistance of their helping spirits and protector-spirits. The latter were said to compel those capable of becoming a shaman to undertake the duty of mediating between humans and the spirits. Once the candidate consented to become a shaman, they would become constant allies in the struggle with hostile supernatural beings and other shamans.

Data concerning shamanic spirits reveal that Turkic Siberians had common ideas regarding the chief protector-spirit of the shaman. This was usually the spirit of a recently deceased shaman, one of the blood relatives of the novice. Among the Altaians, the Kachin, and the Tuvinians, the chief shamanic protector-spirit was the spirit of the ancestral mountain. Similar to this were Yakut beliefs that the primary protector of the shaman might be a lesser-rank celestial deity; Kachin ideas concerning shamans who were patronized by a sky spirit; and the belief of the Todzhin-Tuvinians in the bestowal of the gift of shamanism by the spirit-owner of the taiga which, like the sacred ancestral mountain, was the center of a clan and tribal protector cult. Possibly, these common ideas pertain to an early archaic stratum of Turkic Siberian belief, when shamanism was clan-based. As it became a class religion, emphasis was placed on an ancestral cult of the shamans, who were able to deal not just with clan spirits proper, as was done among the common ancestors of the Turkic-speaking peoples of Siberia. The acknowledgment by all Turkic Siberians of the drum as a magical steed is a legacy from them.

In ancient times, the shamanic drum apparently turned into a wild animal—an elk, a maral (stag), and so on, which "served" the shaman as a means of locomotion. But with the transition to livestock raising, the drum came to be the shaman's horse.

The gradation of shamans into "great," "average," and "weak," which existed among all Siberian peoples, evidently belongs to an early stage of shamanic evolution. The power of the shamans was dictated by the numbers and might of the helping spirits belonging to them. Substantial disparities are found concerning these kinds of animistic ideas of the Turkic-speaking peoples of Siberia. Thus, exclusive to the Yakuts was the belief that each shaman has an *iie-kyyl* (beast-mother), a supernatural being who is sometimes involved in the upbringing of the shamanic *kut*, but is considered to be the shaman's magical double. All misfortunes happening to the *iie-kyyl* were instantly reflected in its master. Such a mythological formulation was common among the Evenk. Its incorporation by the Yakuts is evidently the result of their ethnocultural interaction.

The Southern Altaic shamans dealt with the spirits of the upper world only when helped by the spirits *D'aiyk* and *Suila*, who were sent to earth by *Ul'gen* to protect humans. In the upper world, the shaman was helped by the spirit *Utkuchi*—the mediator between humans and *Ul'gen*. The Southern Altaic shamans descended to the lower world with the help of *Erlik*'s sons. Also "ranked" with the shamanic spirits were deceased relatives who had once been shamans.

A distinguishing feature of Kumandin shamanism is the enlisting of the "dwellers" of the upper and lower worlds to take part in the seance as helping spirits. The Kumandin had a specific belief that shamans possessed celestial horses with which they could journey to the spirits of the upper world, and mythical horses to visit remote places in the middle and the subterranean worlds.

Very singular, but not mutually contradicting ideas have been identified among the Khakass ethnic groups. Thus, protector-spirits of Kachin shamans were the "owners" of the sacred clan mountains. The chief of these was the spirit of Mount Karatag in the Karasyn range. The latter, according to L. P. Potapov, is mentioned in the Yenisei runic inscription on the Kemchik-kai rock [1981, p. 128]. In Sagai beliefs, a recently deceased ancestor, formerly a shaman, became the protector-spirit of a shaman. The new shaman was provided with protector-spirits by *Erlik* and *Ul'gen*. Investigators of Khakass shamanism have succeeded in ascertaining two different horizons here. Among the Kachin, survivals of archaic beliefs of shamanism have been found going back to the cult of clan and tribal tutelary spirits, while a modernization of the conceptions of *Ul'gen* and *Erlik*, formerly regarded as the chiefs of clan tutelary spirits, can be identified among the Sagai. The shamans assigned them the duty of appointing helping spirits. Unfortunately, the fragmentary evidence does not allow a complete elucidation of the views of Khakass ethnic groups regarding shamanic spirits or an accurate clarification of their genesis.

It should be mentioned that Sagai ideas as to spirits belonging to shamans have much in common with the Shor. A curious feature of the animistic ideas of the Shor was the belief that the drum-owner could be the supernatural wife of the shaman.

In Tuvinian animism, V. P. D'iakonova found direct parallels with the Southern Altaians. This includes acknowledgment of *D'aiyk* as the chief helper in the seance to the upper world, the existence of shamans with a protector-spirit in the form of the "owner" of the ancestral sacred mountain and a now-deceased ancestor-shaman.

Among the Todzhin-Tuvinians, judging from the available and by no means complete data, there was no worship of *D'aiyk*. Only the common Turkic ideas as to shamans' helping spirits are in evidence.

Thus, Turkic Siberians have preserved a common ancient stratum of belief in protector-spirits and helpers of shamans, which has been variously transformed in the course of the subsequent development of their historical destinies. A common tendency was formation of a cult of deceased shamans, whose intercession allowed ritual officiants to establish contact with various spirits. The shamans of the Turkic Siberians adapted themselves in many ways to the rituals of early religious forms, imputing new functions to the old deities and convincing the faithful that they were best able to deal with the spirits of all three worlds, by virtue of possessing mighty servants in the form of supernatural beings. The different treatment of the mythical personages associated with the ancient cults also testifies to a relatively later formation of shamanism as a form of religion.

The separation of shamans into a separate social group is doubtless connected with a late phase in the evolution of shamanism and its establishment as the major form of religion of the Turkic-speaking peoples of Siberia. Originally, shamans differed from the mass of their fellows in being possessed by a certain illness, manifested as a disruption of the normal course of life and the influence of certain supernatural beings. Lenin has said that "the frailty of the savage in the struggle with nature gives rise to a belief in gods, devils, miracles, and so forth" [vol. 12, p. 142]. The sufferings of future shamans, like all other diseases, were explained as an attack by spirits. The distinguishing feature of this type of suffering was the possibility of regulating the disease process by controlling a deliberately induced seizure—the autosuggestion seance of the shaman. V. P. D'iakonova is evidently correct  in writing that a group of people characterized by a type of nervous system predisposed to "shamanic" illness was bred for many years [1981b, p. 135]. Those suffering from this complaint not only were able to alleviate it during performance of the rituals, but also frequently mastered a natural hypnotism, allowing them to cure some of their patients.

The "shamanic" illness was hereditary and could be passed along either the father's or the mother's line among Turkic Siberians. Psychological aberration and abnormal behavior of the future shaman were interpreted in different ways. According to the Yakuts, a person occasionally became senseless because his *kut* had been taken by the spirits for "training" and was undergoing various tortures. Southern Turkic Siberians explained fits of insanity of the future shaman as persecution by spirits, requiring his consent to become a shaman. Exclusive to the Tuvinians was the belief that "shamanic" illness began with a rainbow alighting on the person.

After "ascertaining" the shamanic nature of an illness, a person attempted to perform shamanic rituals. Naturally, if any sort of alleviation occurred, he would be convinced of the necessity of becoming a shaman. Siberian shamans elaborated a stereotype for the performance of the shamanic seance, combining recitation of invocations and spells with ritual actions. Various accoutrements were required for the performance. Initially, future shamans employed simple articles invested with religious meaning—a small bow, a linen rag tied to a pole, a drum beater, and so forth.

The most complicated and well-known of the shaman's accoutrements were the drum and the costume, which had developed over a long historical period. Shamanic drums of the Turkic Siberians that are preserved in museums have various shapes—evidently the result of relatively recent ethnocultural contacts. Thus, Yakut and Evenk drums belong to one type, while those of Turkic Southern Siberians have a different appearance. The distinguishing feature of the drums of a number of Turkic ethnic groups is the presence of various images of sacral character. Without going into a circumstantial analysis of the symbolism of these pictures, it should be noted that they were a kind of "calling card" of the shaman, depicting the kinds and number of helping spirits belonging to the shaman and representing scenes from the mythical world.

Most of the few shamanic costumes of Turkic Siberians that are in museum collections date to the turn of the century. Archeological data are extremely sparse; only a single shamanic burial of the eighteenth century has been excavated in Yakutia [Konstantinov, 1971, pp. 41–42]. Because of the fragmentary evidence, only tentative conclusions can be drawn as to the origin of shamanic accoutrements. The absence of a ritual shamanic costume among the Kumandin and the Shor, and the different shapes of pendants on shamanic capes of the Southern Altaians, Khakass, Tuvinians, and Yakuts, testify that special shamanic garb either was a late development or experienced a radical evolution. The archaic use of the costume when shamanizing is indicated by the common Turkic perception of it as a symbolic bird, into which the shaman is transformed while performing the ritual. At the same time, the ritual dress of Turkic Siberian shamans was different even within individual ethnic groups. The shape of the pendants depended on the "power" of the shaman; the number and appearance of the items in the costume differed in each specimen. This aspect of the subject is virtually unstudied. A detailed inventory of all shamanic costumes preserved in museums would enable a characterization of the variations within ethnic groups, which is essential in identifying elements resulting from the various contacts with members of other ethnoses or genetic links.

Preparation of a shaman's basic personal accoutrements was a community event, taking place as a cycle of rituals for the entire clan, with active involvement of the faithful. In performing these rituals, people learned of the advent of a new shaman. It should be noted that, while induction among the Southern Siberian shamans took the form of a ritual of "animation" of the shamanic drum, among the Yakuts at the turn of the century a special group seance was held under the direction of an experienced shaman, who "introduced" the novice to the world of spirits.

 Shamans played a significant role in the life of the Turkic Siberians. From the beginning, they were separated from the common mass as a special group of people, able to enter into personal contact with spirits causing illness and performing rituals that alleviated the actual suffering and certain kinds of illness of humans and animals while carrying out the "will" of the spirits. It must be noted that Turkic Siberians had a rather sophisticated folk medicine. Their healers knew the curative properties of plants, were able to fix dislocations, set bones, and perform at times extremely complicated surgical operations. Quite often shamans and shamanesses were well versed in techniques of folk medicine. This, of course, increased the number of patients cured by them. Of no small importance in their success was adept use of hypnosis and a kind of psychotherapy, mobilizing the will of the patients and directing it to strengthen the body's resistance. The sphere of operations of the shamans gradually widened. They came to be consulted not only for the "healing" of illness, but also in such cases where the customary sacrifices did not "satisfy" tutelary clan spirits. In this way, shamans came to monopolize the functions of the principal officiants of the most important rituals of the cult of clan and tribal tutelary spirits, the hunting cult, and the funerary cult. Accordingly, their social role was greatly augmented. They maintained the legitimacy of economic inequality among clan members, explaining it as the will of the gods. Receiving a sizable payment for a seance, the shamans caused great losses, especially to the poor, by compelling them to make numerous sacrifices of livestock to the spirits. "To be sure, in all religions repentance, sacrifice, and even self-sacrifice (if possible) constitute the very essence of worship and cult" [Marx, Engels, vol. 6, p. 372].

Despite the diversity of rituals performed by shamans, a definite stereotype can be discerned in their execution. In uncomplicated cases, they would pronounce an incantation and make a minor offering. The form of these rituals coincided with the usual offerings to the spirits as performed by all believers. Exclusive to the shaman was the seance—a complicated mystery involving summons to spirits, employment of special accoutrements, and so forth. The order of a seance was identical among Turkic Siberians. Prior to each shamanic seance, a certain preparatory procedure was carried out (invitation of the shaman, manufacture of spirit images, selection of the animal sacrifice, etc.). The ritual itself was performed only at night—from sunset until sunrise. At the beginning, the shaman addressed the local spirits, then summoned his supernatural allies and "identified" the cause of the illness or misfortune with their participation. Next, the shaman either expelled the spirit possessing the patient or journeyed to spirits that had stolen the person's *kut*, conciliated them, and regained possession of it. Upon his return from the spirits, the shaman incorporated the *kut* into the patient. At the end of the ritual, the shaman dismissed his spirits and performed a divination regarding the outcome of the illness. In practice, the shamanic seance was a many-act, colorful, and in some degree theatrical performance. The somber incantations, the descriptions of laborious struggle with hostile spirits—often being refined poetic productions, accompanied by the sound of the drum and the ringing of metallic ornaments—exerted a tremendous influence on the participants of the ritual and confirmed the existence of spirits for believers. It should be emphasized that the shamans themselves believed in the authenticity of their reported dealings with spirits and presumably encountered them face to face. Autosuggestion and hypnosis played an important part in the seance.

The performance of the seance according to a uniform script, the common stylized incantation formulas, and other features existing among Turkic-speaking Siberian peoples may have been inherited from the peoples of Southern Siberia, where shamans may be presumed to have separated into a special social group in the middle of the first century A.D. [Vainshtein, 1961, p. 176]. The features of the seance characteristic of particular ethnic groups resulted from the later evolution of shamanism.

### Editor's Notes

a. The acronym refers to Arkhiv Instituta Vostokovedeniia Akademii Nauk, Leningrad [Institute of Eastern Studies]. Archival references usually include numbers for the *fond* [collection]; *opis'* [guide]; *delo* [document]; and *listy* [pages]. A reverse-side page has *ob.* after the page number.

b. Arkhiv Geograficheskogo Obshchestva [Geographical Society of the Soviet Union], *razriad* [section] 64.

c. This interpretation of neuropsychological illness is widely debated. See the Basilov chapter in this book, and J. Silverman, "Shamans and Acute Schizophrenia," *American Anthropologist*, 1967, vol. 69, pp. 21-31.

d. Arkhiv Akademii Nauk (of the Soviet Union).

e. Alekseev's view that Russian Orthodox conversions were only partially successful is supported by much historical data, including accounts of missionaries. See Iu. Dzhuliani, "O Iakutakh," *Syn Otechestva*, vol. 101, no. 28 (Moscow, 1836); Ksenofontov (1929) and T. V. Zherebina, *Religioznyi synkretizm* (aftoreferat) (Moscow, 1983). See also S. Kan, ed., for a special issue on Christianity in the North, *Arctic Anthropology*, 1987, vol. 24, no. 1.

f. At the turn of the century there was a particularly dramatic religious movement among the Altai Kizhi called Burkhanism, combining shamanic and Lamaist ideas in a new syncretic revitalization, explicitly rejecting Russian Orthodoxy. See L. Krader, "A Nativistic Movement in Western Siberia," *American Anthropologist*, 1956, vol. 58, pp. 282–92; L. I. Sherstova, *Altai Kizhi v kontse XIX–nachale XX v.* (aftoreferat) (Leningrad: Nauka, 1985).

g. Arkhiv Gorno-Altaiskogo Instituta (an Academy of Sciences institute of history, language, and literature).

h. Arkhiv Gosudarstvennogo Muzeia Etnografii Narodov SSSR (archive of the State Museum of Ethnography of the Peoples of the USSR, in Leningrad).

i. Arkhiv Instituta Etnografii (of the Academy of Sciences, Leningrad).

j. In modern form, this *ysyakh* festival is still celebrated in late June, with the start of summer and availability of fermented mare's milk [*kumys*].

## Notes

1. A metaphoric expression in which the human soul is compared to a piece of sacred soil.

2. The *olokh* was a place reached on the shaman's "journey" to the upper or lower world without beforehand stopping to rest. A weak shaman could ascend or descend a distance of three *olokhs*, a strong one nine. Spirits lived at the *olokhs*. The shaman rested at each *olokh*, asking local spirits permission to continue the journey.

3. Shamanic incantations, prayers, imprecations, and the like are a part of Yakut ritual poetry and deserve a special study.

4. See [Konstantinov, 1975, pp. 140–46] for more details.

Translated by Ronald Radzai

# Tuvan Shamanic Folklore

MONGUSH B. KENIN-LOPSAN

Oral folklore has great importance in studying early forms of religious beliefs. The shamanic worldview found expression not only in rituals, but also in folklore. During their seances, Tuvan shamans "voyaged" in the "subterranean" world, the "celestial" world, and the "middle" world, populated by people. The shamans told their listeners of their impressions and actions. It might be said that shamans created worlds through words. Yet shamanic poetry has not yet been investigated as a part of Tuvan folklore.

Folk memory preserves the names of certain authors of shamanic verses, but most of the shamanic texts are anonymous. Indeed, among the shamans were both genuine masters of poetic speech and their imitators. But since shamanic folklore developed in the context of religious tradition, distinct individuality of authorship was not an essential condition for creation. Therefore, the specimens of shamanic folklore that we have recorded at varying times and from different people exhibit mostly typical and similar features. Our task at the present stage is to discover the main themes of shamanic poetry and to analyze their plots and style.

## Composition of the curative seance

The seance—a collective ritual event—was a kind of creative laboratory for the shaman. Verses were conceived during the seance. Examining shamanic texts, we see that the seance is a complex and well-structured event, where one can discern a prologue, exposition, plot, author's digression, culmination, dénouement, and epilogue. This scheme would have varying degrees of completeness in different rituals. The duration of the seance could also vary.

Russian text © 1987 by "Nauka" Publishers. *Obriadovaia praktika i fol'klor tuvinskogo shamanstva Konets XIX–nachalo XX v.* (Novosibirsk: Nauka, 1987, pp. 89–151, 157–63. A publication of the Institute of History, Philology, and Philosophy, Siberian Division, USSR Academy of Sciences.

## Prologue

The curative seance was generally held at the onset of night and before daybreak. After the shaman attired himself in his ritual costume, he took up his drum and rattle, performed the ritual of fumigation with juniper, and began to imitate quietly the voices of birds and beasts—crows, ravens, magpies, eagle-owls, wolves, and bears, so as to select the proper sound for the anaphora or refrain, choose a definite rhythm for the verses, and find the central word or thought that would become the means of healing the patient.[a]

As our informants report, at the start of the seance the shaman spoke of his shamanic duty, of himself. In this way, he introduced himself to the patient and the listeners. For example:

*Aiym, khunym chaazynda*
*Aldai tangdym aldyn o"du—*
*Aldy kyrlyg artysh-bile*
*Aramailap sangym salgash,*
*Artyzhanyp-artyzhanyp,*
*A"ttanyptym, tonnanyptym.*

*Chakpalyg-la charnym chaiyp,*
*Sannaashtyp-la bazhym chainyp,*
*Keuzuldur-le kheureem chaiyp,*
*Keurgen karaam keurup, shiiip,*
*Argalyktyg moinum sunup,*
*Attyg digesh adap keldim.*

(Recorded from Saaia Sambuu)

As my moon, my sun began to rise
I burned the golden herb of my wondrous mountain—
The six-jointed juniper—
Fumigating myself.
And carefully refreshing myself with its aroma,
I then mounted my steed and donned my cloak.

And now I am galloping with my shoulder blades,
Nodding my head with the bird feathers,
Opening and closing the all-seeing eyes,
And dropping my neck in a bow.
And so I come to that which has a name, and so I come to this
    that has become known.

## Search for the cause of sickness

After telling the audience of his duty to help the sick and describing his abilities, the shaman tried to explain the cause of the sickness. He "mingled" with his spirits, psychologically preparing the patient for the upcoming emotional strain, encouraging him, and creating a "case history of the disease." All of this served as a kind of exposition for the "cure." The shaman would say something like the following:

> *Ashpas arty, chuge ashkan?*
> *Keshpes khemni chuge keshken?*
> *Ishpes shemni chuge ishken?*
> *Ketpes khepti chuge ketken?*
>
> (Recorded from Kyrgysa Biurbiu)

> Why did he cross the pass, to where he durst not go?
> Why swim the river, where he durst not swim?
> Why eat the food, which he durst not eat?
> Why wear the clothes, which he durst not wear?

In these lines we see a reflection of the views of the Tuvinians that each person has his own path, swerving from which meant destruction, as well as a special attitude to rivers, passes, and certain kinds of food and clothing. In the present case, the shaman found that the patient committed four "sins," failing to observe the traditional rules, and therefore fell sick. A number of seances would now have to be held to "cleanse" the patient from his "sins."

## The plot of the seance

The shaman "found" the cause of the sickness with the help of his helper-spirits, whom he "dispatched" into various parts of the world. Returning from a lengthy voyage, they were supposed to tell their master everything they had learned.

> *Kaiyyn yndyg bolgulaaryl,*
> *Kaigyyl kylyp choruptaaly,*
> *Changgys chovag kaiaa kalbas,*
> *Chakpalygny chadyptaaly.*

*Kheurlug-Taiga baary chedir*
*Khandyr-sundur choruum-na bar,*
*Kalgyp orungar, chaiaannarym!*
*Karai tyrtyp keurgesh keliil.*
*Kara cherning keugun seukken*
*Kalchan keuktu munupkai-la.*
*Deushtug cherning keugun seukken*
*Keunggur keuktu munupkai-la.*
*Kandyg-kandyg didir siler?*
*Kham-na irem chugaalangar.*
*Kham-na yiash kilengneen-dir.*
*Khaazhylyg ka"ttar edee*
*Kara-dagnyng baarynda*
*Ka"ttar edee belchigeshte*
*Kham-na yiash kilengneen-dir.*
*Kara chirik artyndyva*
*Khaia keurnu bergen-ne-dir.*

(Recorded from Kuzhuget Balgan)

It is strange why this has happened,
We shall go with you to look,
We shall share your grief.
And thou, my soul, spread thy wings.
To the valley of Mount Khorlug-Taiga
I must go,
Go forward, my creatures, with soft steps!
There from the heights we shall watch.
We shall ride the bald blue one,
Who digs the roots from the dark earth.
We shall ride the hornless blue one,
Who tears the grass from the slope.

Of what do you speak, of whom do you speak?
Please speak, my shaman-grandfather,
Yes, the shaman-tree is wrathful.
Truly, the shaman-tree is angry and wrathful,
Standing in the meadow before the Dark Mountain,
Beyond the distant hills,
So beautiful.

Yes, the soul of the patient has gone away for good
To the dark ravine of the dark abyss.


Here, the cause of the sickness is announced as being the wrath of
the tree-shaman.[b] To find this out, the shaman consulted first the
winged *eeren*, or raven, then the "bald" badger, then the "hornless"
bear, then the moth:

> *Kheueurtkuinung keergenchiin,*
> *Kheulegesi argyp kalgan, ooi-ooi.*
> *Sunezini kanchap bargan,*
> *Surdurgenge tutturgan be, ooi-ooi.*
> *Chuuden desken?*
> *Chuuden kortkan? Ooi-ooi.*
> *Duruiaa kushtung ununden be, ooi-ooi.*
> *Erlik oran chetken-dir be, chetpeen-dir be, ooi-ooi.*
> *Choorattyn oranynda doktaagan be, doktaavaan be, ooi-ooi.*
> *Soonaidan surungerem,*
> *Sogun oktan durgen choram, ooi-ooi.*
> *Alys cherge chetkelekte*
> *Atkan o"ktan durgen choram, ooi-ooi.*
> *Algash-tutkash, ekkelinger, ooi-ooi.*
> *Khovui-khovui khovuganym, ooi-ooi, ooi-ooi, ooi-ooi.*
>
> (Recorded from Saaia Sambuu)


How pitiful he has become, this sick man,
Hardly his shadow remains, *ooi-ooi.*
What has happened to his soul?
Has it been caught by the hand of the runner, *ooi-ooi?*
Why did it run away?
What has frightened it? *Ooi-ooi.*
Perhaps it was struck by the voice of the lark, *ooi-ooi?*
Perhaps it has gone to the [underworld] land of Erlik?
    or not gone, *ooi-ooi?*
Perhaps it has stayed in the land of Choorat? or
    not stayed, *ooi-ooi?*
Chase after it.
Fly swifter than an arrow, *ooi-ooi!*

Go swifter than a bullet,
Before it reaches the appointed place, *ooi-ooi*,
Catch and hold the soul and bring it here, *ooi-ooi.*
My little one, my dear little moth, *ooi-ooi, ooi-ooi, ooi-ooi.*

After repeating the exclamation *ooi-ooi* three times, the shaman lifted the drum even higher, gradually ceasing to strike it with the rattle. The mood of the patient was lifted—now he knew that the *eeren* moth had been sent to where his soul was. But the seance would last much longer. The patient was afraid to hear of the possible loss of his soul. An evil spirit now speaks through the mouth of the shaman. He sings a song of the captured soul:

*Chylan shokar, kyyt-kyyt*
*Chyraa shokar, kyyt-kyyt,*
*Chyraa-saiak, kyyt-kyyt.*

*Bazyp olur, kyyt-kyyt,*
*Chychyy tonnug, kyyt-kyyt,*
*Torgu tonnug, kyyt-kyyt,*
*Kaidal irgi, kyyt-kyyt.*

*Khunnug cherning, kyyt-kyyt,*
*Khureng arnyyn, kyyt-kyyt,*
*Khulup alyyl, kyyt-kyyt,*
*Tudup alyyl, kyyt-kyyt.*

*Ailyg cherning, kyyt-kyyt,*
*Arny kyzyl, kyyt-kyyt,*
*Aalynda, kyyt-kyyt,*
*Organ-na boor, kyyt-kyyt.*

*Tangdaa chydar, kyyt-kyyt,*
*Seueugu artsyn, kyyt-kyyt,*
*Tamaa chydar, kyyt-kyyt,*
*Sunezinin, kyyt-kyyt,*
*Surup algash, kyyt-kyyt,*
*Chorui baar men, kyyt-kyyt.*

(Recorded from Saaia Sambuu)[c]

Thou brightly colored one, like a snake, *kyyt-kyyt*,
    thou ambling steed, *kyyt-kyyt*,
Go pacing, *kyyt-kyyt*,
Go ambling, *kyyt-kyyt*.
He wore a serge robe, *kyyt-kyyt*,
He wore a silk robe, *kyyt-kyyt*,
Where is he now, *kyyt-kyyt*.
He was from the land of the sun, *kyyt-kyyt*,
His face was ruddy, *kyyt-kyyt*,
I shall bind him by the hands, *kyyt-kyyt*,
I shall take him alive, *kyyt-kyyt*.
He was from the land of the moon, *kyyt-kyyt*,
His face was red, *kyyt-kyyt*,
He is in his *aal* [settlement], *kyyt-kyyt*,
And there he sits, *kyyt-kyyt*.
Let his bones remain, *kyyt-kyyt*,
In the country where there are mountains, *kyyt-kyyt*,
I must return homeward, *kyyt-kyyt*,
With his captured soul, *kyyt-kyyt*,
I shall drive his soul onward, *kyyt-kyyt*,
It shall lie in the ground, *kyyt-kyyt*.

Thus, the shaman disclosed a page from the case history of the patient's sickness, in keeping with the traditional notions. Having learned of his hopeless situation, the patient asked the shaman to continue the seance.

## The interim seance

The Tuvan shamans practiced the *algysh arazunda alganyr algysh*, a seance held during an intermission of the main seance—a kind of lyrical digression.

Having learned of the presence of a great shaman at a particular camp, anyone from the surrounding *aal* (settlement) could go there to meet with him. Entering the *yurt*, the person tied a white ribbon to the door and asked: "Oh great shaman, I beg you to visit my *aal* and to stay in my native places. I also beg you to foresee that which is not permitted me to know. I ask you to prevent that which threatens my well-being. I ask you to tell me the unknown." Saying these words, the visitor handed the shaman a pipe with tobacco and offered him liquor, *arak*, from his leather flask, and offered a white silk cloth, *kadak*, to the spirits. Interrupting the seance, the shaman smoked the offered pipe and received the offerings. An unexpected interruption would occur— an interim seance within the main seance, devoted to healing the patient. But even if no outsider arrived, the shaman himself could hold an author's digression, serving as a kind of link between the opening and the culmination of the main seance. The digression could have almost any given subject or nature, except that it was based on mythological themes.

> They are beholden to me, they are in debt.
> I have the mandate of my people, *oo-ooi*.
> He has come with white *kadak*, *oo-ooi*.
> He offers bitter tobacco, *oo-ooi*.
> My stout one,
> My black bear, *oo-ooi!*
> And all his children, and all his *aal*
> I ask you to guard, *oo-ooi!*
> Let his dogs not bark, *oo-ooi!*
> Do not chase away his herd, *oo-ooi!*
> Do not trouble the peaceful sleep of his children, *oo-ooi*.
> Is there a fire burning at his house?
> Does a hat appear on a head?
> What has departed? What has arrived? *oo-ooi*.
> Who is creeping on all fours? *oo-ooi*
> My stout one,
> My black bear [*Mashpak kara, Mazhaalaiym*], go and see!

(Here the shaman paused a bit.)

> What did you see? What did you learn?
> Why are you frightened? Why run away?
> Thou—my fearsome honored one, *oo-ooi*.
> You sit on the right side of the *yurt*,
> Your high chest mutters.
> You chew and crunch beetles.
> My fierce black thundering one, *oo-ooi*.[d]
> You chew black worms, *oo-ooi*.

Thus far all is normal,
Thus far life is quiet.
But the camp of the *aal* grows dark,
It will be dangerous in future. *Oo-ooi.*
Sickness will break out,
Be vigilant! Be smart!
Someone will fall sick,
Someone will burn up.
His path is open to the *aza* [spirits], *oo-ooi.*
It is a straight path to the graveyard.
Is this because of the anger of the water and the earth? *oo-ooi.*
Be vigilant! Be smart!

(Recorded from Saaia Sambuu)

The new visitor, hearing the dismal conclusion of the shaman, humbly said: "Whatever is possible, great shaman, must be done for the cure. Not everyone has all-seeing eyes, only you, who have double vision, can do something." Thus the shaman ensured himself a clientele in future. This was a customary technique of all powerful shamans.

**The culmination of the seance**

The culmination was a proclamation (direct or oblique) of the prognosis of the disease. We shall present an example when, in a moment of highest tension, a woman bade farewell to her children, husband, and native land:

My dear, sweet children,
Your mother is sad and forlorn.
And tears flow from my husband's eyes,
When he sees his wife in sadness.
She bids farewell to her people,
She leaves her native *aal* forever.
Her life cannot be saved,
She shall soon go away from here.
To be born and die is the law,
You grow and then you go away—such is life.

Pay it no heed, do not be sad,
For she has sons and daughters.
She has many children, born late,
They will live where she lived.
Yes, she has many children,
They will take the place of their mother.

(Recorded from Kuzhuget Balgan)

## The dénouement of the seance

Apparently, the spirits have at last returned from Kara-Tal, where they have found the true explanation of the patient's condition. The dénouement is at hand.

His life cannot be saved.
It seems he chopped wood on the other side—
A terrible ill has come from there,
Before the winter month is out,

Before the summer moon appears,
He shall be lying in that graveyard.
There, on our northern side,
There, at the entrance to the narrow hollow.
I searched for his departed soul,
I asked for kindness and humbly prayed,
And went beyond the great range Sumber,
But was not able to catch it

Do not say I helped you not,
I was unable to return his soul,
Do not say I did not drive it here—
It is already in chains and shall not return from there.

When one is summoned from the kingdom of Erlik,
Not even the Khan Ezhen can help one.
He, this sick man, has left his native people,
He, this sick man, shall never again appear.

(Recorded from Kuzhuget Balgan)

## Summary

Brevity of information is a characteristic trait of the shamanic seance. The ritual traditionally ended with verses, in which were heard words about fatigue, the difficulties of lengthy travels on the steed (drum), and the victories gained by the shaman with the aid of his helpers over the enemies of the sick person. Here is a characteristic epilogue used by the shaman to end a seance:

> My seance, my action, is coming to an end,
> I wish to return home from the seance.
> Lo, my morning is already beginning,
> And my chestnut steed is also tired.
>
> It is time for me to go home,
> Leading the seance in a lively dance.
> It is time for me to go back to my dark, rundown hut
> Leading the seance in a frenzied dance.
>
> (Recorded from Viktor Kok-ool)

The time of the epilogue was in the morning. Night was ending, and the time had come to return home on the chestnut steed or drum—such was the theme of the shaman's epilogue. At the end of the ritual, the shaman reminded the audience not to forget to invite him on another occasion, to another *aal*.

## Basic themes and techniques of shamanic poetry

Frequently the shaman began the seance praising his predecessor shaman or his first teacher in this difficult art. Occasionally, one might hear an entire autobiographical poem. Praising predecessors, the shaman spoke of the shaman's fame, the geography of the travels of specific ancestors—great shamans, and the native places where his relatives lived from earliest times. For example:

> My dear father Delger, *oo-oo!*
> My grandfather, *aa-aa, oo-oo.*
> From a family of shamans, *oo-oo.*
> I was the youngest, *oo-oo.*
> I am the hereditary grandson of a shaman, *oo-oo,*

The lot of a shaman fell to me, *oo-oo*,
I come from six shamans, *oo-oo*,
I became the youngest shaman, *oo-oo*,
I am the heir of my father's clan, *oo-oo*,
I have already become a far-famed shaman, *kham-na, oo-oo*.

(Recorded from Shokshut Salchak)

One of the basic themes of shamanic folklore was that of the native land. As the shaman gained experience and made long voyages to distant *aals* (occasionally to neighboring countries, especially the Altai Mountains and the steppes of Mongolia), the geography of the folklore of Tuvan shamans naturally broadened. Yet the native land, with which the shamans connected their destiny and associated the mighty force of their helper-spirits, is an object of their pride and an eternal theme of shamanic poetry.

*O-oo-ooo*! *Eeren*—lords of the very foundation,
*O-oo-ooo*! Sovereigns of the mountain ranges,
*O-oo-ooo*! Come hither, one after the other, to me,
*O-oo-ooo*! My treasure, my dear taiga!
*O-oo-ooo*! Show mercy to me!

(Recorded from Kuzhuget Balgan)

"Mingling" with the spirits—the masters of the water, sky, and earth—is evidently one of the oldest customs of the Tuvan shamans. Such rituals are evidently connected with the cult of mountains, water, natural phenomena, etc. The shaman questioned his helper-spirits:

Let us rise from the ground to the skies,
Let us play there, past the seven-colored rainbow.
Let us set out on a steed from the lower world,
Let us rise to the upper world, where Azar is.
Let us play there,
Past the seven-colored golden rainbow.
Riding on the motley-red dragon,
Striking red sparks with a whip,
Giving out peals of thunder,
Oh you, the hail and the rain,
Calling forth the beautiful downpour!

Come, fellows, let us play, knocking down the beautiful larches
with arrows.

(Recorded from Viktor Kok-ool)

Every shaman was supposed to compose songs about his attributes
and trusty spirit-helpers. Here is an example of how the shaman treated
his headgear:

*Ai*, my hat with feathers spread wide,
With partridge feathers, resembling the sun and the moon,
My seven-feather *kaskak* hat,
How do you feel?
Let us fly away, fly together!

(Recorded and translated by S.I. Vainshtein)

Here is an example of how a shaman might praise his headgear:

My yellow hat sways so nicely,
It is made of eagle feathers.
My yellow hat changes colors,
It is made of bird feathers.

or:

My hat of bird skin
Reaches to Kurbustan.

The shamans were convinced that their helper-spirits had a universal
ability to comprehend and mimic the speech of any person, the voices
of birds and animals, and the conversations of spirits. The seance
necessarily included a poetic dialogue between the shaman and his
idols.[e]

It was thought that the shaman was not able to discover the intention
of an evil spirit and understand the cause of the sickness and the fate of
a patient without verses addressed to the *eereni*. For example, the
shaman addressed his main helper— the mirror *kuzungu*:

My *kuzungu* of golden copper
Descended from yellow thunderclouds,
Quickly touched ground,

Splitting a yellow rock with one blow.
My *kuzungu* of red copper
Descended from red thunderclouds.
It flew as a red light,
Breaking a red rock with one blow.

(Recorded from Kenden Khomushku)

During the seance, the shaman created an imaginary history of the disease. The content of these verses was exceptionally diversified and multileveled. For example:

Could this be the curse of a shaman,
Which loudly cries in these *aals*?
Could this be the curse of the *turpan* bird,
That cries in the striped willows?

You say this is from the water and from the earth?
Was she really so frightened and splashed so much?
You say she defiled
The source of the spring?
Then go there and see,
What she did, when and where.

Yes, at the spring
The woman spilled water,
And showed her shame there—
And from this has come her woe.

A spider also lives there,
At night he will creep up to the doomed woman—
And the master of the lake himself, Uspa—
Not his daughter and not his son—
He sent his scout here,
To prevent this from being done.

Yes, they say the girl is sick because
She defiled the sacred water *arzhaan*.
Clean your shame yourselves,
Bless the water of the spring.

Organize a great festival,
Serve brisket and the fatty tail of the sheep.
Let there be archery, wrestling, and races,
And heated competitions, and merry games,
And they will clean the dirt and shame forever.

Your daughter shines with laughter,
But she is seeing an outsider.
With the smoke of the juniper
Cover the tracks of this cursed tramp.
In her belly, in the inner organ,
Already lies a two-month child.
Time will pass, and the day will come,
And I will make your happiness.

Among your herds
There is an ambling colt.
There also lies a chest,
In which is silk for a robe, that too is possessed by the devil.

And in your box
Is silverware.
In one chest, in your chest—
There lies a golden talisman.

Bring all of this
As an offering to the master Uspa.
To the spring, whence you draw your drinking water,
As an offering, please bring silk.
I shall fumigate with juniper, wash with water—
And then your sick daughter will be well.

(Recorded from Seree Khertek)

According to the scenario, *eereni* came to help the sick one at the shaman's request. The shaman appealed to them for advice:

Such is the reason for our talk!
Let us speak, let us smoke,
You must come here and find a solution—
What need be done, what must be done.

You have tried the taste of the milk,
You have tasted the best milk.
I beg you, do not rush away,
Shrouding yourselves with a white cloud.
I beg you to free the sick one,
From the heavy burden of his illness,
Which violently squeezes his chest and does not let him
      breathe freely.
What method, what advice is necessary?
I beg you to tell me, *eereni*.
Where, do you say? Which, do you say?
In what direction is it found?
Where is it hiding? What does it have with itself?
What has occurred, and how has this come about?

(Recorded from Aldyn-Kherel Ondar)

Here is how a shaman asks his helper-spirits to save the life of a man dying from tuberculosis:

*Eereni*, make him spit strongly,
So that the bloody pus comes out in a stream. Do so!
Stop his loud coughing,
Let the bloody foam come out of him. Do so!
Make his belly swell,
So that he belches and does not sit down. Do so!

Disturb him so he sneezes,
So he passes his illness down below,
So that it comes out with the gases. Do so!

(Recorded from Viktor Kok-ool)

The theme of illness in general occupied a major place in shamanic poetry. The motif of forestalling mournful events, the approach of illness, and a person's tragic death was also often sounded.

The shaman constructed his predictions so that listeners became afraid of unknown forces. According to stories of the old people, after a shaman was consulted for a prediction every healthy person felt sick and again appealed to the shaman.[f]

The shamans liked to pose as prophets. The nature of the prediction often depended on the social status of the applicant. To the poor, the shaman made a short prediction, to the rich a more elaborate one. If a patient was rich, the shaman deliberately avoided a clear formulation of the prognosis in order to repeat the seance after a certain time and receive a larger reward.

> Your companion-soul
> Has flown away to the upper world of Kurbustu.
> In the country where it is dwelling,
> There is nothing foul.
> These people have their own *eeren*
> Who makes all the bones of the body shake.
> If you will feed me meat, then I
> Might vanquish such *eeren*.
>
> (Recorded from Viktor Kok-ool)

If the shaman were no longer called upon, he would have no income. In order to enlarge the clientele, a shaman resorted to intimidation:

> A ways from your *aal*
> There is a cave, facing the north.
> There a company of *aza* is gathered—
> They might be dangerous.
> This cave requires a great offering-payment,
> A wicked evil is brewing there.
> A stranger will arrive to visit you,
> He is placing his foot in the stirrup.
> Together with him shall come a spirit from the land of Erlik,
> He is waiting at the roof of your yurt.
>
> (Recorded from Seree Khertek)

Shamanistic followers dreaded the shaman's wrath. Even so, the shaman might become angry. For example, a person who inadvertently "offended" a shamanic spirit-helper by walking in front of its image became his personal enemy. The highest pitch of passion was achieved in rivalry between two shamans. A folklore expedition recorded an imprecation of the former shaman Oorzhak Shokar:

Ah, let the *aza* consume the cursed one,
Let it devour his children,
Let it tear open the bosom of his parents,
May you be eaten piece by piece!

*Oi*, let him have no descendants,
*Oi*, let him be alone, like a stake,
*Oi*, let him be like a withered tree.[1]

Followers believed that if a soul abandoned a person they would take sick and die. The soul of the deceased would visit its native places, where its friends and relatives lived, at least twice: after seven days and after forty-nine days. In visiting the familial hearth, the soul of the deceased, according to Tuvan notions, attempted to tell its kin about itself, to express its displeasure with a particular ungrateful living relative or to impart its last wish to a friend.

If no children were born to a family, this meant in Tuvan belief that the soul of a child was not inhabiting their yurt. The parents of the newlyweds then invited a well-known shaman to summon this soul. Here is a fragment of text of a seance intended to "summon the soul" of an unborn infant:

*Naryyn-naryn! Alaas-alaas!*
And you, multitude of idols,
And you, ancient elders,
And you, sovereigns of Burkhan![g]

And my drum, like a mountain,
And my rattle, like a stone,
And my gray mother's grandmother.
You know how things grow,
You know the life of he who shall die.
My gray-headed ancestors!
You are the protectors of he who is in the cradle,
You bestow good fortune on the infant!

I sing your praises, I sing your praises,
Having prepared delicious food for all of you.

I solemnly bless you,
Giving you a white *kadak*—a silken handkerchief,
A soul of the infants—the golden-headed children,
Playing in the *saizanak* of stones,
I call, I summon and invite.
*Kurai-kurai!* I call the souls of children.

Boys who will carry the flint,
Girls with ribbons—
Call their fortunate souls.
My dark and fearsome *khaiyrakan*,
Who stands at the bedside, near the pillow!
My snakes, my four-sided ones!
My creator, copper-headed old one!
Give us happiness, give us goodness!

(Recorded from Saaia Sambuu)

Or:

Let the souls of tiny children come down
Onto the surface of the milken food.
*Kurai-kurai! Kurai-kurai!*
Children, whose cradles are made of gray willows,
Children who feed at their mother's breast,
Children whose cheeks are round, let your souls come here!
*Kurai-kurai! Kurai-kurai!*

Children, whose cradles are made of willow withies,
Children who lie on the goat skin,
Children, let your souls return here!
*Kurai-kurai! Kurai-kurai!*

(Recorded from Saaia Sambuu)

Fire enjoyed great veneration among shamanic followers. The autumn ritual of fire reverence was supposed to ensure the well-being and good fortune of the family year-round. A "great" shaman was generally invited to the celebration of the hearth.

He has a fast steed—a yellow goat with an apple on its brow,
He has an encirclement—an iron ring,
He has a birch enclosure.

This fire, he is the master of the smoke-darkened idols [*eeleri*].
Be quiet! Be courteous!
*Kurai! Kurai! Kurai!*
He is the well-being of the livestock,
He is the happiness of growing children.
*Kurai! Kurai! Kurai!*

You, O smudged creator idols,
Create a protection, a fence around the hearth,
So that no loss is suffered!
And the souls of boys carrying the flint and knife,
And the souls of girls skilled in the needle and ring,
Protect and guard them.
*Kurai! Kurai! Kurai!*

(Recorded from Aleksei Bair)

In this poem devoted to fire, we notice an intertwining of mythological and real motifs. At first, the shaman describes the general appearance of the domestic hearth. This is a very familiar picture to those
who were born and grew up in the *yurt*: a tripod for the iron kettle, a
square of birch wood around the hearth—all of this is absolutely essential. Every hearth has a domestic animal devoted to it (the "yellow goat
with an apple on its brow"). The hearth has its own protector *eereni*,
which are supposed to prevent the entry of evil spirits into the *yurt*.
Death, disease, birth, misfortune—all depends on fire. "Fire is my god,
fire is my creator," Tuvans say.

The shamanic seances also reflected themes connected with productive activity—the hunt, animal husbandry, and farming. For example,
the shaman Oorzhak Mortui-ool once held a seance at the request of a
hunter. To ensure a successful hunt, the shaman appealed to the tall
mountain range of Khan-Deer. According to a Tuvan legend, once
many animals lived here and the hunters killed so many of them that
their blood flowed in a river, in which the sky was reflected (hence the
name of the locality: Khan-Deer, "Bloody Sky"). Here is the text of the
shaman's propitiatory poem:

I light the censer,
I sprinkle the holy water,
I offer a white and blue ribbon in sacrifice,
To you, my Khan-Deer!

What you wish to give me—
Please give.
What it is rightful for me to take—
Please grant.
If one should come insolently to you—
Let him have no place to hunt,
If one should steal from you—
Give him no riches,
O wealthy Khan-Deer!
Do not conceal
Your wealth under yourself.
Do not hide
Under branches.

Where there is level ground,
Where there is a handsome tree,
There bestow, my wealthy Khan-Deer!
My dark taiga,
You have a thousand dark trees,
You have a hundred hearts,
You have nine pitchers.
My taiga, bestow that with the shiny earrings,
My taiga, bestow that with the bushy tail.
Be good, my taiga,
Guard me, my taiga,
Give me strength, my taiga,
Give my horse strength, my taiga!
*Kurai! Kurai! Kurai!*

(Recorded from Aleksei Bair)

If one of the members of a family took ill, or if the head of the family suffered a misfortune, the shaman was invited to hold a seance in honor of the sacred horse. The shaman conducted the ceremony and composed verses addressed to this animal, so that a horse with its mane decorated by a red ribbon was sanctified.

Whose eyes are like a spyglass?
Whose teeth are like a shell?
Whose breath is like a fog?
Say thy word,

Stretch forth the golden shoe,
Do not be angry,
Do not be distracted,
Be the guardian of your yard,
Never abandon your gates!

I have washed you with holy water—*arzhaan*,
So that your anger disappears.
I have bathed you in the smoke of the juniper—*artysh*,
So your fright disappears.

Do not be angry with your master,
Who fed and raised you.
If you pace in a circle,
My head will be dizzy.

If you get angry,
My throat will choke. And so be good!
I beg of you,
Do not weaken me, be good!

(Recorded from Aleksei Bair)

## The poetics of shamanic folklore

Most of the shamans held the seance in the Tuvan language, although there were some exceptions. Shalyk Darbaa told of the "great" shaman Shadyk who held seances in Tuvan, Mongolian, and Chinese. His only son, Don, was mute. The people said that shaman Shalyk, who was fluent in three languages, spent his whole life in battle with hostile shamans, and though they could not "devour" him they nevertheless took vengeance in his son being born without a tongue.[h] And Saaia Sambuu told how the shaman Kaldar, who died in 1930, migrated from the nearby Altai Mountains to the Mongun-Taiga region in the early twenties. He shamanized only in the Altai language. Another shaman, Askak, also held seances in Altai. According to information obtained from Tash-ool Kungaa, the famous female shaman Kurgak Kyrgys lived beside the rivers Kachyk and Saigal, which are on the border with Mongolia. Her entire life she "serviced" the sick of the Tuvans and Mongols, shamanizing in the Mongolian language.

Even in the same seance, the language often changed. Each of the characters had their own style and speech, with a rich symbolism of sound. This intensified the emotional aspect of the seance. The elder Chimba Lopsan said that if a shaman was cursing his enemy he imitated the raven; summoning rain, he imitated the crow; frightening people, he imitated the wolf or the eagle-owl; uncovering a lie, he imitated the magpie; showing off his power, he imitated the bull; and expressing rapture, the bear. In a word, the shaman could imitate the voices of many wild animals, birds, and domestic animals. According to Soruktu Kyrgys, the female shaman Shimit-Kyrgys also imitated various voices in the same seance. If it turned out that the patient was ill from "meddling of the spirits" of water or earth, the female shaman imitated the voices of the raven, crow, wolf, Siberian stag, billy goat, marmot, and bear. Having decided that the patient was the victim of the anger of domestic animals, Shimit-Kyrgys imitated the voices of the nanny goat, sheep, camel, horse, and dog.

Words and sounds had a definite symbolism. In Tuvan beliefs, if a horse bites his bridle, his master could take ill and die. By imitating the neighing of a horse, the shaman predicted a bad outcome. If the cry of the raven was heard at night, this meant the soul of a person was going away. By imitating the voice of the raven, the shaman predicted the imminent passing of a person with his soul.[i]

Before the start of the seance, the shaman turned to the audience and shouted onomatopoeic words, selecting those needed for the anaphora of the verses; in a quiet voice he conversed with the spirits, choosing a rhythm. Salchak Tamba recalls that the shaman Suiziuk never began by singing verses. First he imitated the raven, the magpie, and the bear; then he performed a shamanic dance; and only after this did he begin the seance.

The Tuvans are great masters in making onomatopoeic words; they have a special throat singing (of the *kargyraa, sygyt,* and *khomei* types):[j]

> *Aa-uu-aa-uui! Kelbes cherge chuge kelding?*
> *Choruvas cherge choraan sen.*
> *Aa-uu, aa-uui! Euzheen-kylyyng algan-dyr sen*
> *Alyryngny algan-dir sen.*
>
> (Recorded from Saaia Sambuu)

*Aa-uu, aa-uu!* Why did you come to the forbidden place?
It seems you have already been where it is not permitted.
*Aa-uu, aa-uu!* You have already taken back your anger,
And you have taken that which need be taken.

The beast about which the shaman is singing is not mentioned here, but it is recognized from the voice, and it is clear to the audience that the shaman is singing about a wolf. The seemingly senseless words, according to our informants, produced an intoxicating effect on the onlookers. The shaman's helpers usually sat at his right and left and echoed the same words.

*Azyg aksyng, oo-ooi,*
*Aazatpa, oo-ooi,*
*Azyg dizhing, ooi-ooi,*
*Shaaratpam, Ooi-ooi.*

(Recorded from Saaia Sambuu)

Your mouth, *oo-ooi,*
Do not open, *oo-ooi,*
Your fangs, *ooi-ooi,*
Do not show, *Ooi-ooi.*

This is how the shaman addressed the helper-spirit, *eeren moosa*, so that he did not reveal his "fearsome outer form" to the people. The words *ooi-ooi* in this case perform a magical function.[2]

The seance began in standard fashion, occasionally with pairs of onomatopoeic words; this is characteristic of an archaic construction. For example:

*Aryyng-aryyn!*
*Alaas-alaas!*
*Aryglanyp,*
*Naryydap aain!*

(Recorded from Seree Khertek)

I wish to be cleansed
And I prepare myself for cleansing!

The Tuvans say: *"Khalak deerge—khalas barbas"* ("Say *khalak*—there will be a sacrifice"). When the shaman conjures a thief, he necessarily uses the "magical" word *khalak*:

*Aa khalak-khalak!*
*Algash baardy, kulugurnu!*
*Aa khalak-khalak!*
*Azalarnyng, aldyn shalba!*
*As khalak-khalak!*
*Ara kirzin, kulugurnu!*

(Recorded from Viktor Kok-ool)

*Aa khalak-khalak!*
He took the cattle, the scoundrel!
*Aa khalak-khalak!*
A golden lasso should [take him] to the devils!
*Aa khalak-khalak!*
Let the scoundrel not reach his home!

The word *khalak-khalak* in this incantation, indicating fresh milk and having lost its independent meaning, plays the part of an interjection and expresses the shaman's hatred of the thief.

Word-symbols could also be placed at the end of a text. It is said there was once a "mighty" shaman Keldir Khirligbei, who liked to sing songs of the daughter of the mythical subterranean king Erlik. At the end of each line of verse were interjectory words of purely abstract semantics:

Erlik's daughter, *shalyr-shalyr,*
My friend, *shalyr-shalyr,*
I would like to come to you, *shalyr-shalyr,*
I would like to meet you, *shalyr-shalyr.*

Never, *shalyr-shalyr,*
Shall I die, *shalyr-shalyr,*
Erlik's daughter is mine, *shalyr-shalyr,*
She is my friend, *shalyr-shalyr.*

(Recorded from Saaia Sambuu)

Onomatopoeic words of the *shalyr-shalyr* type are often found in shamanic verse and designate a loud rustling sound.[3]

By its very nature, shamanic verse is musical. We find striking parallels in the use of interjections and onomatopoeic words in ancient folk songs and shamanic texts. Here is a folk song:

> *Kuu dagnyng baaryndan, konggurgai,*
> *Kuduk kassa ugmein kanchaar, konggurgai,*
> *Kuskun kara uruglarny, konggurgai,*
> *Kudalaza albain kanchaar, konggurgai.*[4]

> If you dig underneath the mountain Kuu, *konggurgai,*
> There will be a well, *konggurgai,*
> If you woo girls with tresses like a raven's wing, *konggurgai,*
> They will become women, *konggurgai.*

Another song, a recent one, is called "*Dembildei.*" The composer, Saaia Biurbee, wrote the music for it to the words of the national poet of the Tuvan ASSR, Sergei Piurbiu.

> *Orai kezhee syldys karaa chetchip-tip,*
> *Salgyn bolchaang euiu keep-tip, ezhikei,*
> *Oglaa-saryg dynyn tyrtyp, chutkui-dur.*
> *Salgyn-bile charzhyptar-dyr, dembildei.*
> *Dembil, dembil, dembildei.*[5]

> In the late sky the eyes of the stars appear,
> My dear, the hour of the meeting has come.
> The restless piebald horse is anxious to go,
> Let us fly, speeding with the wind, *dembildei,*
> *Dembil, dembil, dembildei.*

In these two examples, we find a succession of onomatopoeic words of exceptional vivacity. Such words intensified the rhythmical sounds of shamanic incantations, and they also beautify the melody of modern songs. Rasul Gamzatov has written on the rhythmical, poetic, and melodious nature of words of this type. The word "*dolalai*" that he uses and the Tuvan "*dembildei*" or "*agarooi*" are identical in their function:

I, composing verse, sometimes sing:
*Dolalai, dolalai, dolalai.*[6]

Obviously, word-symbols, word-music, and word-interjections participate in creating the rhythm of song and cannot be replaced by any other words of purely lexical meaning.

We shall present some examples characterizing the riches and diversity of the figurative-expressive means of the language of shamanic poetry. A classic example of the use of epithet is the following text:

> *Kalchaa dalai keustup deldi,*
> *Kanchalyyly, chalgynnygbai?*
> *Chadgynnarym chadyptain che,*
> *Chalbaraashtyng kiripteeli.*
>
> (Recorded from Salchak Tamba)

Lo, the raging sea, has appeared,
What shall we do, wingèd one?
Let us stretch out our wings
And make a prayer.

Such was the song of the popular shaman Siuziuk in the Kaa-Khemsk region during his seance. Addressing his raven idol [helper spirit-image] shaman Siuziuk created an image of a mythological sea, to which only he and his helper could fly. Or an example of simile:

My aorta, my liver have dried up.
Like a snake in a hollow,
I am the shaman Burbu, I am the pock-marked shaman.
I ask for good things from the benefactor,
I ask for mercy with my seance,
So that death will go away forever.

(Recorded from Arkadii Bazyr-Taraa)

The true meaning of what was sung in the shaman's verse could only be understood by knowing the historical and lexical meaning of each word. For example, the shaman could talk at length about his *eereni* without naming them. Whoever knew the shaman's helpers would understand what he was singing about. Allegory was a favorite technique of the Tuvan shamans. We present an example:

Have you indeed come to take him away?
Have you indeed come from his *aal*?
He has gone from the yurt and stands beyond
    the threshold,
He is looking back, there he stands.
What must I do for it to be well?

                 (Recorded from Salchak Tamba)

The poet Salchak Tamba, who provided this text, was present in his youth at a seance of the female shaman Kham-Kadai. She was "curing" a man who could not get up from his bed and she was talking to someone. After the seance the female shaman explained: "A very strong *buk* (evil spirit—M.K.-L.) has appeared in this *aal*. I wrested him away from the sick man and chased him from the *yurt*. But he went out and is standing there, beyond the threshold, he is standing and looking at the sick man. However much I chased the *buk*, he does not want to go any further. He wants to take the one he came for."

The shaman might speak in his verses of a living person as though he were dead. He might sing of a long-deceased person as of one who has come from afar to take someone back with him. The shaman might speak of a tree, a spring of water, a mountain, as of a living being. Many examples of personification can be found in shamanic folklore. Here is a fragment from the seance of a shaman appealing to the high mountains Khattyg-Taiga and Buura-Taiga:

My Khattyg-Taiga!
My shamaness—my Buura!
Look, listen!
When you, the watchful one, when you, the careful one,
With your storm, with your rain
Let the plague pass by,
I humbly beg of you.

               (Recorded from Arkadii Bazyr-Taraa)

The shamans liked to exalt their helper-spirits. For example, a shaman spoke about the meaning of his small wooden raven *eeren*:

He flies swiftly—
The flute sounds piercingly.

On his wings is an inscription,
On his tail is drawn an ornament,
He flies to where the beast with red blood dwells,
He ascends to the zenith,
Such thou art, my slender, my black raven.
You are carried easily through the air,
My black raven, hungry raven!
You are my black scout, you are my white scout.
I beg you to come to me, to come nigh!
[*Arai-la beer, oon-na beer!*]

Descend from the skies,
Drop on my head with a dance.
There, between my shoulder blades, hang little bells,
They are of bronze, amuse yourself with them!
On my shoulders are little bells—
They are black, they are masculine.
Play to the sound of these bells.
[*Konggalarnyng, unu-bile oinazhyngar!*]

In this poem the shaman created an extremely vivid and poetic image of the raven: it flies headlong, it cuts the air with its wings, it soars in the skies, it lightly descends to earth. All that is on the earth and in the sky is subservient to the raven-spirit.

Shamans could conjure with special respect for *albys* [witches; Russian *ved'ma*]:

Under the lowering skies, under the storm clouds,
Above the spreading trees
My golden *albys* fly,
My *albys* fly with a rustle, with a noise,
Each one has a forked tongue.
My amber-golden ones, my all-powerful ones,
With forked tongues.
You are sharper than an awl,
More clever than a spy.

(Recorded from Aleksei Bair)

In the images of the *albys*, we see legendary creatures, but to the shaman the *albys* were real forces.

The shamanic rituals made use of *chazhyg*, a pitcher of holy water, and *san*, or juniper, which was strewn on a flat stone, resembling a small plate. How the shaman exalted these in verse can be seen from the following example:

> *Eei-ei!*
> At the beginning of the moon, at the beginning of the
>     sun, *oo-oo-oo!*
> At the very dawn of this day, *oo-oo-oo!*
> *Eei-ei!*
> I offer holy water, like a large sea, *oo-oo-oo!*
> I burn juniper, like a large mountain, *oo-oo-oo!*
>
> (Recorded from Salchak Shokshut)

Here, the pitcher of holy water is called a sea and the handful of juniper is compared to a mountain. There are many such examples of exaggeration of the qualities and dimensions of attributes in shamanic mythology.

In the lexicon of shamanic poetry one can find words that have gone out of the word fund of the modern Tuvan language. Here is an example of the words used by a shaman in creating a portrait of his white *eeren*:

> His *baryndak* is of white silk,
> His *ovaadai* is of lynx and sable skin,
> His food is wormwood,
> His *chegedek* is of white *kadak*,
> His food is the aspen tree,
> His *chegedek* is of yellow *kadak*.
>
> (Recorded from Aleksei Bair)

Here, *baryndak* is a handkerchief, *ovaadai* a hat, *chegedek* a vest. It should be noted that certain words and phraseological combinations employed in shamanic texts are also missing from dictionaries, in particular the *Tuvan-Russian Phraseological Dictionary*.[7]

A primary characteristic of shamanic verse is the repetition of an identical number of vowel sounds in a line. The quatrain is the basic unit of shamanic poetry. In rhythm, the shamanic verse has an equal number of syllables. The strict alternation of interjections at the beginning and end of the line sets the rhythm.

The oldest determinants of the sound organization of the shamanic seance were interjections, which are totally absent from modern Tuvan poetry. Without the musical instrument of the drum, without the music composed by the shaman himself, and without his performance of it, these archaic determinants lose their emotional force. We shall present several examples in which the most characteristic rhythmical determinants of shamanic song are easily seen.

The use of interjections at the start of a line:

> Alas. Alas. I have been to Erlik's land.
> Alas. Alas. I am very tired, I have suffered much.
> Alas. Alas. I have been in Aza's land.
> Alas. Alas. I am very hungry, I wish to drink.
>
> > (Recorded from Arkadii Bazyr-Taraa)

The use of interjections at the end of the line:

> The red mountain range, *doot-doot*,
> Where I shall lie, *doot-doot*,
> The red blossom, *doot-doot*,
> Which I have eaten, *doot-doot*.
>
> > (Recorded from Saaia Sambuu)

Example of four-syllable verse:

> *Dunggurlugnung*
> *Duvu changgys.*
> *Orbalygnyng*
> *Oruu changgys.*
>
> > (Recorded from Dezhit Tozhu)

> He who has the drum,
> Only one bottom.
> He who has the rattle,
> Only one road.

Example of eight-syllable verse:

> *Kalgan-bargan chuvelerni*
> *Katap ergeesh, kanchaar onu.*

*Eulgen-bargan chuvelerge*
*Eurgul kylyp kanchaar onu.*

(Recorded from Kuzhuget Balgan)

One need not return to those,
Who have gone away forever.
One need not honor the dead,
Who are long since deceased.

Example of twelve-syllable verse:

*Artysh, shaanak chydy dolgan bedik taigam,*
*Arzhaan sugnung uner deuzu ulug synym,*
*Azhy-teuldun amy-tynyn alyr deeshting,*
*Artysh, shaanak, agy-kanggy kypsyp tur men.*

(Recorded from Viktor Kok-ool)

My high taiga full of the scent of the juniper and heather,
My high mountain, where the water *arzhaan* takes its source,
In order to save the life of small children,
I burn the juniper, heather, and wormwood.

An identical number of syllables in syntactic parallelism functions as a rhythmical determinant of shamanic verse. The singer (shaman) places primary attention on the first syllable of the line and thereafter on the parallel harmony of vowels in couplets (according to the type of the proverb). Thus, the full vigor of shamanic verse depended on the rhythmical alternation of vowels. As an illustration, we take one stanza of shamanic poetry:

*Aalyngarnyng kedeezinde*
*Aksy dedir ulug kui bar,*
*Aza-chetker ynda chyylgan—*
*Alys baryp ondaktyg-dyr.*

(Recorded from Seree Khertek)

In the back of your *aal*
There is a cave, facing north.
There a company of devils is gathered—
In future they may be dangerous.

The scheme of harmony of the vowels in the above stanza is as follows:

aa-y/a-y e-ee/i-e
a-y e-i u-u u/a
a-a/e-e y-a yy-a
a-y a-y o-a y-y.

Here, we observe the equal number of syllables in parallel syntacti-cal lines. This is an important feature of shamanic versification. Eight-syllable stanzas are the most common, four- and six-syllable stanzas considerably rarer. Five-, seven-, and ten-syllable stanzas are almost never used. The words and the order of presentation in our example preserve the archaic form of syntactical parallelism: the vowels of the first line harmonize with the vowels of the second, those of the third with the vowels of the fourth. The principle of equality of symbols in paired couplets and quatrains dictates the rhythmicity of shamanic po-etry. Tuvan shamanic verse is synharmonic in nature, based on rhyth-mical syntactical parallelism.

An essential organizer of the sounds of shamanic versification was lexical or phonetic refrain, anaphora. To the characteristic sounds of shamanic verse, anaphora was not merely a repetition of words or syntactical constructs, but also a means of unification of sounds at the beginning of sentences, verses, and stanzas.

A classical example of a shamanic text:

> *Kady taakpy tyrtyzhaaly,*
> *Kady araga izhizheeli,*
> *Changys a"tka ushkazhyyly,*
> *Changys tonga khoigazhyyly.*
> *Dyngnaan chuve chazhyrbaaly,*
> *Typkan chuve kamnaaly.*[8]

Let us smoke tobacco together,
Let us drink *arak* together,
We shall travel on the same steed,
We shall wear the same coat,
We shall not conceal the tidings heard,
We shall guard that which is found![9]

In this example, the verbal parallelism initiated by the words *kady* and *changys* is accompanied by a rhythmical highlighting of these parallel terms. Every composer of shamanic song considered a uniform beginning of his speech to be an essential condition, not paying attention to the random repetition of words or sounds in the middle and at the end of lines. Anaphora is the basic technique of shamanic versification. We shall present several examples characterizing anaphora as the organizing principle of shamanic versification.

An example of sound anaphora:

> *Idiingerning khonchuzunda*
> *Iii dangza taakpy bar-dyr.*
> *Ishtingerde, khyrnyngarda*
> *Iii-le ailyg urug bar-dyr.*

> (Recorded from Viktor Kok-ool)

> There, tucked in behind the shoe,
> Is tobacco enough for two pipes.
> There, in your belly,
> Is a two-month child.

Each line begins with the same vowel, "i," on which the shaman placed special emphasis during the seance. Lexical anaphora, intensifying the role of rhythm in the verse, imparts a sing-song quality:

> *Kyzyl kyrny kyrlai kakkash,*
> *Kyzyl charyk askyn keureel.*
> *Kyzyl khany ynda teuktur,*
> *Kyzyl tyny ynda kalyr.*

> Along the red slope we shall gallop,
> There we shall see the mouth of the red ravine,
> Red blood turns crimson there,
> It bids farewell to the red breath there.[10]

Here, lexical anaphora of the same word is used by the shaman to highlight the beginning of the lines and hold the listeners' attention.

Anaphora of paired words is seldom found in shamanic verse. We have an example of such anaphora from the seance of Kham-ool, the hero of a play by V. Kok-ool:

Softly-softly sit,
Let the boys and girls gather round.


A peculiar technique of shamanic versification is strophic anaphora. The eminent expert in Tuvan folklore, B.K. Mongush,[k] has provided me with a characteristic specimen of strophic anaphora:

*Agarooi!*
My *kuzungu* of golden bronze,
It is a gift of the skies.
It is the terror of six men,
It took its breath from six sheep.
*Agarooi!*
My *kuzungu* of iron bronze.
It is the gift of devils.
It is the terror of seven men,
It took its breath from seven sheep.


When we speak of anaphoric parallelism, we mean syntactical parallelism. Many examples of syntactical anaphora can be found in shamanic folklore. For example:

*Chedi kudai shavyzy men,*
*Chedi khamnyng cheeni men,*
*Aldy kudai shavyzy men,*
*Aldy khamnyng anynaa men.*

(Recorded from Kenden Kuular)


I am the follower of seven skies,
I am the grandson of seven shamans.
I am the follower of six skies,
I am the youngest of six shamans.


Alliteration is a powerful means of vocal expressiveness of shamanic verse. If the shaman began one line with a consonant, he would start the parallel line with the same consonant.

*Beudei kara chadyrymche*
*Beueuldei khamnap chanain yngai.*
*Samdar kara chadyrymche*
*Samnai khamnap chanain yngai!*

(Recorded from Viktor Kok-ool)

It is time for me to return home,
Leading the seance in the wild dance.
It is time for me to return to my rundown, my dark hut,
Leading the seance in the wild dance.

In this example, the first and second lines begin with the consonant "b," while the third and fourth begin with the consonant "s." Thus, our analysis shows that shamanic verse, in its composition, is anaphoric verse.

There is no rhythm, in the full meaning of this term, in shamanic poetry. Instead, the principal form of metrical composition is atrophic epiphora. This appears as a repetition of the same vocal combinations, sometimes words or combinations of words. One should emphasize the special role of epiphora at the end of syntactically parallel lines. For example:

*Terek bashtap kagaalyngar,*
*Tereng suglap kezheelinger,*
*Oorug bashtap kagaalyngar,*
*Ottuk-dashtap alyynyngar.*

(Recorded from Viktor Kok-ool)

Over the tops of the poplars we shall fly,
The deep rivers we shall swim across,
Over the tall mountains we shall roam,
Flintstone we shall gather.

The identical (consonant) endings of the lines and verbs of identical rhythmical meaning are quite characteristic of shamanic verse. A repetition of morphologically identical endings is also found in the form of nouns, singular or plural:

*Ailar, sholban karaktyymny,*
*Aldyn, meunggun syrgalyymny,*

*Kydyr-kydyr karaktyymny,*
*Kyzyl khureng shyrailyymny.*

(Recorded from Viktor Kok-ool)

Her eyes resemble the moon and the morning star,
She has golden and silver earrings,
Her eyelids have delicate creases,
Her face is of ruddy amber.

The words for eyes, earrings, and face have the same declensions, which intensifies the phonic rhythm, in which the long vowel "y" is most clearly delineated.

Anaphora at the start of lines is a conscious choice of sounds or words. The coincidence of sounds at the end of lines of verse, as I.V. Stebleva correctly writes, is forced, and therefore not creative.[11] The epiphora of shamanic verse is not a rhythmoid, much less a rhythm. It arises by chance as a result of the coincidence of terminal sounds of identical grammatical forms, as a compulsory euphonic technique.

Alliteration and assonances as constituent elements of root anaphora are an organic part of the general organization of shamanic versification, where the archaic order of words is preserved in its primordial form. The expressive force of the root syllable has not been suppressed here by the influence of other languages. The principal element of the vocal organization of shamanic verse, as shown by our analysis, was the root syllable. The most important for a characterization of shamanic verse are the active role of the beginning of the word, the passive role of the end of the word in each line, the presence of a constant accent, the tendency to balancing of syllables in parallel lines of verse, the archaic construction of the sentences, and the major role of synharmonism as the basic rhythmical law of shamanic verse. Thus, the form of shamanic poetry, according to V. M. Zhirmunskii, was based on rhythmical-syntactical parallelism, characteristic of the ancient epic style of the Turkic peoples;[12] but with strict observance of vowel harmony. Shamanic verse is anaphoric in composition and synharmonic in rhythmics.

## Editor's notes

a. The author's use of the masculine for shamans and their dress is preserved here, although ahead it is clear that some Tuvan shamans were women. It should be noted that some still are (personal communication V.Iu. Suzukei, Tuvan ethno-musicologist, August 1992). See also V. Iu. Suzukei, "Shamanizm i muzykal'nyi fol'klor Tuvintsev," in A. I. Gogolev, A. P. Reshetnikova, K. N. Romanova, P. A. Sleptsov, Z.F. Semenova, eds. *Shamanizm kak religiia (Tezisy dokladov mezhdunarodnoi nauchnoi konferentsii)* (Yakutsk: "Iakutsk" Gosudarstvennyi Universitet, 1992), pp. 57–58.

b. Word order is preserved here, so that the meaning of "tree-shaman" is differentiated from the more general concept of a shamanic, or world-tree. See for context: Mircea Eliade, *Shamanism* (Princeton: University of Princeton Press, 1972), pp. 37–42, 70–71, 271–82; Vilmos Diöszegi, "Tuva Shamanism," *Acta Etnografiia*, 1962, vol. 11, pp. 143–90.

c. Subsequent poems translated here were also provided in the original text in the Tuvan modified Cyrillic, with Russian translations. Readers interested in linguistic subtleties of the highly alliterative poetry should consult the original text. Where discussion of word musicality makes transliteration crucial, it is provided. Tuvan used Mongolian and Tibetan scripts into the 1930s. In 1930, a modern Tuvan Latin alphabet script was also devised. This was changed into Cyrillic in 1943, and is now the subject of political debate.

d. Poetic license seems to have been taken in Kenin-Lopsan's Russian translation, for he uses the refrain "*oo-ooi*" more in the Russian poem than the Tuvan original. More significant, he twice glosses as "idol" two phrases that are metaphorical, referring to the bear helper-spirit as "honored one" and "thunderer." Euphemisms for the bear are widespread throughout Siberia and also in Slavic tradition.

e. "Idols" is used in the original, although the terms "spirit images" or "ancestral images" have less pejorative meaning and are more specific. *Eeren*, which also means spirit, appears most frequently in the Tuvan incantations, glossed as *idol* or *idol-bog* by Kenin-Lopsan but kept here as *eeren*.

f. For other, more positive, dimensions to the psychology of consumers of shamanism, see S. Shirokogoroff, *Psychomental Complex of the Tungus* (London: Routledge & Kegan Paul, 1935); M. M. Balzer, "Introduction," in *Shamanism: Soviet Studies of Traditional Religion in Siberia and Central Asia* (Armonk, NY: M.E. Sharpe, 1990), pp. vii–xviii; Lola Romanucci-Ross, Daniel Moerman, and Lawrence Tancredi, eds., *The Anthropology of Medicine* (New York: Bergin and Garvey, 1991).

g. This refers to Burkhan, a Mongolic name for a manifestation of the Buddha worshipped in Burkhanism, called *ak di'an* or the "white faith." It developed among the nearby Altai-Kizhi at the start of the century, and can be interpreted as an ethnic revitalization or "nativistic" religion, syncretizing aspects of shamanism and Dzhungar Lamaism. See Liudmilla I. Sherstova, "Shamanizm i Burkhanizm: Dinamika vzaimootnoshenii," in A.I. Gogolev, et al., eds., *Shamanizm kak religiia*, p. 86; Lawrence Krader, "A Nativistic Movement in Western Siberia," *American Anthropologist*, 1956, vol. 58, pp. 282–92.

h. Sadly, this idea of revenge of hostile shamans or their helper-spirits on family members of shamans has not died, and is widespread through much of Siberia, judging from discussions on this with Khanty (Ob-Ugrian Ostiak), Sakha (Turkic Yakut), and Nanai (Amur River Goldy) consultants. Related to a perceived need for protection, the Tuvan words for *kham*, seance, and to guard, *khamna-*, probably have the same root, also widespread.

i. The raven holds a special place in the ranks of shamanic helper-spirits among many of the Eastern Siberian peoples, and also in Northwest Coast Alaskan traditions. The Sakha also specifically associate the raven with messages of death.

j. A Tuvan throat master is able to sound like more than one person singing at once by creating deep, gutteral resonances through a highly controlled system of song types. The echoing magic of this music (created in and for the mountains of the Altai) can be heard on the Melodiia record (D–030773–74) "Melodii Tuvy," and 9307-40017-2 in the Smithsonian/Folkways series, produced by ethnomusicologist Ted Levin. Throat singing has been part of the Tuvan cultural revival, with groups led by activist-singers such as Genadii Chash, to whom I am grateful for insights into Tuvan culture. See *Soveshchanie po problemam razvitiia khomeiia* (Kyzyl: Ministerstvo kul'tury, 1988).

k. Borakh K. Mongush is the author's father.

## Notes

1. "Rukopisnyi fond Tuvinskogo NIIIaLI," t. 57, d. 250, l. 15.

2. A similar technique was used by the author in the poem "End of the Shaman," the main character of which, the shaman Shagar, begins a strophic anaphora with the onomatopoeic interjection *agarooi*:

> *Agarooi!*
> Pour out your rage,
> Sounding like the rain,
> Yet do not hurl at me
> The lightning-snake!
> *Agarooi!*
> Water is needed,
> Celestial chief,
> Send the rain
> Speedily here!

(Translation Iu. Razumovskii)

See M.B. Kenin-Lopsan, *Selected Works* in 2 vol. (in Tuvinian) (Kyzyl, 1975), vol. 1, p. 203; idem, *Kinovar'* (Kyzyl, 1973), p. 115.

3. F.G. Iskhakov and A.A. Pal'mbakh, *Grammatika tuvinskogo iazyka: fonetika i morfologiia* (Moscow, 1961), p. 462.

4. "Tyva ulustung yrlary" (Tuvan folk songs), musical arrangement by Maksim Munzuk, texts gathered by Kara-Kys Munzuk (Kyzyl, 1973), p. 37.

5. Biurbe Saaia, *Kush-azhylga maktal* (Glory to Labor!), in Tuvan (Kyzyl, 1967), p. 37.

6. R. Gamzatov, *Chetki let* (Moscow, 1973), p. 213.

7. Ia. Sh. Khertek, *Tuvinsko-russkii frazeologicheskii slovar'*, ed. D.A. Tatarintsev (Kyzyl, 1975).

8. *Obraztsy narodnoi literatury tiurkskikh plemen, izdannye V.V. Radlovym* (St. Petersburg, 1907), pt. 9. Dialects of the Uriankhai (Soiot), Abakan Tatars, and Kargas. Texts collected and revised by N.F. Katanov, p. 48.

9. Ibid., p. 45.

10. D.P. Potapov, "Materialy po izucheniiu etnografii tuvinskikh raionov Mongun-Taiga i Kara-Kholia," *Tr. TKAE* (Moscow-Leningrad, 1960), no. 1, p. 223.

11. I.V. Stebleva, *Poeziia tiurkov VI–VII vekov* (Moscow, 1965), p. 39.

12. V.M. Zhirmunskii, *Tiurkskii geroicheskii epos* (Leningrad, 1974), p. 580.

## List of informants

(The complete list of informants is given in the supplement to the manuscript dissertation: M. B. Kenin-Lopsan, "Siuzhety i praktika tuvinskogo shaman-stva: Opyt istoriko-etnograficheskoi rekonstruktsii," GPB im. Lenina, disser-tation collection.)

Aldyn-Kherel Ondar (1892–1980?), born in Man-Churek of Siut-Khol' (Dzun-Khemchik) region, lived his last years in the village of Chyraa-Bazhy, Dzun-Khemchik region, a great expert in Tuvan mythology.

Bazyr-Taraa Arkadii Dambaevich (b. 1917), born in Ezhim, Ulug-Khem re-gion, lives in the village of Khaiyrakan of the same region, took part in the First Republican Gathering of National Poets and Musicians.

Bair Aleksei Shirinmeevich (1904–85), born in Aldyy-Ishkin of Dzun-Khemchik region, very familiar with Mongolian and Russian languages.

Balgan Kuzhuget Lenchaevich (b. 1913), born in Tele-Gol, Bai-Taiga region, a wood carver. Recording taken in the village of Kara-Khol'.

Biurbiu Kyrggys Oidupovich (b. 1936), born in Torgalyg, Oviur region. Now lives in Kyzyl, Baitaiga region.

Dazhy-Bilbin Khovalyg Balchyi-oolovich (1905–80?), resident of the village of Torgalyg, Ulug-Khem region, storyteller, very familiar with Russian and Mongolian languages, knew many *algyshy*.

Dezhit Tozhu Lopsan uruu (b. 1912, former female shaman), born in Sorug-Chazy, Kaa-Khem region, now lives in the village of Kungurtuk, Kyzyl re-gion. A great expert in shamanic folklore.

Dongak Barykaan Kuralbai uruu (1898–1975), born in Bedik-Khavak, Dzun-Khemchik region. The first poetess of Tuva, writing in Mongolian, an expert in Tuvan folklore. Recording taken in the village of Khon-dergei, Dzun-Khemchik region.

Dulush Chamyian Kalbak oglu (b. 1914), born in Kara-Sug sumona Tarlag, Pii-Khem region, a teller of folk tales.
Dulush Sharap, born in Khaiyrakan, Ulug-Khem region.

Kok-ool Viktor Shogzhapovich (1906–80), born in Torgalyg, Oviur region, a great expert in shamanic folklore, dramatist, actor, writer.

Kungaa Tash-ool Buu oglu (b. 1940), born in Sergek-Khem, formerly Erza, now Kyzyl region. Was raised among reindeer herders and hunters of the Tepe-Khol' state farm, near the Mongolian border.

Kuular Badat Davyndai oglu (1906–74), hunter and expert in Tuvan oral folklore. Born in Teve-Khaia, Dzun-Khemchik region. Recording taken in the village of Khondergei, Dzun-Khemchik region.

Kuular Kendenchik Sembil oglu (1904–75), born in Ak-Aksy, Siut-Khol' region, a remarkable performer of shamanic *algyshy*, an expert in shamanic folklore.

Kuular Sengil Davyndai oglu (1903–73), a hunter and expert in folk songs, proverbs, and legends.

Kuular Chanzan-ool Bolunmai oglu (b. 1901), born in Aiangaty, Barun-Khemchik region, storyteller.

Kyrgys Soruktu Samdanai oglu (1901–?), born in Ol-Aryg sumona, Mezhegei-Tanda region, lived in the village of Erzin, could do guttural singing.

Lopsan Chimba Sendelchikovich (b. 1910), born in Ush-Terek, Barun-Khemchik region.

Mongush Belek Mandylaazhyk oglu (b. 1894), born in Ulaan-Byra, Dzun-Khemchik region.

Mongush Bora-khoo Kendegei oglu (1892–1970), born in Teve-Khaia, Dzun-Khemchik region, hunter, storyteller.

Mongush Opai Angyrban oglu (b. 1900), born in Shemi, Dzun-Khemchik region.

Mongush Sendinmaa Shiizhek uruu (1895–1962), born in Ush-Tei, Khondergei village council, Dzun-Khemchik region, storyteller.

Oiun Seden Khuragandai oglu (b. 1907), born in Khaialyg-Odek, across the Chargy mountains, on the right bank of the river Ulug-Khem, a former lama, very familiar with Tibetan.

Saaia Seren Sotpa oglu (b. 1927), born in Ergi-Barlyk, Barun-Khemchik region. Recording made in the village of Khondergei.

Sambuu Saaia Chuvurekovich (1908–86), born in Migur-Aksy, Mongun-Taiga region, Distinguished Cultural Worker of the Tuvan ASSR, a great expert in Tuvan folklore.

Saryg-ool Stepan Agbanovich (1908–83), born in Torgalyg, Oviur region, National Writer of the Tuvan ASSR, a great expert in oral folklore.

Sat Sotpa Oiduu oglu (1901–76), born in Orten-Tei, Barun-Khemchik region, storyteller, a remarkable expert in the old ways of the Tuvans. Recording made in the village of Khondergei, Dzun-Khemchik region.

Seree Khortek Burulbaaevich (b. 1924), born in Kara-Tal, Bai-Taiga region, an expert in Tuvan folklore, writer.

Solaan Duger Segbe oglu (b. 1902), born in Tere-Khol', former shaman. Recording made in the village of Kungurtuk, Kyzyl region.

Siukterek Tadar Endan uruu (b. 1918), born in Baian-kol, former Pii-Khem, now Kyzyl region.

Tagba Boris Uvazhaevich (b. 1906), born in Erzhei, Kaa-Khem region, an expert in Tuvan ethnography.

Tamba Salchak Odekeevich (1918–83), born in Oshtan, Kaa-Khem region, journalist, poet, and folklorist.

Tarzhaa Khertek Naiyrovich (b. 1905), born in Koop-Sook, Bai-Taiga region, teacher, a great expert in Tuvan ethnography, fluent in Mongolian and Russian.

Toibukhaa Khertek Koshtaiovich (1917–81), artist, a great expert in Tuvan folklore.

Shalyk Darbaa (b. 1912), born in Bai-Tal, Tes-Khem region, an expert in the old ways of the Tuvans and Mongols.

Shokshui Salchak Sunduevich (1906–72), born in Mongun-Taiga region, hunter, storyteller, well versed in Mongolian. Recording made in the village of Mugur-Aksy, Bai-Taiga region.

Choodu Chorbaa Donduula oglu (b. 1912), born in Terektig, Tes-Khem region.

Translated by Ronald Radzai

# Healing Techniques
# Among Evén Shamans

ANATOLY ALEKSEEV

This account concerns the Evén, a Tungus people also formerly known as the Lamut, who live in northeastern Siberia. According to the traditional Evén view, the world was divided into three mental spheres: the Upper World, the Middle World, and the Lower World. Shamans were the mediators acting between those three worlds. In the present paper, I shall try to reveal the methods and techniques for treating humans and animals used by the Evén shamans as those methods have been related to me by my informants in the village of Sebian-Kuel in the north of the Sakha Republic (Yakutia). Basilov [1984, p. 13] has written:

> It is not easy to enumerate briefly all the shaman's duties. These duties were wide and varied. The shaman asked the gods and spirits for prosperity and health, for the fecundity of humans and animals, for good hunting and good weather. When misfortune occurred, the shaman asked the spirits for help. As well as protecting his fellow-tribesmen while they were alive, he accompanied their souls to the other world. It was also his business to diagnose the causes of diseases and to treat them. He could learn from the spirits what would happen to a person in the future, and the location of lost people, animals, and things. In general, the competence of the shaman extended to all cases where the intervention of supernatural forces was suspected.

In connection with this, one of the important functions of the Evén shaman was to protect people from the influence of the evil spirits of Argi (*arinkolduk* and *ibd 'irilduk*) of the Lower World, as well as to aid his people in times of epidemics and misfortunes.[a] According to the traditional Evén view, "the principle of a shaman's treatment is the belief in the connection between illness and the activity of spirits. The diagnosis and the method of treatment as based on this belief" [Basilov, 1984, p. 17].

---

To achieve this, the shamans performed various ritual seances [*kamlanie*]. The purpose of those seances was to avert or to treat human diseases and reindeer plague under the difficult conditions of nomadic life whenever practical aid was needed by the family, kin, or tribe. In particular, hunters needed help if they were dogged by unsuccessful hunting. Therefore, the shaman's seance had different meanings according to its purpose. The seance was a special conversation, a communication between the shaman and various spirits of the Upper and Lower Worlds. The Evén believed that different diseases were caused by evil spirits that enter human beings, or that "the disease could result from the fact that the soul had been abducted by the spirits. In this case, one must defeat them and drive them out" [Basilov, 1984, p. 17].

The shaman was sent for only after all ordinary forms and methods of folk medicine had been tried. The functions of physicians were performed by herbalists, native healers, even by adult family members (mostly the old men). For treatment, various drugs of vegetable and animal origins were applied. The antlers of young reindeers (*n'imet*) were used as a general restorative remedy. After singeing the velvet of the antlers on a bonfire, the Evéns scraped off the singed parts with a sharp knife and then ate them. Especially valuable was the blood from inside the antler, which was sucked. Other widely used tonic medicines were the *oir* fern and "golden root" (*ginseng*), infusions of which were taken for three, twelve, or forty days according to the seriousness of the disease. Poplar buds [*sul*] were used as a painkiller. For liver and stomach diseases, and for jaundice, dysentery, rheumatism, painful joints, abscesses, and ulcers, they used bear's gall and the stomach secretion of the muskdeer, as well as other medicines of vegetable and animal origins.

If a disease could not be healed by traditional folk medicine, the family had to call the shaman. It is surprising that, as the former shaman Stepan Spiridonovich Krivoshapkin said, "the shaman knew in advance what the disease was. To heal the patient, the shaman performed one or another specific seance." At the same time, "shamanic ritual healing is an archaic form of psychotherapy. As distinct from the modern doctor, with his psychotherapeutic techniques, the shaman does not act in his own name. Behind the shaman stand higher forces. It is not he who heals, but spirits or gods more powerful than people. The patient's belief in the shaman's ability to restore his health is reinforced by the ritual. The shamanic session as a whole is intended to demonstrate the power of the shaman and of his spirits" [Basilov, 1984, p. 24].

At the end of the seance, the shaman uttered magical incantations. Sometimes he added purifying rituals including the cleansing of pollution by fire or fumigation by wild rosemary or azalea [*höngkös*]. It is well known that during prerevolutionary times in northern Siberia, many people died from smallpox. Sometimes whole clans perished. The Evén believed that the evil spirit of smallpox appeared on the migration routes of reindeer herders in the form of a woman with red hair like a European. Usually she arrived with travelers sitting on a sledge at the back of their caravan. The people did not notice her, but the shaman saw and knew that the evil spirit of smallpox had come to their place "to pay a social call." The shaman prepared himself for "combat." Most shamans were unable to fight alone against the smallpox spirit, which assumed the form of a huge red bull and rushed at the shaman. If a strong shaman of the lineage [*marka*] won in this "combat," he saved his kinsmen from that dangerous disease; if he lost, all his kinsmen, including the shaman himself, would die, with the exception of two relatives who remained alive to bury the dead. Sometimes, in order to expel the smallpox spirit, two or three shamans performed a special seance together.

Shamans also used a special *kud'ai* deer to treat seriously ill relatives. "Every Evén used to have a *kud'ai* deer of his own," explained Stepan Spiridonovich. "From among many reindeer, the shaman specially chose the *kud'ai* as the protector of a particular person. Not every deer could become a *kud'ai*, only a deer with a divine mark, white or piebald, and only those that had a *tigök*."

A *tigök* is the ball of hair that can sometimes be found on a reindeer's neck. From that ball, the Evén made a hair rope for the *dolburge* [a ritual gate] (see below). This ball was kept in a special saddlebag called a *herukle*, since it was believed that it brought happiness to the owner of the *kud'ai* and to his family, well-being to the deer, and luck to the hunters. This kind of deer had been probably put on the Earth by a celestial deity called *kud'ai*, or by the deity of the Sun, or Evén by the supreme deity Hövki. It was a person's protector. "When someone, man, woman, or child, is ill, the shaman orders the sacred reindeer to be brought. If someone's back is aching, then the shaman treats it with a light puff of the sacred shamanic reindeer on the exact spot that aches."

The shamanic *kud'ai* deer was able to heal his owner and even to rescue him from death. According to Stepan Spiridonovich, "there were instances when a *kud'ai* could even die while protecting its owner, that is, sacrifice itself in order to rescue its master." When a *kud'ai* died suddenly for whatever reason, it was strictly forbidden to touch it, and even more strictly forbidden to eat its flesh. The dead deer was left where it lay. "And when I was seriously ill," said the former shaman, "the great shaman Dygdaa Khabyrylla placed two *kud'ai* at the entrance of our tent, one white and one piebald, and then performed a healing rite. The spirit of disease was transferred to the two *kud'ai* and the shaman let them go free. That's how I recovered." Old men told me that "the *kud'ai* was used for treatment as follows: near the tent [*chum*] where the sick man lay, the shaman tied up one or two deer (depending on the seriousness of the disease), either piebald [*buvdi*] or white [*geltaldi*], which had to be young. The sick man was then brought out of the tent and the deer allowed to breathe on his forehead, face, and chest. The shaman then fumigated the sick man and the deer with azalea or wild rosemary smoke, directing the smoke three times to the left and three times to the right with the aid of a small carpet [*dahi*] sewn from the skin of a reindeer's head. Then the sick man was made to spit on the muzzle of the *kud'ai* three times, and after that the *kud'ai* was set free. It was believed that the disease was passed to the reindeer with the saliva. From that moment, nobody had the right to use the *kud'ai* for the ordinary needs of the nomadic economy. It was even more strictly forbidden to cut the *kud'ai*'s antlers or to brand it. The *kud'ai* remained free till the end of its days.

If an evil spirit of disease from the Lower World attacked a human being, the shaman applied the following method of treatment. He performed a seance in order to transfer the spirit of the disease into a pair of wooden birds. The shaman started his seance late at night, near a bonfire. In front of the sick man's tent he attached the wooden birds, painted red, to two sticks. According to the former shaman S. S. Krivoshapkin, the birds were made by another according to the shaman's orders. These birds were loons [*okingee*] or hawks [*gyakai*]. As the result of the seance, the shaman made the birds fly to the celestial world, having previously transferred the evil spirit of disease into them. If the birds disappeared during the seance, the sick man recovered. Once the spirit of disease was divided into two parts and sent to the heavens, it could not return.

One of the most effective shamanistic methods of healing was to send the soul [*'An'ian*] of a sick man to the celestial world [*n'am-*

*nantaldula*]. This healing ritual was called *boi 'aianman tootuke 'ek*. The shamans believed that this ritual was called for when a disease spirit from the Lower World had attacked a person. In this case, a classic principle of opposition is clearly revealed: the Upper World is opposed to the Lower World. For these purposes, the shaman used a special construction made from willow twigs, called *höbök*. First he cut the twigs to 70–90 cm; then each twig was split into two parts, with the upper parts of each twig kept intact. After the twigs were pulled to one side, they were stuck into the ground [compare Okladnikov, 1949].

In all probability, this dome-shaped construction represents a simple model of the world. This disk-shaped device, called *indaan* in the Evén language, is made of wood, and has a round hole in the middle. A similar device, used by the Evénki reindeer herders of Manchuria in northern China was photographed in 1931 by the anthropologist Ethel-John Lindgren [1935, p. 177]. The female shaman [*udaghan*] of the Manchurian Evénki used almost exactly the same methods related to me by the Evén shaman in northern Yakutia.

Stepan Spiridonovich explained to me that

> the *höbök* and *indaan* represented a symbol of the Universe. The symbol of the Universe in the Evén language is *nelbeen omno*, while the *indaan* as a symbol of heaven is called *n'amnaldam*, and as a symbol of the Sun, *n'øltin*. Having built the *höbök* in a glade and placed the *indaan* inside it, the shaman, together with the old men, took some of the sick person's hair and laid it on the *indaan* inside it. The Evén believed that one of the souls of a person [*khan'ian*] is in the hair. By means of the seance, the shaman sent the soul of the sick person to heaven, since it was believed that the spirits from the Lower World could not fly up to the Upper World, far less stay there and cause evil and pain in a person's soul. In heaven, the disease quickly left the person's soul and the person recovered. After the seance, the *höbök* was left in place.

According to many informants, the same ritual was applied by the shaman to the reindeer herd [*dölmiche*]. This ritual was called *orom töötukehek*, that is, sending the souls of reindeer to the celestial country lying between heaven and earth. The Evén consider that reindeer are a gift from the Supreme god Hövki and from the God of Sun and that they are therefore celestial and solar animals.

The shamans performed the *orom töötukehek* ritual in the last days of June, believing that doing so they could avert widespread necrobacteriosis among the reindeer. It was believed that the deers' souls, having reached heaven, received the blessing of the Supreme God Hövki and then returned to the Middle World (i.e., to the earth) perfectly "clean." According to the stories told by old men, the ritual was performed as follows: the shaman, together with the old men, made the *höbök* from willow twigs, and all the deer ropes called *hular* [*uhilbu*] were placed inside it. Having collected all the ropes in a circle, they hung it inside the *höbök* [*nelbeene*]. Not far from the *höbök*, a small gate called the *delburge* was placed. The *delburge* consisted of two young larches, rope made from the *tuguk* hair of the *kud'ai* deer and from the hairs under the reindeer's neck (*neeielde*). Between the two trees, the *delburge* (the rope to which the reindeer under-neck hair was fastened) was stretched. The ritual has changed over time; instead of the hair they now hang colored pieces of cloth. But this has not changed the general idea of the ritual. Two young trees and the *delburge* signify the celestial gate through which the deer must pass to reach the celestial world, the realm of purity and well-being. And through the *höbök* the shaman raised the deer rope [*hular*] up to the celestial world, so that the evil spirits of necrobacteriosis would enter the rope, become separated from the deer, and leave them alone. Under the *delburge*, a bonfire was kindled, and then rosemary or rhododendron was thrown in the fire, for their smoke possessed bactericidal properties. All those actions were performed to purify the deers' souls from pollution through fire before the souls reached the celestial world.

The ritual was performed in the following sequence. The shaman started his seance. The shaman's assistants and the old men slowly led the deer to the gate [*delburge*] and let them pass through the gate to heaven in a single file. The deer had to move against the current of a river or stream for it was believed that water always flowed down from mountain peaks, and heaven is located higher than mountain peaks. According to the Evén, when water flowed down it flowed to the Lower World. If the *delburge* had been placed downstream and the deer had been sent through the gate down with the current of the river, it would mean that all of them would die from the disease and would go to the Lower World. Therefore, before beginning that ritual, the Evén always emphasized the place from where the river (*okaat*) flowed.

Usually, even after the ritual, individual cases of the reindeer disease called *kopïtka* (necrobacteriosis) still sometimes occurred, but there were no instances of mass outbreaks any more. In order to prevent epidemics, the shamans exposed those deer to treatment as follows. The shaman with the assistance of his helper spirits could see "the bacteria" (the worms) of that disease with their own eyes. They could even pick up those worms with their fingers, kill them, and thus heal the deer. The shaman was not allowed to reveal how he actually healed deer suffering from necrobacteriosis, since if he revealed his secret he would have been punished by his helper-spirits. Sometimes, the shaman sucked the microbes from the wound on the reindeer's sore leg and spat three times on the wound. After all that, the treatment is considered to be finished and the deer recovered.

An ordinary reindeer herder was not allowed to suck pus from the wound on the sore leg of the deer, for he might have died from that disease. I was taught by other shamans and helper-spirits how to treat reindeer and humans suffering from various diseases. For each disease, the methods and techniques are different.

Informants also said that if a disease, for instance necrobacteriosis, had resulted in the death of a deer, the shaman would perform the following ritual. During a thunderstorm, he showed the dead reindeer and the sore leg to the lightning and the thunder [*avdri*], asking 'Inken, the spirit of lightning and thunder, to take Argi, the evil spirit of disease and death, with him. This was to be done to avert a necrobacterios epidemic and murrain among the deer. Sometime the shaman asked the Sun to take the spirit of the disease with it. Before asking the Sun, the shaman cut off a dead deer's leg and hung it in the sunshine for three days. When three days had passed, the adult members of the nomad camp, led by the shaman, asked the Sun to take away the disease, to have mercy on the deer, and thus to save them from the influence of the evil spirit of that disease. After all had been completed, the leg was taken down and burned on a bonfire, with the shaman repeating that the spirit should disappear and leave the deer alone.

It is quite usual for reindeer to suffer from pneumonia in summer. It is very hot in the mountains in the afternoon and very cold at night, when the temperature may fall to $+3° - +5°C$. Sometimes it snows in the mountains, or *mondi* may occur (it rains for a long time, the sky is covered with clouds, and it becomes cool). As a result of protracted rains followed rapidly by a warm spell, the deer suffer from pneumonia. The shamans used to treat those deer by the following method: with their hands they "opened" the hair on a deer's wither and spat into it three times. If the deer's joints also hurt, the shaman spat under its tail. Thus shamans treated humans and animals using various methods and techniques, according to the spirit of disease and death.

According to the shaman's outlook, the health of their kinsmen and reindeer depended not only on a person but also on the place where the nomadic camp was situated. Therefore, the old men chose the site for the nomadic camp (*orikit*). The site had to be favorable both for humans and for animals. Usually, it was a clearing (*kuuntok*) on the bank of a stream or river. The ground should not be swampy, so that people would feel comfortable and in harmony with nature. Places with swamps and ravines were considered geopathogenic zones. To pitch a nomadic camp in such places was dangerous for the health of both humans and animals. The Evén believed that the evil spirits of disease and death [*hargi*] came up through swamps and ravines to the earth's surface. The old men never pitched their camp in the middle of a swamp [*bule*], in a boggy area [*dottoordu*], or in an area full of dried-out trees [*borin toordu*]. Dried trees were believed to impart an energy from the earth that was unfavorable for the human organism. Such places were also considered geopathogenic. The door of a *chum* (tent) should point downstream, while a person should sleep with the head pointing against the current. The Evén believed that if they slept with their heads pointing against the current, the water would not wash away the person's "thoughts" and "health" into the Lower World. In other words, the person would always feel comfortable and healthy.

Sometimes Evén shamans felt ill. According to stories told by the shaman S.S. Krivoshapkin and the reindeer herder E.M. Kolesova (the author's mother), shamans sometimes suffered from various diseases if they had not performed a seance for a long time. In order to recover, they placed an iron rod or a knife in the fire, or asked someone else to do it, and after making it red-hot, took it out with their hands and licked it. My mother told me a story about a female shaman and her son Pyotr. In late 1970, they worked together in the same herding camp. One day the shaman fell ill and asked my mother to make some iron red-hot in the fire and give it to her. The shaman took the red-hot iron and began to lick it, producing a hissing sound, and kept licking it until it became cold. She said that her soul had at last been calmed, fell asleep, and awoke the next morning quite healthy. The same thing happened with her son.

To summarize, Evén shamans were the protectors of their kinsmen's souls in the Middle World. They protected people from the influence of evil forces in nature, and if these evil forces of disease and death had done any harm, the shaman would save people from their influence. Shamans used various methods and techniques of healing and restored the balance of forces between humans and nature.

### Editor's note

a. Although the Evén shamans are referred to here using the male pronoun, Evén healers, including shamans, could also be women, as is clear by the end of this chapter.

## Informants (Evéns from the village of Sebian-Kuel in the Sakha Republic (Yakutia))

Stepan Spiridonovich Krivoshapkin, Naku clan, born in 1913, shaman.

Pyotr Stepanovich Krivoshapkin, Kirgembis clan, born in 1940, reindeer-hunter.

Evdokiia Mikhailovna Kolesova, Tigiasir clan, born in 1920.

Vasilii Pavlovich Keimetinov, Keimeti clan, born in 1918.

Translated by Sergei Muravev and Piers Vitebsky

# Part II.

# Wedding Theory and Field Data

# The Teleut Ritual *Chymyr*

## Exorcism and Explanation

Dmitri A. Funk

"After us there will be shamans
Like unto the *chymyrchy*-whisperers"
—(From the mystery to Adam of the
Teleut shaman Kanakai)

At the beginning of the twentieth century, Teleut shamans [*kam*] carried out grandiose seances [*kamlaniia*] to contact the first-ancestor–deity, Adam. One of the stages of the path that, according to Teleut notions, was completed by the *kam* was marked by a *tamga*, a mark on a pine tree growing at the base of heaven.[1] The *kam* dramatized an arrow shot from its bow and held a drum [*buben* (frame drum)] in the left hand. Taking aim, he quickly ran a beater [*kolotushka*] across the drum, as though releasing the arrow toward the target.[a] Having "shot," the shaman sang with regret about how the *tamga* of the ancient *kam* are still clearly visible after all this time on the pine tree, but the closer the shamans stand to our time, the less clearly are their marks visible, or their arrows do not even reach the pine tree at all:

> *Körzögör myny kalyng cherü:*
> *Ozogy udyldyng tamgazyn*
> *T'ash karagai poiyna*
> *Palta tobozin kidire sokkonyn.*
> *Any ezhe udyldyng*
> *Salgan tamgazyn körzögör—*
> *T'ash karagai poiyna*
> *Palta mizin kidire sokkondii*
>
> . . . . . . . . . . . . . . . . . . . .
> *T'ash karagai kaizyrygyn*
> *Soio sogup chygyptyr.*
>
> . . . . . . . . . . . . . . . . . . . .

Russian text © 1995 by the Russian Academy of Sciences, N. N. Miklukho-Maklai Institute of Ethnology and Anthropology, and D. A. Funk. "*Chymyr*—Teleutskii obriad izgnaniia zlogo dukha (novye materialy)," *Etnograficheskoe obozrenie*, 1995, no. 4 (July–August), pp. 107–14. This work was completed with the aid of the Russian Humanitarian Scientific Fund grant no. 96–01–00352.

*Tiskin poi t'etpei tüshtür.*
. . . . . . . . . . . . . . . . . . . .
*Armakchy poi t'etpei tüshtür.*
*Any ezhe bis udyldyng*
*Salgan tamgabis körzögör.*
*T'ash karagai poiyna*
*T'uukta kelbei turganyn.*


Behold this mighty host:
The *tamga* of the ancient shamans
All the way into the young pine tree,
Like an axe all the way to
the head, has struck.
The shamans following
Behold the *tamga*—
Into the young pine tree
[It] has struck as though with the sharp edge of the axe.
. . . . . . . . . . . . . . . . . . . .
[Only] the bark of the young pine tree
Stripping off, piercing, has it passed through.
. . . . . . . . . . . . . . . . . . . .
[The *tamga*] has fallen, not having reached [the pine tree
    by such a great distance as the length] of a rein.
. . . . . . . . . . . . . . . . . . . .
[The *tamga*] has fallen, not having reached [the pine tree
    by such a great distance as the length] of a lasso.
The next, by us—the shamans'
Superimposed *tamga* behold.
To the young pine tree [not even]
Close do they reach in flight.


The picture of the decline of shamanism was concluded with a prophesy:

*Pisting kinibistegi udyldar*
*Chymyrchydang* [*teng*][2] *polor!*

The shamans—our descendants
Shall be like unto the *chymyrchy*![3]

So who are the *chymyrchy*? What did they engage in? Why did the shamans consider them to be a "lower order" in comparison with the true *kam*? Are such specialists found among the Teleut today? We shall attempt to answer some of these questions.

In published works is a sole mention of the existence among the Teleut of the *chymyr* ritual, directed at the exorcism from a sick person of an evil spirit, the *üzüt*. A. V. Anokhin's "Dusha i ee svoistva po predstavleniiu teleutov" [The Soul and Its Properties According to the Notion of the Teleut] provides the following information.[4]

For a long time after the burial of a person (or, more accurately, the corporeal shell), prior to migration to the "land of the *üzüt*," a certain posthumous substance continued to exist on earth, having received among the Teleut, as among many other Turkic peoples of the Saiano-Altai, the general "generic" name *üzüt*. In some research, the *üzüt* is included in the list of "souls"; in others, it approaches the Russian concept of *pokoinik* [the deceased], although it is hardly likely that an explanation of this "essence" can be found through such analogies.

According to Teleut views, one of the most characteristic peculiarities of the *üzüt* is to cause harm to the living. Wanting some company, the *üzüt* can make its way into a house, select an "interlocutor," and penetrate the stomach through the mouth. After this visit, the person could be racked with stomachaches; in such cases, a specialist in the exorcism of an *üzüt* needed to be called.

> The specialist makes a small wooden scoop [*lopatka*] and places burning hot coals with ashes on it. On the coals is placed flour, oil, and tobacco. What results is a smoking mixture [smudge] with [spirit-] discouraging smoke. The ritual called *chymyr* is performed with this smudge over the ill person in bed. It consists of the following. The invited person, while fumigating the ill person, reads out a prayer, quietly at first, somewhat louder in the middle, and at the end attaining a frenzied, frightening shout. With the last words, the person performing the ritual runs to the threshold and casually throws the scoop with the concluding words: "*shau—ili ai, tatai*" [begone, get lost!].

Anokhin wrote about the exorcism of an *üzüt* from a kettle during the distillation of wine as a particular instance of the harm-causing activities of the *üzüt*, to reveal the application range of the *chymyr* ritual: if less wine resulted than expected, this was explained by the

settling of an *üzüt* in the kettle.[5] This information was supplemented by
the text of "a prayer pronounced over a sick person." The published
text need not be repeated; more important is the [Teleut] original used
by Anokhin. In Anokhin's archive, I discovered a manuscript titled
"*Chymyr*," written in an unknown hand, dated 9 June 1911 (Cheluk-
hoevskii ulus).[6]

*Shilii-ai!**

*Chymyr, chymyr* (10 times)

*Kandu üzüt, kara iek[7] ne?*

[Is the illness from] an ill-intentioned *üzüt* or from a black *iek*?

*Chymyr* (4 times)

*Toluk saiyn tolgondyng ba?*
*Aral saiyn ailandyng ba?*
*Kuiun bolup kuiburdung ba?*
*Salkyn bolup saabyryldyng ba?*

Did you hang around all of the corners?
Did you tangle your way through all of the groves?
Having become a whirlwind, did you spin?
Having become the wind, did you whirl around?

*Chymyr* (10 times)

*Jakshy etkening jazyk boldy,*
*Iigi etkening ilek boldy.*

Your good deeds have become crimes,
Two of your deeds have become a joking matter.

*Chymyr* (6 times)

*Ak taikany azhyp kelding be?*
*Agyn suudy kechip kelding be?*

---

*The literal meaning of the exclamation is not known to me.

Having crossed over a white mountain, did you come?
Having swum through the flowing water, did you come?

*Chymyr* (10 times)

*Ady, jolyn aidynyp otur,*
*Tizhin bile puulalba,*
*Tilin byla chichilip otur.*

Your name, your path, begin to tell
Do not tie yourself up with your teeth,
Begin to free up your tongue.

*Chymyr* (6 times)

*Jazhyl otko jangzairym,*
*Kyzyl otko kystairym.*
*Jyda myngang jymyrarym,*
*Kylysh byla kymyrarym.*
To the green fire I will press you,
To the red fire I will squeeze you.
With a spear I will strike [you],
With a sword I will smash you.

*Chymyr* (15 times, loudly)

*Kök temirge kystairym,*
*Jar piiikke jangzairym,*
*Suu terengge kystairym.*

To the green iron I will squeeze [you],
To a deep ravine I will press [you],
Into the deep water I will shove [you].

*Chymyr* (6 times)

*Kapshygaiga kaabylyp otur,*
*Ady-bazhyn aidynyp otur.*

Hurrying yourself up,
Begin to tell about your name and kin.

*Chymyr* (2 times)

*Kesken seeng agazhyna*[8]
*Temdegende jajanyna,*
*Alyp bargan aldang*[9] *byla,*
*Jip bargan jimekching byla.*

[Go] to the coffin that has been carved out for you,
To the grave which has been measured out to fit you,
With the spirit of death that has taken you,
With the devourer that has eaten you—go.

*Chymyr* (10 times)

*Idim bolzo, kabagan,*
*Üiüm bolzo, suzegen,*
*Aigyrym bolzo, tebegen.*
*Ady, jolyn aidynyp otur, chymyr!*
My dog bites,
My cow butts,
My stallion kicks.
Your name, your path, begin to relate, *chymyr!*

*Shau!!!*

I will not stop to explicate; some questions readers may have will be answered below in the discussion of other texts. Rather, I will address a few of the questions formulated at the beginning of this article.

Judging by the information cited by Anokhin, the *chymyr* ritual was performed by a "specialist." Knowing the significance of the *chy*-affix (a word-forming affix signifying a profession), it is not difficult to understand that in the mystery addressed to Adam, relevant were specialists at conducting the *chymyr* ritual, that is, *chymyr-chy[lar]*. Their principal duty was to exorcize evil spirits-*üzüt* with the help of a relatively uncomplicated series of ritual acts and, accompanying them, incantations [*zaklinaniia*] with an "international" three-part structure[10] (in Anokhin's terms: "quietly," "louder," and "frenzied, frightening shout"). New materials about the ritual and about the people who perform it were gathered by me in the 1980s and 1990s during ethnographic trips to the Teleut of Kemerovo Oblast (Russian Federation).

Usually, the Teleut do not include the term *chymyr* among those words that can and should be translated into another language. Nevertheless, a possible translation of it into Russian as "a whisper, whispering" was not disputed. The word-forms to be found in dictionaries that are the closest to *chymyr* would be: *chym*—quietly, quieter; and *chymyra*—to whisper.[11] Taking into consideration the obvious close semantic connection of these words with the term *chymyr* and the specific features of the use of this term in a ritual context, we can assume that *chymyr* can most adequately be translated into Russian with the adverb *tikho* [quietly], or with the phrase "everything's going to be all right, be careful, don't be afraid," addressed by the *chymyrchy* to the evil spirit for the purpose of not frightening the latter and of attaining, in the end, the revelation of the *üzüt*'s name.

In the opinion of the Teleut, including actual specialists in the exorcism of the *üzüt*, *chymyrchy* are categorically not shamans. It goes without saying that, like shamans, they possess some kind of powers, a certain level of clairvoyance (without, at the same time, being professional *kösmöksi*—clairvoyants); they are capable of entering into contact with "uncleanness," and they know the texts of incantations. A specific feature of *chymyrchy*, as compared with shamans, is considered to be their "narrow specialization," the application of their abilities in commonplace situations, and the absence of the indispensable attributes of a *kam*—the drum and the beater.

Now, as before, judging by the recollections of my elderly informants,[12] people able to drive out evil spirits from sick people fulfill their "duties" by invitation.

The most widespread, general symptoms of the settling of an *üzüt* in a person are sharp or protracted pains in the belly or stomach, as well as a weak pulse and nausea. Having made a preliminary determination of the cause of the indisposition, the sick person or a relative goes to the *chymyrchy* for assistance. The *chymyrchy* comes to the sick person without fail and usually confirms the diagnosis and exorcizes the *üzüt*, generally in one session.

Despite the negative attitude of officials in recent decades toward any religion whatsoever, many rituals and texts accompanying them within so-called everyday [*bytovoi*] shamanism have been preserved fairly completely among the Teleut to this day. This assertion applies, in part, to the *chymyr* ritual as well.

On 26 July 1988, in the village of Teleuty (Middle-Teleut ulus), my long-time acquaintance P. P. Porosenkova (1902–91; *née* Todysheva, Mundus *seok*, Kandy-iuty *yurt*) at my request dictated into a recorder the text that she usually used when invited to perform the *chymyr* ritual. According to her preliminary explanations, at first she attempted to ascertain which evil spirit had penetrated the sick person, and the path that this *üzüt* had taken. After this, she had to guess the name of the *üzüt*, or to find it out from [the *üzüt*] by means of trickery, in order to obtain complete power over it. Only after this could the ritual be concluded—exorcizing this evil force back to the "land of the *üzüt*." The final part of the text is pronounced at an accelerated tempo and a higher pitch. Of course such a simplified, superficial explanation has a deep-seated subtext: in actual situations, the *chymyrchy* really could heal a sick person.

The text I recorded turned out to be the longest of all those known before. In addition to the texts from the archive and from Anokhin's article, several *chymyr* lines were published in the newspaper *Altaidyng cholmony* (17 March 1990) in a recording by A. P. Alaganchakova. Unfortunately, even my recording is not without flaws. First of all, the ritual was carried out in an artificial situation; consequently, the *üzüt* was not named in the text. The pronouncement of the text was an act of memory, and not its reproduction for an occasion. Second, for many reasons, text deciphering was begun four years after the fact, after Porosenkova's death, and thus a number of questions remain without satisfactory answers.

*Chymyr, chymyr, chymyr!*

*Kandu üzüt, kara iek?*
*T'oloi al ioloktyng ba?*
*Udra polzo, uchradyng ba?*
*Kuiun polyp kuibur t'ürding ba?*
*T'el polyp t'elbir kelding ba?*
*At aldynang chaaptyng ba?*
*Art kiiinineng kuudung ba?*

[Is the illness from] an evil *üzüt* or from a black *iek*?
Did you walk along roads?

Did you walk toward a meeting?
Did you spin like a whirlwind?
Did you blow like the wind?
Did you run in front of a horse?
Did you try to catch up from behind?

*Chymyr, chymyr!*

*Özök aiak örüldüng ba?*
*Öpkö t'ürek kabylding ba?*

Did you try to get underfoot?
Did you stick to the lungs and the heart?

*Chymyr, chymyr, chymyr!*

*Ashtang ala ashtadyng ba?*
*Suudang ala suusap kelding ba?*

Did you lack food to eat?
Did you lack water to drink?

*Chymyr, chymyr!*

*Ashtang ala ashtap kelgen polzo—*
*Kürek pazhy küldü ash—*
*Küle tuda myna kap!*
*Ashtang ala ashtap kelzeng,*
*Ailü ierdeng ochkonyna*
*Ala tuda mynang kap—*
*Ailü suudy pöl(ö) alsyn!*
*Suudang polzo, suusap kelding—*
*Kürek pazhy küldü ash—*

If for lack of food you have come to eat—
At the end of the scoop is bread in ashes—
Smiling, grab it!
If you came for food to eat,
From the land under the moon of peaceful rest (?)
Grab it here—

Let lunar water be shared!
If for lack of water you have come to drink—
At the end of the scoop is bread in ashes—

*Chymyr, chymyr!*

*Küle tuda myna kap!*
*Tong köksündi[13] pöl(ö) alsyn!*
*Kuiun polyp kuibur t'ürding ba?*
*Iel polyp t'elbir kelding ba?*
*At aldynang chaaptyng ba?*
*Art kiiinineng kuup kelding ba?*

Smiling, grab it!
Let the firm breast be shared!
Did you spin like a whirlwind?
Did you come blowing like the wind?
Did you run in front of a horse?
Did you try to catch up from behind?

*Chymyr, chymyr!*

*Kaia polzo, körböi par!*
*Kalcha polzo, pakpai par!*
*Aina polzo, aikyrarym!*
*Iekti polzo, iekkererim![14]*
*Idim polzo, kabagan!*
*Üiüm polzo, susegen!*
*Kelgen t'olyng ianylba!*
*Kechken suung temdenbe!*
*Kesken polzyng t'eringe*

Without looking back, go!
Do not shoot with the eyes, without turning around, go!
If [you are] an *aina*—I will drive [you] away! If [you are] a *iek*—
            I will expel [you]!
My dog—bites!
My cow—butts!
Do not confuse the path wherefrom you came!

Do not confuse the river across which you swam!
Go to that land where all has been cut down.

*Chymyr, chymyr!*

*Kemdegende agazhynga!*
*Kaia polzo, körgüspessim,*
*Kalcha polzo, paktyrbassym!*
*Ashtang ala ash tatpassym!*
*Ailü t'erdi achkynyna!*
*Ala tuda mynang kap—*
*Ai köksündi pöl(ö) alsyn!*
*Suudang ala suusap kelgen polzyng*
*Kündü t'erdeng küzelü[15] ash*
*Küle tuda mynang kap!*

The tree measured out [to fit you]!
If you look back, I will not show you,
If you squint your eyes, I will not turn around!
[Choosing] from the food, I will feed you![16]
Peaceful rest has come to the land under the moon!
Grab here—
Let the lunar breast be shared!
If for lack of water you have wanted to drink,
Baked bread of the sunny land,
Smiling, grab it!

*Chymyr, chymyr!*

*Tong köksündi pöl(ö) alsyn!*
*Al taikady ash kelding ba?*
*Agyn suudy kechip kelding ba?*
*Kuiun polyp kuibyr kelding ba?*
*Iel polyp t'elbir kelding ba?*

Let the strong breast be shared!
Did you cross over a high mountain?
Having swum through the flowing water,
    did you come?

Like a whirlwind spinning, did you come?
Like the wind blowing, did you come?

*Chymyr, chymyr!*

*Kaia polzo, körgüspesim!*
*Kalcha polzo, paktyrbasym!*
*Aina polzo, aikyratam!*
*Iekti polzo, iekkeretim!*
*Uuzym polzo, ieldü!*

If you look back, I will not show you,
If you squint your eyes, I will not turn around!
If [you are] an *aina*—I will drive [you] away!
If [you are] a *iek*—I will expel [you]!
In my mouth is the wind![17]

*Chymyr, chymyr!*

*Alakanym atu!*
*Kaia polzo, körgüspeem!*
*Kalcha polzo, paktyrbaam!*
The palm of my hand is an "*atu*" [has fire?]![18]
If you look back, I will not show you,
If you squint your eyes, I will not turn around!

*Chymyr, chymyr!*

*Kelgen t'olyng ianylba!*
*Kechken suung kemdenbe!*
*Kesken polzo, t'eringe*
*Kemdegende agazhynga!*
*Kara t'ering kasyngan,*
*Katu agazhyng chamyngan!*
*Idim polzo, kabagan!*

Do not confuse the path wherefrom you came!
Do not confuse the river across which you swam!
Go to that land where all has been cut down

The tree measured out [to fit you]!
[Go to the place where] your black land was dug up,
[Where] your hard tree was rough-hewn!
My dog—bites!

*Chymyr, chymyr!*

*Üiüm polzo, süsegen!*
*Aina polzo, aikyratam!*
*Iekti polzo, iekkeretim!*
*Kaia körböi kalcha pakpai par!*
*Kuiun polyp kuibur kelding ba?*
*Iel polyp t'elbir kelding ba?*
*Al taikady ash kelding ba?*
*Agyn suudy kechip kelding ba?*
My cow—butts!
If [you are] an *aina*—I will drive [you] away!
If [you are] a *iek*—I will expel [you]!
Without looking back, without turning around, go!
Like a whirlwind spinning, did you come?
Like the wind blowing, did you come?
Did you cross over an unassailable mountain?
Having swum through the flowing water, did you come?

*Chymyr, chymyr!*

*Özök aiak kabyldyng ba?*
*Öpkö t'ürek örüldüng ba?*
*Aina edip aikyrarym!*
*Iek edip iekkererim!*
*Kaia polzo, pakpai par!*
*Kalcha polzo, körböi par!*
*Kelgen t'olyng ianylba!*
*Kechken suung kemdenbe!*
*Aina polzo, aikyratam!*
*T'ekti polzo, t'ekkeretim!*
*Alakanym atu,*
*Uuzym polzu, ieldü!*
*Aina polzo, aikyratam!*

*T'ekti polzo, t'ekkeretim!*
*Kaia polzo, körgüspem!*
*Kalcha polzo, paktyrbam!*

Did you stick underfoot?
Did you stick to the lungs and the heart?
Thinking that [you are] an *aina*—I will drive [you] away!
Thinking that [you are] a *iek*—I will expel [you]!
Without looking back, without turning around, go!
Squint [your] eyes, do not look, [but] go!
Do not confuse the path wherefrom you came!
Do not confuse the river across which you swam!
If [you are] an *aina*—I will drive [you] away!
If [you are] a *iek*—I will expel [you]!
The palm of my hand is an "*atu*" (?),
In my mouth is the wind!
If [you are] an *aina*—I will drive [you] away!
If [you are] a *iek*—I will expel [you]!
If you look back, I will not show you,
If you squint [your] eyes, I will not turn around![b]

This incantation can be considered "standard" with respect to a whole range of indicators. The logical structure, the size of the lines, and the use of standard "formulas" unite it both with the Anokhin texts and with all of the different variations of performance by *chymyrchy*-specialists in existence today. Nevertheless, this is but one side of the modern condition of the Teleut ritual tradition.

Parallel to the gradual disappearance of "professional *üzüt*-fighters," the Teleut began the tradition of recording texts of everyday shamanic folklore on paper. The greatest variety of texts is encountered, among them the *chymyr*. The texts of the first group are generally intended only for performance on specific occasions (not necessarily aloud) together with ritual actions; the "written texts" are usually intended not only as "crib-notes" in ritual conduct, but even become instructions during the incantation. As an example, I can refer to my own attempt to ask that such a text be read, on 30 August 1992 in the village of Shanda. This created significant complications for the owners of the manuscript.[c] As an illustration of such "written texts," I will cite it here (with corrected spelling, naturally):

*Kandu üzüt, kara t'ek!*
*Kelgen t'olyng t'anylba!*
*Kechken suung temdenbe!*
*Ailü t'erdeng airyi kalgan,*
*Arbys-kaanga chachyl kalgan!*
*Ady-t'olyng aidynbasym,*
*Aina chylap aikyrarym,*
*Kyzyl otko kystairym,*
*T'azhyl otko t'angzairym!*
*Tolyk saiyn tolgondyng ba?*
*Aral saiyn ailandyng ba?*
*Kesken polzo, agazhynga*
*Kemdegen polzo, tobragynga!*
*Kaia polzo, paktyrbam,*
*Kalcha polzo, körgüspem,*
*Itu toshtop otkyrerim,*
*Üzüt t'olynga chogyrarym,*
*Kara tashka pasyrarym,*
*Köp t'olynga kokyrarym.*


Evil *üzüt*, black *iek*—
Do not confuse the path along which you came!
Do not confuse the river across which you swam!
Having separated yourself from the land under the moon,
Return to Arbys-khan!
Your name-path I will not name,
[If you are] like an *aina*—I will drive [you] away,
To the red fire I will squeeze [you],
To the green fire I will press [you]!
Did you hang around all of the corners?
Did you tangle your way through all of the groves?
[Go] to the tree that has been chopped down [for you],
Measured out [to fit you], [go into that] clay-earth of yours!
If you look back, I will not turn around,
If you squint your eyes, I will act like [I haven't noticed]!
. . . . . . . . . . . . . . . . . . . . .
To the *üzüt* path I will prepare [for you],
To the black stone I will squeeze [you],
On many paths with ashes I will scatter [you].

Such texts are widespread. The principal function of papers with "magic words" is for [personal] safekeeping. They can be kept at home, usually in a dresser, and they can be taken on a distant journey. Given the history of the spread and existence of Orthodoxy among the Teleut, an attempt to find the roots of the phenomenon in Christian ritual and even in the religious practice of the Soviet period appears completely plausible. The texts of Christian prayers recorded on sheets of paper and handed out as a protection to young people going on journeys far from home, to serve in the army, and so forth are relevant here. Nonetheless, the possibility that the Teleut came to this independently can likewise not be ruled out.

In the most general outlines, such are new materials gathered by me on the Teleut *chymyr* ritual and on the *chymyrchy* who perform it. Although questions remain, the representative character of the texts published nevertheless allows us to outline principal directions for future research.

Virtually everything that a culturologist can do needs doing: making many recordings of the ritual and its ancient variants with all technological means, and searching for parallels in the culture of neighboring nationalities. Indeed, the Shor have a ritual of *üzüt* exorcism, and its text apparently can to be regarded as the closest such parallel.[19] In addition, the participation of specialists of another kind, capable not only of recording words or movements, but also of permeating the essence of the phenomenon, is required to assess the *chymyrchy* phenomenon. I remind the reader that as the result of the actions of a *chymyrchy*, an ill person often became well.

## Editor's notes

a. The word for shaman used here, *kam*, is common among southern Turkic peoples, and from it derived the word for séance, *kamlanie*, that came into the Russian language. In Turkic languages, a common word for human or father is *adam* or *agham*.

The use of *tamg* as clan identification marks is common among both Turkic and Ugrian peoples. The masculine gender for the *kam* is left here, for this passage refers to a specific séance. As is made clear below, Teleut shamans and other spiritual-medical practitioners were and are both men and women. See also Dmitri A. Funk, *Teleuty* (Moscow: Rossiiskaia Akademiia Nauk, 1992, 2 vols., in the series "Narody i Kul'tury," XVII); D. A. Funk, ed., *Shamanizm i rannie religioznye predstavleniia* (Moscow: Rossiiskaia Akademiia Nauk, 1995); A. M. Sagalaev and I. V. Oktiabr'skaia, *Traditsionnoe mirovozrenie tiurkov Iuzhnoi*

*Sibiri. Znak i ritual* (Novosibirsk: Nauka, 1990); and N. A. Alekseev, *Shamanizm tiurkoiazychnykh narodov Sibiri* (Novosibirsk: Nauka, 1984).

b. These passages have been glossed into English using both the (Turkic) Teleut and Russian texts provided. In a few cases, where the Teleut was grammatically and poetically repetitive, the English reflects this even if the Russian does not, for example, "if you look back, I will not show you; if you squint [your] eyes, I will not turn around." Part of the task of a shaman in many séances of northern peoples is to cajole spirits into leaving patients. The language here, declaimed in a variety of registers and tones (from whisper to shout), reflects a psychologically fascinating balance between cajoling and threatening that may well have also had a psychological effect of calming the patient.

c. The implication here, familiar to ethnographers of Siberia, is that one should not read such passages lightly, for mere ethnographic purposes, since reading the text aloud can attract spirit attention.

# Notes

1. This article is the second in a series of publications on modern shamanism among the Teleut. For the first publication, see: D. A. Funk, "Sovremennyi bytovoi shamanskii fol'klor teleutov. 1. Novye zapisi," *Rossiiskii etnograf. Etnologicheskii al'manakh* (Moscow, 1995).

2. In the original, the text reads "*chymyrchydan kal polor*"; the word "*kal*" is crossed out, and another word is written above it illegibly in the hand of A. F. Khlopotin. After consultations with native speakers, I considered it possible to substitute the word *teng*, which does not change the meaning of the phrase.

3. The text is cited according to: A. V. Anokhin, *Misteriia Adamu* . . . Archive of the Museum of Anthropology and Ethnography [St. Petersburg], fond 11, opis 1, del 149, list 108 reverse side, 109, 109 reverse side. The texts of the original and of the translation have been edited.

4. A. V. Anokhin, "Dusha i ee svoistva po predstavleniiu teleutov," *Sbornik Muzeia Antropologii i Etnografii*, vol. 8 (Leningrad, 1929), pp. 253–69.

5. Ibid., pp. 263–65.

6. Archive of the Museum of Anthropology and Ethnography [St. Petersburg], fond 11, opis 1, del 32, list 4–5 reverse side.

7. *Iek/t'ek*—is one of the "generic" names for evil spirits along with "*aina*," "*körmös*," and others, most frequently translated into the Russian language with the word "*chёrt*" [devil].

8. Many folklore and ritual texts, as well as the stories of elderly Teleut, have preserved knowledge about the use in the past of hollowed-out larch-wood trough-coffins (*kemduu*).

9. A. V. Anokhin transformed the "*Aldang*" in the original into "*Aldachy/Aldachyng*" during the publication of the text. See: A. V. Anokhin, "Dusha i ee svoistva," pp. 264–65. The latter form permitted S. E. Malov to express an interesting opinion about the verb form for -*dacy*, bringing the Teleut language closer to Kipchak, as well as to find a parallel to the Teleut *Aldachy* in the Karaim (*Aldadz*) (See: S. E. Malov, "Neskol'ko zamechanii k stat'e A. V. Anokhina 'Dusha i ee svoistva po predstavleniiu teleutov,' " *Sbornik Muzeia Antropologii i Etnografii*, vol. 8 (Leningrad, 1929), pp. 332–33).

10. See, for example, concerning the tripartite structure of incantations among the Slavs: V. A. Kharitonova, *Zagovorno-zaklinatel'naia poeziia vostochnykh slavian* (L'vov, 1992); idem, "Zagovorno-zaklinatel'nyi akt v narodnoi kul'ture vostochnykh slavian," *Etnograficheskoe obozrenie*, 1993, no. 4, pp. 91–106.

11. *Oirotsko-russkii slovar'* (Moscow, 1947), pp. 183, 187.

12. In addition to P. P. Porosenkova, these are A. M. Porosenkova (*née* Andriushkina), born 1913, Mundus *seok*, city of Novokuznetsk; A. K. Alagyzova (Uskoeva), born 1936, Merkit *seok*, village of Shanda; V. S. Khlopotina (Shadeeva, 1900–1991, Tumat *seok*, village of Chelukhoevo; V. N. Chelukhoev, born 1931, Iyty *seok*, village of Chelukhoevo, and others. I likewise express my gratitude to U. A. Chelukhoev (*née* Iktina, born 1922, Iuty *seok*, village of Chelukhoevo) for assistance in the deciphering of indistinctly pronounced phrases in the tape recording of the text of the incantation cited subsequently.

13. Allegorical designation for a person.

14. Despite the existence of the dictionary form *d'eek kör*—"to look with disgust, with hatred, to detest' " (*Oirotsko-russkii slovar'*, p. 51), I considered it possible, based on the actual sound of this word and its assumed meaning, judging by the context, to cite it in the published text in the forms "*iekkererim*," "*iekkeretin*" (I will exorcize, I will be exorcizing). One should likewise take note of the difference in the way the words *iek/t'ek* and *ieek/t'eek* are spoken and written. As distinct from the Altai language (or from those meanings which ended up getting recorded in the *Oirotsko-russkii slovar'*), in Teleut, the first applies exclusively to the designation of an evil spirit, while the second signifies a braided sash.

15. Compare: *küzerge*—to stir up coals or ashes.

16. Literally "I will not let you hunger."

17. That is, "I possess sacral power." For detailed ethnological analysis of the notions of the Saiano-Altaic Turkic peoples concerning this power *jel/jelbik/jelbi* etc., see: L. P. Potapov, *Altaiskii shamanizm* (Moscow, 1991), pp. 67–69, 76–82, and others.

18. It is possible that this is the indistinctly pronounced word *ottu*—"with fire."

19. N. P. Dyrenkova, recordings, translation, introductory article, and notes, *Shorskii fol'klor* (Moscow/Leningrad, 1940), pp. 342–45. Texts 107, 108.

Translated by Stephan Lang

# Appendix:
# An Ethnographic E-Mail Dialogue

### On the persistence or possible revival of the *chymyr* ritual and its relation to cultural revival and Teleut ethnicity

Today, as in the 1980s and the first half of the 1990s, when I have been able to observe changes through my own fieldwork, the *chymyr* ritual seems to be in its own special block of traditional beliefs, which the Teleut themselves categorize as "our faith." In this category, in addition to the *chymyr*, are rituals of offerings [literally feedings] to *emegender* (female elder images)—small figurines that are family, birthing mother, and child protectors; rituals of offerings to *somdor* (four to fifteen birch saplings) placed near the home each Troitsa [Russian Orthodox spring holiday] in honor of specially revered spirits; rituals of offerings to *ot-ene* (mother fire), especially during weddings; various rituals called *alas*, including appeals to *maj-ene*, the protector of children; incantations against cholera, *kor-ene* (or mother-cholera), and smallpox, *ene-kizhi* (or mother-person). Also part of this category are certain specific shamanic conceptions of the soul. The whole category to some degree works as a buttress for the preservation of ethnic identification [*samoidentifikatsiia*] of the Teleut. Concerning the special role of these or other rituals in the revitalization of culture, and the self-awareness [*samosoznaniia*] of the Teleut, it seems to me that this is not so coherent. The modern process of rebirth is so politicized that cultural questions as a rule are just not specifically addressed.

### On repression of shamanic and other rituals

Your suggestion that the séances of *kam* [full shamans] were more repressed than the *chymyr* practitioners is quite true. *Kam* were also more repressed than practitioners of *alas*, rituals of purification through fire [smudging], *jadachy*, specialists to guide the weather, or *kosmokchy*, clairvoyants, as well as others. The whole so-called everyday [*bytovyi*] level of shamanistic and still earlier beliefs seems to have

---

Dmitri Funk's July 4, 1996 answers to the editor's questions.

been more hidden, and thus more alive and resistent, more protected from official propaganda and repression. I've discussed and provided samples of contemporary texts related to other Teleut rituals elsewhere (see note 1). I should add that discussion of repression refers to suppressing open séances, characteristic for the country as a whole, and not the actual physical repression of shamans, since the last Teleut *kam* died their own natural deaths.

## On gender dimensions of cultural preservation

On the issue that specifically women may have managed to preserve the everyday shamanism—this is not clear because no evidence indicates that *chymyrchy* were more often women than men. Another aspect, however, may be the statistic that women live longer than men. There are very few male elders [*stariky*] among the Teleut, and those who know something [of sacred matters] are still fewer. It should be added that men were exclusively responsible for the birch sapling *somdor* offering ritual, but I had to get my material only from women. Such is life!

## On the incident in Shanda village concerning written exorcisms

This is about the family of my good long-term Teleut acquaintance Anna Kirilovna Alagzyzova, one of the last master weavers and very knowledgeable on traditional songs. When I asked about current ritual practitioners, she dug out of a store-bought cabinet two completely written pages of text for *chymyr* and *alas* rituals. Both texts were written on the principle "what I hear is what I write"—that is, with a number of mistakes. When I copied the text, I immediately encountered words I did not know and asked for help. Anna K. and her daughter pored over the text and it was clear that they too did not understand quite a few places. But each had been written by Anna K. herself! "Why do you keep such 'memory joggers' if they are not understandable on reading?" I asked. "Well, yes. You never know what might happen, what might be needed suddenly. And indeed, the soul is somehow calmer when you are away from home and you know they are there. They are somehow guarding [*steregut*] the home," was the answer.

Translated by M. M. Balzer

# The Archaic Epic and Its Relationship to Ritual
## *from Ritual and Folklore in Siberian Shamanism*

ELENA S. NOVIK

## Introductory Remarks

In this section we shall discuss the relationships between rituals and folklore texts. We have shown that the syntagmatic structure of ritual arises or may arise apart from direct reliance on a folkloric plot, as a realization of communicative relationships of varying dimension.*a* Does this mean that the folkloric plot arises as a direct reflection of the ritual plot? The answer to this question will largely allow solution of a whole range of other problems confronting the ethnographer wishing to use folklore as a historical source, and the folklorist studying the principles of folklore plot formation.

As early as 1946, V. Ia. Propp pointed out that "complete concurrence of ritual and custom with fable" is very seldom found. Much more often a different relationship prevails, which he termed the "rethinking of ritual," when a separate element or group of elements of the ritual, "having become unnecessary or incomprehensible by reason of historical changes," is replaced by another, whereby a deformation of the ritual occurs. "We should regard as a particular case of rethinking," he writes, "the preservation of all forms of the ritual, although the fable assigns it an opposite meaning or signification, an inverted interpretation. Such instances we shall term inversion" [Propp, 1946, p. 13]. Propp treats both "rethinking" and "inversion" in a diachronic aspect, arriving at the conclusion that the "plot [of the fable] arises not in an evolutionary manner by direct reflection of reality, but by negation of this reality. The plot corresponds to the antithesis of reality" [ibid., p. 14]. Divergences and discrepancies between ritual and its reflection in folklore he explains in conformity

Russian text © 1984 by "Nauka" Publishers. *Obriad i fol'klor v Sibirskom shamanizme: Opyt sopostavleniia struktur* (Moscow: Glavnaia redaktsiia Vostochnoi literatury Izdatel'stva Nauka, 1984), Part 3, pp. 223–79.

with his idea of the demotion of former idols: the once well-meaning and generous figures of mythology fall into oblivion, and are then repudiated and ridiculed; in connection with a decline of belief in spirit-owners, they are transformed from givers of blessings into evil monsters, with whom the hero wages battle [Propp, 1953]. This idea has aroused objections on the part of E. M. Meletinskii, who points out that, in the archaic epic, "monsters from the other world are not always disenthroned owners and doing battle with them does not show the downfall of animistic beliefs" [Meletinskii, 1963, p. 18].

Propp regarded the relationships between ritual and folklore as exclusively genetic: he compared the rituals with classical genres —the magical fable and the heroic epos, even though between these and their roots in ritual comes the dense stratum of "archaic epic"— myths, legends, traditions, customary accounts, and "mini-histories" [*bylinchiki*]—synchronously related to the ritual institutions and current beliefs. These genres, it would appear, should also be consulted in the present case, in order to trace the transformations experienced by ritual once it has entered the realm of folkloric narration. Furthermore, since religious and mythological conceptions are in fact based largely on the oral poetic tradition, analysis of these texts may throw light on the mechanisms of formation of both religious beliefs and narrative constructions, not yet crystallized into those rigid plots characteristic of the higher genres of narrative folklore, which reduce their underlying mythological concepts and transform them into the conventional mythology of the fable. Finally, since both strata of folklore are often intimately related in the Siberian region, the results from analysis of the subjects of archaic prose could be used subsequently for more detailed study of the ways in which rituals are interpreted in such advanced folkloric genres as the magical fable and the sung *bogatyr* [heroic] fable—the direct precursor of the heroic epos.

For a synchronous examination of the relationships between ritual and folkloric narration, it would seem necessary to consider, first of all, the functioning of the narratives within the ritual, when they are incorporated into a particular ritual complex. The materials presented above, however, make us doubt the wisdom of this approach to explaining the mechanisms of composition of folkloric plots. Indeed, direct comparison of ritual and storytelling presented us with two basic types of situation: 1) incorporation of fragments or even entire stories with completed plot into the fabric of ritual, and 2) reproduction or, at very least, an intention of reproduction of myth in the course of a ritual.

The former of these occurred, for example, in shamanic seances, when the shaman while summoning the spirits would expound the history of his calling, including episodes from the life of a particular spirit or relating the biographies of his ancestors. It has already been mentioned that shamanic genealogies, legends of voyages, feats, accounts of initiatory ordeals, etiological myths and the like are used in this case as a fabric, a plan of expression (along with other nonverbal means) of contact established with the spirits.[b] With respect to their role in the structure of the ritual, they represent only one of the codes. There may be other alternatives—actions, implements, and so on. For example, the account of the shaman's initiation is supposed to convince the spirits that the conjuring shaman is entitled to their help, and therefore after the account the spirits are expected to "respond" to the summons. But the same purpose may be achieved by other means: the noise of the drum, into which the spirits come, or the refreshments prepared for them by the participants in the ritual.

The alternation of verbal and nonverbal means of establishing communication leads us to classify the storytelling during the course of the ritual with the superficial, and not the deep-lying level of ritual text. Usually the account covers only an individual episode or group of episodes of the ritual (for example, the account of the shaman's journey to the world of the spirits accomplishes the second syntagmatic unit of the seance). As for the plot structure itself, constituting the intrinsic nature of folkloric storytelling, this is usually easy to disrupt: either the story is greatly shortened or it is transformed entirely into a cue (often sung), addressed to a partner. As a result, the integral plot of the text is replaced by a fragment, a reference to an individual episode, a citation, an allusion.

We encountered the second situation in the Evenk *ikenipke* ritual, corresponding to the myths of the cosmic hunt, in the animal-escorting ceremonies, which may be compared to myths of a dying and resurrecting beast, or in the shamanic initiations revolving around shamanic legends as to the teaching of the neophyte's soul in the land of the spirits, the re-creation of his body, and so on.

Here, it would seem, there is reason to expect that the plot foundation of the narrative will be preserved. Yet this is not so. First of all, it is very difficult to determine which specific version of the myth (and folkloric narrative is always in the form of a series of versions) is intended by the officiants of the ritual. Thus, the majority of versions of the myth of the cosmic hunt tell of the origin of the Great Bear constellation as the result of a rivalry among three hunters (occasionally they are representatives of different ethnic groups, such as a Ket, a Russian, and an Evenk), pursuing a giant elk. A closer connection with the calendar mystery of the *ikenipke* is revealed by those texts that relate how the prodigious elk Kheglen captured the sun and was pursued by the *bogatyr* Main-Mangi, who killed the animal, released the sun, and became its guardian and the giver of light, the source of warmth and life [cf. Anisimov, 1959, pp. 12–13]. However, in this case also, it is not appropriate to speak of a direct dramatization of myth: in the *ikenipke* ritual the collective of people headed by the shaman pursue the cosmic elk—giver of life and prosperity, but the main conflict of the myth—the battle for the sun—is not portrayed. Of course, we may presume that this ceremony is based on some other unattested or lost version of the myth, corresponding more precisely to the main features of the ritual. But even in such cases when the investigator possesses the text of a myth known with certainty to be the intention of the officiants of the ritual, the discrepancies between the scheme of its syntagmatic unfolding and the plot of the narrative are very considerable.

Thus, A. M. Zolotarev records a special tale of the Ul'ch—the *duente sudalini* (literally, the "trail of the taiga person," i.e., the bear), which the Ul'ch themselves viewed as a kind of scenario of the bear festival and took pains to follow unswervingly. This myth tells how the sister of two brothers, after having a dream, sets off into the forest, marries the forest human-bear, gives birth to twin bear cubs and sends them to her brothers "for food." The older cub, humiliated by the perfidious treatment of the wife of one of the hunters, dies and returns to the "people of the taiga." Yet even here he cannot stay, being required to make a purificatory voyage to the spirit-owner of the mountains. There ensues a series of obstacles, which the hero overcomes on this trip [cf. Zolotarev, 1939, p. 178 *et seq.*].

But the ritual of the bear festival involves the people removing a bear cub from its den, rearing it in a cage, carefully observing ritualistic rules for its handling, then killing it on a special platform and eating it during the course of ceremonial exchanges with members of other clans, chiefly the clan of the sons-in-law. And although a variety of episodes of the holiday indeed "symbolize and portray this trail that the bear must follow in journeying to its parents" [Zolotarev, 1939, p. 127], the main twists in the plot of the myth (such as the sister's going into the forest, her transformation into a bear, the birth of the twins, the insult offered to one of the bear cubs during its suckling, and even many vicissitudes of the journey itself) are not directly reflected in the ritual. Orienting themselves to the deeper meaning of the myth and dramatizing it with ritualistic means, i.e., employing the narrative as a plan for the details of the ritual, the participants of the bear festival nevertheless pay special attention to such purely ritualistic elements as the "gifts" the bear transfers to the "people of the taiga" and a careful differentiation of the parts of the carcass, which are consumed in strict conformity with age-sex and social divisions of the collective in a manner reminiscent of the potlatch.ᶜ

Thus, even here the ritualistic scheme does not follow the plot of the narrative, but arranges it in accordance with the rules of its own development: the syntagmatic structure, dictated by the divisions of the social and natural realm, is accomplished in the ritual primarily through interactions and exchanges between these segments, but does not reproduce the scheme of the syntagmatic development of the plot of the story.

Hence, the functioning of narratives within the ritual, whether it is a case of incorporation of the story into the texture of the ritual (where it serves as a plan of expression) or an effort to reproduce the story during the course of the ritual (where it serves as a plan of the details), only allows us to establish the fact of transformation, the fundamental reversibility of the plans of detail and of expression, but does not provide the possibility of discerning the manner of formation of the folkloric plot, for once translated into the "language of ritual," the stories lose their plot organization.

It therefore seems more productive to consider a different situation, when ritual is translated into the "language of folklore," i.e., when it appears as the focus of the story. Such a situation, however, is very seldom encountered. In his time, B. N. Putilov noted that epic production usually "does not contain (or contains hardly any) ethnographical descriptions *per se*. They are created during the course of the storytelling, having a functional nature suited to the situation. . . . Descriptions that do not advance the plot or that fall outside the given plot situation are not included in the epos. The ritual receives a corresponding treatment" [Putilov, 1974, p. 78].

As a rare example of the ritual scheme dictating the structure of a folklore plot, he presents epic songs about match-making, taking it as certain that they "contain not just a reflection, but an enduring structural expression of the most characteristic features of the nuptial relations of the clan system: exogamy, with its characteristic practice of finding a wife outside the groom's social microcosm, with the existence of permanent nuptial relations between clans, and so forth; the various ordeals of the groom that accompany marriage; the special role of two parties in the ritual—the party of the groom and the party of the bride, and so forth'' [ibid., p. 79].

Although the main conclusions reached by Putilov in comparing the nuptial ritual and the songs of match-making are basically beyond reproach, this comparison itself is not very apt. In particular, it may be suspected that the structural coincidences are a direct result of reflection of the nuptial ceremonies in the epos. Such an assumption is certain, given the statements of Putilov himself that ''the classic forms of the heroic epos are genetically related to the typologically earlier forms—the so-called archaic epic''; and ''the classic epos does not grow from ritual, it is created by virtue of transformations of older epic forms'' [ibid., p. 76].

Meanwhile, the archaic epic itself demonstrates that those plots pertaining to match-making and the wedding do not even reproduce the nuptial ceremony as such. Examples include many stories of conjugal relations between people and animals, in which it is told how, as a result of concluding such conjugal agreements, a hunter himself or relatives of a woman, having married a human-bear, a human-tiger, a human-fish, or the like, acquire power over the forces of nature and thus obtain enduring success in the hunt. The plot composition and semantic paradigm aspects of such stories have been analyzed in great detail by E. M. Meletinskii on the example of the Koryak myths and stories about the marriages of the sons and daughters of Raven [cf. Meletinskii, 1979, p. 71]. In all texts of this type, the ''conclusion of marriage'' serves merely as a *means* of establishing contact between human and objects of the hunt, a code whereby this contact is recorded, but in no way the subject of description. It is instructive that these stories, in addition to the establishment of romantic or matrimonial relations, also contain other codes: mutual favors and exchange of valuables between hunter and beast (the man saves a tiger or bear from a snake, removes a thorn, or the like, and in gratitude receives success in the hunt; the bear saves a lost hunter, allowing him to spend the winter in his den, for which he receives a gift of dogs, and so forth).

On the contrary, in those stories dealing with the conclusion of matrimonial agreements between two exogamous communities, this element is most often portrayed as a treacherous attack. Even in cases where the text directly mentions an exchange of women between two groups [cf., e.g., Vasilevich, 1936, no. 60–66], one of the groups is portrayed as cannibals, who try to sacrifice or eat outright the girl given as wife, who saves herself by fleeing. Thus, the situation of the conclusion of matrimonial agreements in this case is encoded by a food code, i.e., a picture is created that is directly opposite that in stories about marriages with animals.

And even though the texts of both these groups differ substantially in their plot structure from that of the advanced epic, which is in exact agreement with the structure of the nuptial ceremony, we still may not suppose that the epos is oriented more to the ceremony than to stories resembling the above, or that the structural coincidences in this case result from a clear purpose of reproducing the ceremony, and not from the influence of the epic canon itself, which proposes to portray the epic biography of the hero and only for this reason reflects certain of the main conflicts of the rites of passage, including the nuptial rite.

It follows that one must select, from the multitude of archaic epics, texts about which there is no doubt that they are not only connected with ritual in some way, but also directly describe it. We have just such a situation in the so-called "shamanic legends," in which the hero is the shaman, i.e., the person especially appointed to discharge ritual functions. Therefore, they may serve as convenient laboratory material enabling detailed study of how ritual is interpreted by folkloric tradition, especially since the shamanic seances possessed a plot structure facilitating their comparison with the narratives. The fact that ritual appears in these texts as the focus of the story makes it possible to examine the relationship between ritual and folklore not in a genetic sense, but to employ the shamanic legends as a kind of "description" of the ritual in the language of folklore, and thereby attempt to produce a key to the deciphering of certain purely folkloric motifs.

Before examining the plots of shamanic legends, we should make a number of stipulations concerning the genre. The genre affiliation of these texts is far from clear: there are shamanic myths, and traditions about legendary shamans of the past, and histories of shamanic initiations, and accounts of the competitions between shamans, shamanic journeys, sleight-of-hand, miracles, and so forth. Collectors refer to them as fables, myths, customary accounts, genealogical or historical traditions, legends, "mini-histories," or the like. The unifying factor here is usually considered to be the figure of the central hero—the shaman—while the genre features themselves may vary quite freely.

Incidentally, the situation is similar in trying to determine the genre of stories not associated with the figure of the shaman, including some recorded as "fables" by students of the Siberian archaic epic. At the same time, efforts to classify them under the headings "animal," "hunting," "magical" or "ordinary" meet with insurmountable resistance from the material itself, which in terms of composition is again very hard to describe with the current indexes of folkloric plot. It seems that, while openly acknowledging that genres cannot be distinguished in the archaic epic, the diachronic study of folklore is still involuntarily oriented to those genre forms that are known from other, more recent epic traditions. At the same time, elements pertinent to the Siberian region go unnoticed, especially the rather distinct partitioning of all narratives into *authentic and nonauthentic* or imaginary tales. Here, in essence, a clear logical mistake is committed, replacing the opposition *authentic/imagined*, consistently employed by those transmitting the folklore, with the opposition *real/fantastic* (as it appears to the European mind), which, of course, agrees neither with the orientation of the transmitters nor the esthetics of folklore.

Here, for example, are extracts from the preface to the collection "Fables and Myths of the Oroch" [Avrorin and Lebedeva, 1967]. Characterizing the differences between the main genre varieties of the Oroch narrative folklore—the *nimapu*, *sokhori*, and *telumu*—the compilers make the following remarks: "The *nimapu* and the *sokhori* are distinguished not by genre, but simply by their genesis [the Oroch classify fables borrowed from other peoples as *sokhori*—E.N.]. Both of these are distinguished from the genre of *telumu* as productions with *imaginary, fantastic* [my emphasis—E.N.] plots versus productions based on authentic reality, not only objectively real, but also 'real' in terms of the religious beliefs of the Oroch." And further: "The Oroch classification based on opposition of *fantasy and reality* [my emphasis—E.N.] cannot be taken as absolute. It comes more from the incentives, the final purpose in creating the folkloric productions, than from the nature of their content. . . . In giving our classification of the genres of Oroch folklore, we acknowledge the positive elements of the opposition just considered, but take as our basis, quite naturally, a different principle, that which underlies the scientific classification of the productions of literature—differences in content and the consequent artistic form" [Avrorin and Lebedeva, 1967, p. 26].

As a result, the sections of this collection follow the traditional classification of folkloric studies oriented toward literary criticism: the material is divided into "fables about animals," "ordinary fables," "heroic fables," while the category of myth—that is, texts that are "authentic" from the standpoint of the Oroch—includes a considerable number of *nimapu*, i.e., productions that the Oroch themselves regarded as "nonauthentic." Thus, replacing the opposition *authentic/imagined* with the opposition *reality/fantasy* deprives this classification of its grounding, since the "nature of the content" of the particular text, from the standpoint of the transmitters of folklore, becomes distorted, and not accessible to study.

To be fair, it must be mentioned that V. A. Avrorin and E. P. Lebedeva, while not folklore specialists, as they themselves declare, have assembled a superb and in fact the first sufficiently complete collection of Oroch folklore (in 1978 we published another collection, supplementing the first: "Oroch Texts and Vocabulary"); and furthermore, in their commentaries they frequently (though unfortunately not always) report how the Oroch themselves categorize the particular text, while such information is often lacking entirely from many publications on Siberian folklore. Their statements are presented here solely to demonstrate how strong is the pressure exerted by the established patterns even on profound and thoughtful scholars.

In working with the Siberian archaic epic, one must constantly realize that, no matter how fantastic the events of the story, no matter how similar their plot to the classical fables, we have no grounds for regarding them as "fables," if the informant assigns them to the category of authentic histories.

In this respect, our task is somewhat facilitated by the fact that folklorists quite unanimously accord the status of shamanic legends to such texts as are regarded by the transmitters of folklore as authentic, despite the fantastic nature of their content. Hence the most common designation of these stories as "legends," which shall also be used hereafter as a working definition for the entire group of texts concerning shamans, and not a particular genre. In actuality, as already stated, the shamanic legends include texts of different genre—from the myth to the mini-history, i.e., they occupy in nonfabulous prose a position similar to that occupied by seances in the ritual tradition, encompassing different levels of ritual. The fact that shamanic legends constitute texts of different genre may allow subsequent use of this material for the genre distribution of other divisions of the archaic epic as well.

## The Poetics of the Shamanic Legends

### Genre characteristics of the accounts
### regarding shamans

Exactly what are the genre parameters of shamanic legends? In his day, E. M. Meletinskii proposed using a whole array of distinguishing features to differentiate between myth and fable, among which he identified two main groups. The first characterizes the production from the standpoint of transmitters of folklore. Here, in addition to the already-mentioned feature of *authenticity/nonauthenticity*, are such factors important to our subject as *ritualism/nonritualism* of the text, its *sanctity/nonsanctity*, and the *ethnographic-particular/conventional-poetic* type of imagination. This first group of features is complemented by the second, corresponding to the "content of the production itself—its themes, heroes, the time of the action, the result of the action," specifically: *mythical hero/nonmythical*; *mythological* (prehistorical) *time of the action/fabulous* (outside historical time); *presence of etiology/its absence* (or ornamental etiology); *collective* (cosmicity) *of the object portrayed/its individuality* [cf. Meletinskii, 1970, p. 142].

Using this scheme, we can identify distinguishing features of the shamanic legends. The first group of features basically coincide with the characteristics of myth: account authenticity naturally leads to ethnographic specificity of the imagination and the possibility of using the text for ritual purposes, concomitant with its sanctity.

As for the second group, the following is worthy of note. Accounts about shamans can be assigned not only to the mythological time of the first creation (Tm), as can myth, but also to the historical (or rather, the quasihistorical) past (Ti) or even to the present or recent past (Tn), but not, of course, to the conventional time of the fable. In other words, it is useful to employ an entire scale of times to define the genre of the stories about shamans: Tm—the time of myth, Ti—the time of tradition, Tn—the time of the customary account or mini-history.[1]

Although a definition of the shamanic account genre as myth, tradition, or mini-history has, for us, an aspect of metalanguage, within the epic tradition itself it is sometimes possible to find correspondences.

Thus, for example, the Chukchi divide narratives into the *tottomgatken pynylty*—"accounts of the time of creation" (cf. myths), *akalyletken pynylty*—"accounts of the time of discord" (cf. historical traditions), and *lye pynyl*—"true accounts" (cf. customary accounts), all of which are contrasted with the nonauthentic (from their perspective) stories, or *lymnyl* (cf. fables). The Nivkhi distinguish myths, *tylgund* (according to Shternberg, from the word *tyland*—"remote," "long ago"!), and traditions, concerning more recent events, *keraind*. G. M. Vasilevich reports that the Evenk, "representing the historical course of the group's existence by legends and traditions, distinguished the periods of *nimngakan*, very remote, 'when the earth started to be formed'; *bulemekit*, a period of wars and dispersal of the reindeer-breeders; and the period of formation of the present groups. . . . The Evenk defined all events with respect to these three periods" [Vasilevich, 1969, p. 191]. It is important to underscore the fact that the term *nimngakan* means not only a period of time, but also a genre of story—myth—and is contrasted with narratives of the genre *ulgur*—stories of happenings preserved in the memory of the living, i.e., customary accounts of recent events [see Vasilevich, 1969, p. 195; Romanova and Myreeva, 1971, p. 12], both genres encompassing accounts taken as authentic.

In other cases, the assignment of the texts to myth, tradition, or customary account is not directly supported in the terminology of the people, which contains only a more general division of the epic into authentic and fictitious narrative. However, it may be presumed that the transmitters of the tradition, in these cases as well, employed a similar time scale, but marked it out in a different fashion, e.g., with the name of the principal hero, or by correlating the stories with the figure of the culture hero (myth), the founder of the clan (tradition), or a neighbor (mini-history).

Just such a situation occurs, perhaps, in the beginnings of the Koryak myths: "This was the time when Great Raven lived," "This was the time when Great Raven and his people lived," "This was the time when the self-creating father of the maker lived." In the monograph of Meletinskii "The Paleoasiatic Mythological Epos," from which these examples are taken, it is shown that, although the Koryak Raven Kuikynniaku, unlike the Raven of Chukotkan myths, is not a creator (he does not procure the earth from the bottom of the sea or the heavenly bodies, does not create the mountains and rivers, and so on, as does the Chukotkan Kurkyl'), and although the Koryak altogether lack the genre of "creation accounts," and the raven epos belongs to the group of *lymnyl*, the texts regarding Raven and his family are indeed myths, and their plot organization results from a markedly mythological semantics [Meletinskii, 1979, ch. 2].

Among the Evenk we find accounts of Un'iany [see Vasilevich, 1936, pp. 41–44 and 245], outwardly little different from the tales about a struggle with a prodigious opponent. This character, however, was regarded as the protecting spirit of the shaman Maieli [see Suslov, 1931, p. 101], from which it may be concluded that these texts should be assigned to the group of clan legends.

The particular temporal locus of the shaman account thus correlates both with a dimension of the main character: being a culture hero with the attributes of a great (the first) shaman in the myth, a venerable ancestor in the legend, and finally a particular shaman contemporaneous with the narrator in the mini-epic; and with a dimension of the topography of the action, unfolding respectively in the cosmos (myth), on defined clan territory (legend), or in a particular locality (customary account).

Action, in turn, is correlated with a type of etiological finale, relating an event in the account to the present state of affairs. For the shamanic myth (as well as myth in general), this is an explanation of the current state of elements in the natural world and the culture; for the legend, genealogical and toponymic aspects pertain, the history of the origin of a particular hallowed precinct or ritual object (including the history of the origin of a venerated shaman); for the mini-history, the expounding of a moral lesson, the explanation of fortunes or misfortunes that have become "ever since then" the lot of the narrator or his relatives.

All these features (the time of the action, the place, the nature of the hero, and the etiology), specifying the genre parameters of the text, *appear directly in the narrative*, constituting more or less constant elements of its plot structure and occupying a strictly defined place: in the *initial* part, it is related "when" and "where" the events transpire, and a description of the characters is given, while in the *final* part comes the etiological conclusion. But these elements, comprising a framework for twists in the plot itself, may easily be omitted; for this very reason, the above-identified correlations of features appear extremely significant to us, since they allow the investigator to determine the genre of the text, even when certain of these characteristics are missing.

## The portrayal of the seance
## in shamanic legends

One other characteristic is important to our theme concerning those shamanic legends that may be described as tales of bygone days, mini-histories, or customary accounts. Among them are both *memorates*, i.e., recollections by eyewitnesses of seances that were held in their presence, and *fabulates*, where the main emphasis lies on the vicissitudes of conflicts in the plot. The boundaries between these forms, generally speaking, are rather fluid and not conscientiously perceived by the narrators themselves (in any case, folk terminology in no way distinguishes them). However, a differentiation between them will be highly productive in explaining the lines of formation of the narrative constructions within the immediate realm of the narration, as noted in particular by E. V. Pomerantseva [1975]. Relying mainly on characteristics of storytelling technique, she demonstrated that the desire to explain the circumstances of an individual case in the greatest possible detail results in an account being overgrown with trivial features and psychological motivations, thereby transforming memorates into fabulates. We shall attempt to employ the differences between memorates and fabulates to clarify what happens to ritual when it is recounted by the transmitters of tradition themselves. This may also elucidate certain mechanisms in the composition of folklore plots.

The task is facilitated by the fact that our entire material, with respect to subject matter, falls into two rather distinct groups: 1) legends of miracles, contests, and feats of the shamans; 2) legends of the birth of the first shamans, the obtaining of the shamanic gift, a kind of "biography" of the great shamans of the past, and so on. Thus, the material correlates with the basic forms of shamanic ritual (the first with the seances of the shamans and their contests of strength, the second with ceremonies of shamanic initiation and rituals of worship of shamans who have become cult objects).

We shall deal only with the legends of the first group, which describe seances most fully and consistently, and shall compare their texts with the invariant seance structure that has been identified in the first part of the book.

Recall that the deeper structure of the seance is a sequence of three main blocs, which are realized in three code versions: "transferral of a communication," "transferral of power," and "transferral of valuables." The actor structure, i.e., the collection of roles, consists of three pairs of actors: "giver-receiver," "helper-antagonist," and "subject-object" (this structure, as pointed out, covers the chief categories of character in shamanic beliefs: the "giver" is the spirit-owners, the "receiver" is the shaman, the "antagonist" is the evil spirits, the "helper" is the shaman's spirits and the protectors of the hearth, the "subject" is the person who requests the seance, the "object" is the soul, a piece of property, or the like). And finally, the plot structure of the seance resulting from the syntagmatic unfolding of the blocs of the deeper structure along the identical lines of "exchange of information," "exchange of power," and "exchange of valuables," has been described as a sequence of functional relations between 1) the requestor of the seance and the shaman; 2) the shaman with his helping spirits and the addressee of the seance (i.e., one of the characters in the current belief system); 3) the object obtained (valuable) and the requestor of the seance.

Let us now examine how this original scheme becomes refracted in shamanic legends. In terming the structure of the seance "original," we do not mean a genetic derivation of the shamanic legends from these rituals (as will be demonstrated below, their plots in no way duplicate the plots of the seances), but merely intend to use their structure as the most illustrative and syntagmatically developed, as opposed to the other rituals, for comparison with narrative plots.

As a beginning, let us consider a memorate in which an eyewitness describes the seance, as it were, from without. For example, the collection of A. P. Dul'zon has the story "How the Shaman Cures the Sick."

> A man takes ill. He is old. All the time he is sick. His son goes to the shaman. "You should shamanize for father," he says. "I will do so." Then people come to him, bring a drum, spread skins on the floor, and start beating. The drum sounds. The shaman arrives, goes up to the sick man, and shamanizes. The shaman hangs a rag on him. He also hangs a rag in back. The shaman shamanizes on and on. He shamanizes, beating the drum, and then sits down and smokes. He finishes smoking. Again he shamanizes. He shamanizes, beats the drum, stops whirling about, sits down and smokes. The people begin to talk to him. The shaman talks. "Now I will shamanize for you, and you will get better." The shaman shamanizes and the people help. He is done shamanizing. "I have shamanized for you and you have been cured. After this you will still feel bad. Two days will pass, and on the third day you will go out into the street" [Dul'zon, no. 122].

There is no mention in this text of the spirit of illness. The narrator's main attention is devoted to such events as the "invitation" of the shaman and his "predictions," while all other actions are described only superficially: "beats the drum," "whirls about," "hangs up a rag," and so on.

E. A. Kreinovich records a similar memorate among the Nivkhi.

Epkun told the shaman Koin"yt that his son was sick and invited him to come and sing and cure his son, and Koin"yt did not refuse. He brought the drum to the dwelling of Epkun and hung up trinkets. The Nivkhi cut down some shrubs and brought them to the dwelling and shaved an *inau*. From the *inau* they made a binding for his head, they made spectacles and tied them to the head binding [the "spectacles" are placed on the forehead of the shaman—E.K.]. They made a binding for his neck from the *inau*, they made him a belt from the *inau*. They bound up all his joints with the *inau*: they bound the left knee, they bound the right knee; they bound the left ankle, they bound the right ankle; they bound the left elbow, they bound the right elbow; they bound the left wrist, they bound the right wrist [the bindings are not placed on the joint itself, but slightly higher—E.K.]. Next they placed ledum and spruce in a cup and poured water into it. This is water for the helping spirits of the shaman to drink, so they say. They placed *sarana* and *t'irkh* roots into a cup and set it on the edge of the hearth, for the helping spirits of the shaman to eat. They set fire to the ledum and spruce, they fumigated his head binding of *inau*, placing it on his head, they fumigated his belt with the trinkets, they warmed his drum over this fire [of the ledum and spruce— E.K.]. Then he stood up and began to sing [i.e., shamanize—E.K.]. After shamanizing, he said: "The mountain people desire Epkun's dog. If he kills a dog for the mountain people, the sick one will recover—so they have said." No sooner was the dog killed than his son felt better on the very next day. After that, he recovered completely [Kreinovich, 1973, pp. 442–43].

Here, as we see, the main attention is given to a detailed description of the preparations in which the narrator himself took part. In the only instance when he speaks about the purpose of the preparations, mentioning the helping spirits for whom a cup with refreshment is offered, he gives a kind of "reference" to the prevailing opinion on this subject ("so they say"). But the signification of the seance as an "agreement" between the shaman Koin"yt and the mountain spirits regarding a sacrifice is placed in the mouth of the shaman himself.

It is possible that at least some of these memorate accounts are of artificial origin, i.e., rather than being specimens of traditional folkloric prose they are provoked by the questioning of ethnographers, who explained how the seance was conducted in the past. This is suggested, in particular, by the abundance of ritual details, which are seldom found in such quantity in the narratives, and also by the fact (which should be especially emphasized) that there is often no plot whatsoever in such texts (cf. the above account from the Ket, published by Dul'-zon). A somewhat different situation occurs when the account describes a particular event (as in the legend presented by Kreinovich): the plot then follows quite accurately the conjunctures of the ritual.

Such is the account, for example, of [R. A.] Silkin, an Enets, recorded by B. O. Dolgikh, relating how the shaman Diabadea saved a sick boy of the Muggadi clan by performing the *pu pozu* [stone gates] ritual over him [see Dolgikh, 1962, pp. 153–57]. This presents in great detail the history of how the younger son of the Enets Karitua took sick, how his elder son went for the shaman, indicating who of the Muggadi clan was a helper-*tetaguzi* during the seance, what instructions the shaman gave to the participants of the ritual, what was its general course, what the shaman foretold after the seance, what gifts he received from Karitua, and so forth.

Such memorates sometimes even approach ethnographers' own descriptions of the seances.[2] Beyond question, they are of great scientific value, especially when the narrator provides a substantive interpretation along with mentioning actions of the ritual, portraying the seance not only "from without," but also "from within," in the eyes of the shaman himself, as it were. In these cases, the ethnographer obtains additional information to establish the significance of the ritual operations, and the folklorist has an opportunity to discern how a particular ethnographic feature develops into a folklore motif, since the ritual is placed here "as a focus" of the narrative.

Even with respect to such texts, however, both ethnographer and folklorist should display the utmost caution, since the shifting of "external" and "internal" perspectives of the ritual quite often results in distortions that obscure the true relationship between ritual and narrative "reality." We shall present two examples.

From the already-mentioned Enets informant Silkin, B. O. Dolgikh recorded an account of how the shaman Narzale of the Nenets clan Iadnia cured the Enets Tebk, who resided in the same tent [*chum*] as the narrator (i.e., this account should be classed in the genre of the mini-history). The plot structure of this memorate comes not so much from the internal conjunctures of the seance (as in the Enets specimen above), as from the structure of the story itself: at the request of relatives, the narrator first brings to the sick man the shaman Pasu, whose ritual manipulations and sacrifices did not bring success, and only the shaman Narzale was able to save the dying one, at the cost of his own life.

The purpose of a more or less detailed exposition of the ritual side of the seance is replaced here by a desire to recount a specific *instance*, i.e., to convey the drama of the situation in which the seance was held. After the first shaman's failure, the second, having shamanized for a while, admits that he also is unable to "catch the soul" of the sick man, and asks first to be pierced with an ice pick, and then to be choked. In the text under examination, two somewhat differing interpretations are given for these "shamanic tricks" (to which we shall return). The first is provided by shaman Narzale himself: "I then began to shamanize and did not kill the reindeer. Pasu [the first shaman—E.N.] needlessly killed the reindeer. Instead of the reindeer, I cut my own head with the leash, as one chokes a reindeer. I stabbed myself, as though piercing it in this way. It is the illness that I was stabbing. Had I not stabbed and choked myself, the sick one would not have recovered" [Dolgikh, 1962, p. 106]. Further on in the story it is told how Narzale, after receiving presents, went away, and sometime later Silkin and his neighbors learned that the shaman had been killed by a bear. Commenting on his death, the relatives of the cured man came to the following conclusion: "The bear killed him because he gave up his own soul for the sick man. Did he not choke himself here and give up his soul for the sick man? He said to the *kacha* [the spirit of illness—B.D.] 'take my soul instead of the sick one.' That is why he died. Why else should a bear come out of its lair in the winter and kill him?" [ibid., pp. 106–7].[d]

As we see, although both interpretations agree with the deeper meaning that characterizes the central core of the seances (the shaman explains his actions as "doing battle" with the spirit of illness, the relatives as an "exchange" of the soul of the sick man for an object of value, in which capacity they regard the life of the shaman himself in this instance), the story as a whole cannot be taken as a strictly documentary record of the ritual, even though it describes a perfectly defined, particular case, including many details of custom and ritual, while the narrator himself is an active participant in the described events. This account by Silkin is interesting not so much because it contains authentic information on how the seance is conducted, as because it brings out in high relief the way the goal of a *cause-and-effect* explanation for events is reached. The shaman's misadventure, placed in context with his actions during the seance, is incorporated into the plot of the story, which, while generally agreeing with the plot of the seance, differs from it in having the last bloc given a negative light in the text: after the function ''rewarding the shaman'' for saving the sick man comes the function ''death of the shaman'' from the vengeance of the spirits.

Silkin's story gives both views on the shaman's manipulations, and so this slight deformation of the ritual is readily apparent. The matter is complicated, however, if the ''external'' view of the ritual by the narrator is omitted (or absent), and the main attention is given to presenting the mere events. Furthermore, this same opportunity of saving the sick man by exchanging his soul for the soul of a sacrifice, including the soul of another person, is frequently used in many legends. For example, a Yakut legend recorded by Ksenofontov tells how a great shaman, living ''in ancient times, in the age of the forefathers,'' was able to resurrect a dead man by giving to the evil spirit the soul of a man living 150 versts away, who ''was going to die in three years' time. Whether he dies now or in three years''—observes the shaman—''is of no great import'' [Ksenofontov, 1930, p. 91]. The actions of the shaman here are justified by the narrator and even lauded, but in other texts such ''exchanges'' may be ascribed to ''evil,'' ''black'' shamans.

M. N. Khangalov has published several legends in which the residents of a nomad camp, learning that a shaman of ill repute had come to a wealthy neighbor who was sick, and therefore anticipating an attempt on his part to save the sick man at the cost of one of their lives, take precautionary measures, so that the shaman is unable to succeed and the sick man dies [see Khangalov, 1959, pp. 208–9]. In these legends, the first segment (harm) is actually developed as a seance during which the shaman-mediator offers (or tries to offer) the spirit of illness a ransom in the form of a human sacrifice (the Buryat call this *dol"o*, i.e., ''replacement''). Curiously, such legends sometimes directly portray a seance during which the shaman sacrifices one of the members of the household of a wealthy patient [see ibid., pp. 206–7]. Khangalov himself, on the basis of these legends, is inclined to declare, along with his informants, that ''in olden times'' the custom of human sacrifice (the *khun dol"o* ritual) existed among the Buryat—a conclusion that does not follow from such sources, since these legends could arise simply from folklore modification.

The foregoing examples should demonstrate a progressive departure from direct depiction of the ritual, first into the realm of ideas (in the present case, the idea of "exchange" as a way to "remedy the harm"), then into the realm of beliefs (the belief in shamans able to cause harm), and finally, into the realm of pure narration, rendering the image of human sacrifice *after the model* of a common ritual. In other words, legends telling of human sacrifices performed in the past use, as their means of expression (the sacrifice image), precisely those accounts with content concerning the exchange of a patient's soul for the soul of another person (the offering of his soul is tantamount to killing him), while these latter *transform* the situation of the ritual itself, in which one item of value (the soul of the patient) is exchanged for other valuables (the soul of a sacrificed animal, presents, refreshments, etc.).[3]

That the folklore text portrays both the means of expression and the seance content can be proved by comparing two other legends regarding a shaman's battle with a spirit of illness, published by Khangalov.

The first tells how the shamaness Arzut destroyed an evil spirit [*ada*] that had been "eating up" the children of a certain Buryat in the *ulus* [locality] Tangut.

> The shamaness ordered that meat and *salamata* be prepared and placed in a *domb* on the right side of the yurt, the shamaness herself standing outside the yurt, while on the inside a *shidekhen* [horsehair rope] was stretched around the entire yurt, except the door.[e] Four strong men drank themselves drunk, and the shamaness also feigned drunkenness, whereupon the *ada* entered the yurt through the open doors, which the shamaness instantly blocked with the horsehair rope, so the *ada* could no longer leave the yurt. The shamaness ordered the four men to grab her by the arms when they realized she had caught something. The shamaness began to shamanize, and indeed she seized something on the eastern side of the yurt; she was flung from side to side, as though fighting with someone, but the sturdy men took her by the arms and hands, holding her body, and passed a sharp knife between her two arms, whereupon there was a sudden smell of onions and something like fish scales was seen; at the same time, a creature resembling a polecat, but without any fur, appeared mysteriously, and they killed it [Khangalov, 1958, p. 334].

Here, the seance is portrayed quite "realistically": the structure of the text is such that the meaning of the shamaness's ritual actions is perfectly clear. The pitcher with refreshment is intended to entice the spirit, the imitation of a drunken condition to lull its watchfulness, the rope to close the exit, the tossing from side to side portrays the struggle with the captured spirit, and the cutting of the hitherto unseen *ada* with the knife results in its becoming a creature that all can see, whose destruction signifies victory over the malefactor.

In the second legend, instead of an external description of the ritual, the shaman's battle with the *ada* is presented as follows:

> From the *ulus* Ushat of the first *babaer* clan of the Kudinsk depart-ment, the great shaman Zamkhan once traveled to a certain wealthy Buryat of the Verkhnelensk department, who had three wives. The shaman saw thirteen *ada* in his house. The host requested the shaman to deliver his home from the uninvited guests, who were killing all his children. The shaman ordered that the next day roast meat and *salamata* should be placed in a *domb* [a wooden pitcher for *tarasun*], and promised to come. Arriving in the yurt the next day, the shaman himself assumed the form of an *ada* and observed that all thirteen *ada* were sitting in the *domb*. Relishing the tasty food, the *ada* said: "How good are our father and mother." Noticing the shaman, i.e., a new *ada*, they asked: "Where do you come from?" The shaman responded: "I have been wandering from house to house and looking into the cups." And he joined their company. One *ada* sat on top and kept watch, while the others stayed in the *domb*. Zamkhan also ate the *salamata* and meat. But when his turn arrived to keep watch on top, he slammed the lid on all thirteen *ada* and ordered the vessel to be taken out in the field and burned [ibid., p. 333].

In this legend, only the general framework of the text coincides with the ritual: the preparation of the pitcher with refreshment and its burn-ing in the field; while all other actions of the shaman are given in pure storytelling fashion—as a "tricking" of the trusting *ada*. Even the single ritualistic feature—the pitcher—is used here not only as a means of luring the *ada* with refreshment and an implement for their capture, but also as the scene of action; instead of the feigned drunkenness of the shamaness in the first story, we have here a "transformation" of the shaman into an *ada*; the pantomime of the "struggle" of the shamaness corresponds to the "dialogue" and the shaman's deceptive partaking

of the meal with the spirits. In this legend, the viewpoint of the requestor of the seance is virtually absent, being entirely replaced by the
viewpoint of the shaman, which, in turn, also encompasses the viewpoint of the spirits, of whom the shaman pretends to be one. The
provoking of the *ada* to act in a way favorable to the requestor, also the
point of the seance, is presented very vividly here, but there is almost
no external description of the ritual, unlike the first legend, which
portrays it in all major parts. Both legends, let us stress, could be
assigned to the genre of the customary account: both report the names
of the shamans and the requestors of the seance, and the names of the
*ulus* where the described events took place.

As an intermediate case in which the plot development of the story is
accompanied by a change of viewpoint, consider a Nganasan text published by B. O. Dolgikh [Dolgikh, 1976, no. 23]. This tells how two
shamans attempted to revive the daughter of the shaman Porbin, who
was living in the same *chum* [tent] with a widow and her two sons. The
shaman Porbin sends these boys to ask for help from a young shaman,
not being confident of his own powers. In the meantime, he begins the
seance himself. The legend states:

> When the young shaman arrived, the *chum* of the old man was
> already filled with guests. The old man was lying on the floor, his
> head in the direction of the tundra, *because he had already departed
> for the nether world.* He is breathing heavily and shaking his head,
> exactly as a reindeer on the run. *The shaman always imitates a
> reindeer in this way when going to the nether world.* The young
> shaman then lay down beside the elder and began to tell what he was
> seeing in a quiet voice. One of the guests sat down near his head,
> listening and repeating his words for the others.

The explanations of the narrator disclosing the meaning of the ritual
actions (shown emphasized above) are then replaced by a description of
the journey of the young shaman to the world of the dead, depicted
through his own eyes, while the story is also taken up in his own
person: "I came to the nether land. A large and very rapid river is now
before me. The old shaman stands on the shore in front of this river and
cannot cross." Leaving him at the river, the young shaman continues
his voyage alone. On the way, he meets the deceased father of the boys
living in the *chum* where the seance is being held and engages him in
conversation. Learning that his family is impoverished, he promises to

give them reindeer when the shaman returns to his "own" world. At length, the youngster gains access to a secret chest in the *chum* of the dead and says: "Five hearts lie in it. Four of them are completely black. One is still half white. I think that this is the heart of the old man's daughter. I have placed this heart in my pocket. (*All the guests saw that the recumbent shaman put something into his pocket.*) I am now going back. Again I meet the father of the two boys. He gives me two reindeer-calves—a buck and a doe. I tie them to the thongs of my parka. (The guests see that the shaman is tying knots in the thongs of his parka.)"

The subsequent presentation of the events happening to the shaman in the world of the dead is told in his own person and accompanied by very circumstantial remarks of the narrator, tending to suggest that the entire text should be viewed as the testimony of an eyewitness—one of the participants of the seance. Yet this is not so. The account doubtless uses recollections of particular seances, but is not a memorate in the direct sense. Even though the plot of the legend in large measure follows the plot composition of the seance as a voyage of the shaman to the world of the spirits, and the events are attributed to specific persons—the Porbin family, to which Dolgikh's informant also belonged—it describes an entirely fantastic situation—the reviving of a dead girl.*ʲ* In this respect, the ending of the story is also of interest: the young shaman, to the beat of the drum, revives the daughter of the old shaman, gives to the widow's sons the tufts of red and white wool received from their dead father, symbolizing future prosperity, and as reward for the seance obtains not only the customary reindeer of Nganasan ritual practice, but also the rescued girl as a wife. The story concludes with an etiological motif: "Since that time, shamans receive girls and reindeer as payment for their shamanism," in which, as throughout the narrative, a purely ritual element (obtaining reindeer as reward) is combined with a folkloric motif proper (marrying a rescued girl).

The ethnographic authenticity of the latter custom (as well as the mention of human sacrifice practiced "in olden times" in the previous Buryat legends) cannot be admitted without further proof, i.e., solely on the basis of such accounts, since the motif of marriage occurs here as a logical conclusion to the story.

Let us investigate how this happens. The circle of actors in this story is somewhat larger than that in the seances: it includes not only the requestor of the seance, the shaman, and the spirits, but also a spectator, or witness of the events; further, the latter character is not the same as the narrator (as in the memorate), although his perspective is also recorded in the text.

As a result, the plot of the legend is no longer a simple following of the seance plot, but arises as an enactment of all these relationships.

Thus, the standpoint of the narrator in this particular legend is recorded in the plot merely by assigning the events to the life of one of his ancestors, and also in the etiological ending, i.e., in the compositional outline of the story. The viewpoint of the spectator or witness of the occurrence is not that of the narrator, yet is also recorded in the characters of the boys living in the same *chum* with the elder Porbin and is expressed by the incidental remarks as to what the hero is doing during the seance (cf. the Enets legend of the shaman Narzale, related by Silkin, in which the standpoint of the narrator coincides with that of the witness). These boys, however, being the object of the narrator's description, appear here as participants both in the seance and in the story, and therefore the characterization of them at the start of the narrative ("the widow's sons," "poor") becomes one of the plot-forming elements: suffering "want," they hereby become also the requestors of the seance, for whom the shaman obtains the souls of reindeer from their deceased father. An identical defocusing of perspective also occurs in the character of the shaman Porbin, who attempts to revive his daughter: he is characterized as both shaman and a person experiencing "want," i.e., a requestor, and in the latter capacity he must appeal for help to a young shaman living nearby, who in turn not only plays the part of an intermediary between the requestor and the spirits, but also becomes the hero of the fabulate: all the major events are described from his standpoint.

The resolution of all these conflicts is what generates the plot of the legend, which first tells of the parallel seance of the two shamans, after which one of them abandons his attempts to penetrate the other world, while the other continues the voyage and attains objects—reindeer wool, assuring the enrichment of the orphan boys, and the heart of the girl whom he revives. However, this "attainment," making it possible to "supply the want" of the requestors, does not resolve the purely narrative conflict between the old and the young shaman, arising in the course of the story. Since this legend does not deal with a rivalry (such legends do exist and will be considered below), the character of the young shaman instead arises as a mere reduplication of the old shaman, who is pushed by the development of the tale into the role of the requestor. The proposal to take the daughter as his wife is a logical resolution of this duplication and at the same time allows identification of the young shaman as the hero of the fabulate. Therefore, the etiological ending, i.e., the conclusion from the standpoint of the narrator, is also primarily a summarization of the outcome of the events described in the legend, but does not generalize the facts of ritual practices, as might appear at first glance (in the commentary on the legend, Dolgikh stresses in particular the tendency of this informant to draw moralizing conclusions from his narratives).[4]

The motif of a shaman marrying the girl rescued by him in another Nganasan legend [Dolgikh, 1976, no. 24], very similar to the preceding, is even more fantastic in ordinary respect but even more logical in respect of the narrative.

> The action begins with an episode identical to the previous text: an old shaman brings to his tent the body of his daughter, dead and buried, and attempts to revive her. He sends his son (there is no other characterization of this personage, and he does not figure in the later account) to a shaman living nearby for help, while himself beginning to shamanize. The future hero is depicted here as a very young child ("he only just started to walk"), which entails the inclusion of further episodes (persuading his parents to allow the child to shamanize and a scene where the young shaman is playing with other children), prior to his voyage to the world of the spirits. The voyage itself is presented in the person of the hero, who encounters on the way first the old shaman, who has halted before a river and lacks the strength to cross, and then (on the other shore) two old men, who ask him for help in reaching the land of the dead. The child promises to make them a "shortcut" on the way back. The conflicts occurring in the world of the dead between the shaman and the daughters of the owner of the subterranean ice, Syrady-barb, are developed with particular detail in the story. Having reached their tent, the shaman makes the mistake of allowing them to comb his hair (i.e., instead of rendering them a service, he accepts a service from them). As a result, he is unable to leave their house, and only the cunning of his helper-spirits, who send a storm and thus distract the women (they must leave the tent to secure the *niuki*, which the wind is carrying away) allows him to steal the heart of the dead girl and run away. On

the road back, he helps the old men and learns from them that ice maidens will kill his parents in revenge for the trickery and theft (i.e., as in the above-given Enets account, the shaman's "victory" over the evil spirits turns into a "misfortune" for himself). Returning to his "own world," the shaman revives the daughter of the old man, who in fact offers his daughter as wife to the boy as remuneration, this being pointed out in the text: "Well, my lad! You are wrong to say: my father will go, my mother will go. Come and take my daughter!" This feature is accompanied by a commentary of the narrator, though not of an etiological nature: "Even though this child-shaman was little, he took the wife. He will become a man afterwards." This variant entirely lacks an etiological ending as such, although the legend concludes with a typical narrator's remark, vouching for the validity of the whole account: "This is no fable, but the old ways. The old shaman and the child-shaman were both *avamskie samodi*" (as the Nganasan termed themselves and the Enets).

In this legend, the genealogical connection between the narrator and the old shaman is left out, as is the character of the eyewitness (we note that the text also lacks parallel descriptions of the ritual actions and statements as to their meaning). The legend is seemingly close to the structure of the seance in its role and compositional structure, although the focus of attention is not indeed the outward appearance of the ritual, which is given even less consideration than that of the previous examples, but the vicissitudes of the voyage of the child-shaman and his encounters with the spirits. These determine the development of the plot, concluding not only with a "supplying of the want" of the requestor, but also with a "loss" (of his parents) and an "acquisition" (of a wife) by the young shaman, which transforms him from a mere intermediary (which is what he is in the ritual) into the hero of the fabulate.

Thus, the traditional accounts, even when affixed to wholly specific events in the life of the narrator or rendering events from the recent past (i.e., externally preserving the features of memorate), are fabulates, where the main attention is given not to portraying the ritual as such, but to the relationships between the shaman and other actors in the account. It is these that govern the development of the plot, even in such cases where it appears to follow faithfully the plot of the seance, or is closely connected in theme.

## Transformations among legend plots

In seances, plot elements were built mainly by placing a series of intermediate characters into the relationship. "requestor of seance—required item of value." Matters are completely different in the legends, where conflicts forming the plot may arise between any given pair of actors. In fact, the plot of certain stories is based on conflicts between a common person and the shaman (cf. the first bloc of seances), while all other relationships enacted in the seance are left alone. Other legends describe a collision of a shaman with an opponent, still others only his voyage, and so forth. As a matter of fact, we are dealing here not with accounts of seances, but with accounts of shamans, in which their activity is given either a positive or a negative valuation, which is what generates the plot of the fabulate. Let us examine how this occurs.

Whereas the first bloc enacting the relation "requestor of seance—shaman" appears in the ritual as "request—consent" and is often surrounded by special ceremonies, a number of stories portray it as different, often *logically contradictory versions*. For example, it is reported that a certain person does not "request," and "does not believe in" the power of the shaman (he ridicules the shaman, greets him impolitely, refuses him a courtesy, or in some way "*violates*" the customary rules of deportment with a shaman). In response to the insult, the shaman performs actions that allow him to demonstrate his power. In certain texts, these are presented as a "seance" (described with more or less ritual particulars), while in others the seance is reduced to a single action or "miracle," accomplished by the shaman. And while these miracles are often similar in kind to the functions performed by the shaman in his ritual practice, the seance itself is not mentioned in the story. For example, in spite of the skepticism of the onlookers, the shaman saves a sick man not by making a sacrifice or fighting with the spirit of disease, but simply by blowing in his face [see Ksenofontov, 1930, pp. 84–85]; or obtains food, not from the spirit-owners, but simply by smacking his lips [see ibid., p. 85]; or the like. Other miracles may also be regarded as a reduction of syntagmatic links: instead of the "summoning—response" of the spirits as in the seance, the legends often speak of the shaman's ability to "turn" into animals, fly in the form of a bird, and so on.

Having proved his power by such a miracle, the shaman either punishes the profane one ("misfortune" for the requestor) or merely frightens him by demonstrating his power and compelling respect, then showing mercy (''salvation'' of the transgressor).

The plot structure of these legends also happens to consist of three main blocs; however, it is quite obvious that this does not result from direct following of the seance plot structure, but merely reproduces the underlying structure, itself based on a logic of interaction, syntagmatically unfolding in the sequence of ''action > counteraction > result.''

Such accounts may be further expanded by *stringing together links of like function*, thus producing a story with cumulative cycles describing miracles once performed by a certain famous shaman. However, it is important to stress that neither *repetition* nor *reduction* violate the tripartite syntagmatic structure of the text and only vary the plot within these limits.

But if one of the blocs is omitted (in the present case, the first, in which the shaman is himself subjected to a trial on the part of his ill-wishers), instead of a plot-organized account we have the bipartite composition of a popular belief, ascribing the ability to work wonders to a particular venerated shaman.[5]

Another technique of plot development involves one of the blocs being *expanded into a hierarchically organized series*. For example, on the way to a patient a shaman is exposed to ridicule from relatives. In response to their lack of confidence, he makes an image of a fish out of birch bark, brings it to life, and sticks it into a tree above the campsite of his companions. The fish begins to wriggle so much that the entire site is covered with snow. Next time, the shaman sends a wooden wolf to chase and return escaping horses. Here the ''miracle'' is achieved by means of special agents—fish and wolf. The episodes of their ''fabrication'' are comparable to ''preparation of the ritual images'' in a seance plot composition, but in the legend they are not confined to the seance (once arrived at the home of the requestor, the shaman performs a successful seance, but the seance preparations are not even described), instead serving as only one of the means to demonstrate the shaman's force. They constitute a preliminary plot movement, when the shaman is identified as the hero of the fabulate, and in this respect contrast with episodes in which he performs his main feat—the saving of a dying woman [see Ksenofontov, 1930, pp. 86–88].

Varying of the ''requestor—shaman'' relation by a reversal of predicates may also result in *redistribution of roles*. For example, instead of a ''request'' for help, a shaman is given an ''order'': a greedy or obstinate man compels him to bring down from the sky a wife, mowers for the fields, servants, or the like. The shaman fulfills the demand, but the arrival of the celestial spirits results in the demise of the requestor [see Popov, 1937, pp. 62–64; Ergis, 1960, nos. 139, 140, 142; Popov, 1936b, pp. 207–13]. Here, the requestor plays the part of the shaman's opponent, which results in an inversion of the entire plot structure. Instead of a ''misfortune'' of the requestor, there is a ''misfortune'' of the shaman (he is whipped and taunted until he consents to shamanize). The second bloc—the shaman's voyage to the spirits—is intended to remedy this very misfortune, although outwardly it coincides with the demand to ''supply the want'' of the requestor. Fulfillment of the demand is in fact the shaman's vengeance for the humiliation suffered. Instead of a ''rewarding of the shaman,'' there is a ''destruction of the requestor.''

Although these legends are often associated with historical persons (both shaman and wealthy man are the forebears of certain specific clan subdivisions; current destruction or decline of this clan then is explained as the outcome of punishment by celestial spirits), it is quite apparent that the account in the present case does not portray a particular seance (even though the seance itself is described in great detail by certain texts). Nor is there an ''ideological rethinking,'' resulting from loss of faith in the might of the shamans. On the contrary, this is affirmed in every way. The legends about the vengeance of a shaman result not from shifting of ideology, but pure folkloric variation, the role of the shaman's opponent being played not by an evil spirit (as in the seance), but by a person who has done harm to the shaman or those under his protection. It is instructive that this opponent in a number of texts is also interpreted as a ''foreigner'' on the superficial level (being assigned to a different clan subdivision or a different ethnic collective), i.e., his personal characteristics are closely tied up with his role.

Such legends often revolve around the personality of a particular renowned shaman [see, e.g., Ksenofontov, 1929b, pp. 43-49; Okladnikov, 1949, p. 87; Popov, 1936a, pp. 214-18; and many others] and apart from the cumulative principle of building elements of like function (as already discussed) this process may bear the nature of a biography, i.e., recounting his deeds from birth to death.[6]

Last of all, the temporal characteristics of shamanic miracle legends are interesting: the heroes are generally shamans already dead. Often the text openly declares that ''in olden times'' such shamans existed, who were able to pierce themselves with an ice pick, remove their head, turn into animals, produce a flood in the yurt, and the like, but "nowadays" such shamans "are no more." The miracles themselves, under the impact of modern understanding, are occasionally explained by the informants as "tricks" or the result of "hypnosis." In other cases, the accounts of miracles are assigned to particular persons, recently deceased, and therefore these legends include many alleged histories.

An inversion of the stories about wonder-working shamans is the extensive group of legends about shamans who bring harm [see, e.g., Dolgikh, 1962, pp. 182–87; Ksenofontov, 1930, pp. 34–35, 78; Khudiakov, 1969, pp. 305–6; Ksenofontov, 1977, nos. 159, 167, 230; and so on]. Their plot, again, is based on conflicts between the shaman and a common person, but the main predicate linking this pair in the seances along lines of "saving of the requestor by the shaman" appears here with opposite meaning: "doing of damage by the shaman."

Certain of these, such as an Enets customary account published by Dolgikh, also portray a seance "in reverse": a Sel'kup shaman or *mitakhaza* (sorcerer), instead of "swallowing" the spirit of disease, "spits out" a patient's soul that he had himself swallowed in response to a refusal by the Enets family, who had come to the Sel'kup trading reindeer for fish, to present him with a live reindeer, offering only the meat and hide. The Enets elder, in accordance with ritual practice, rewards the shaman for saving his son, extracting his promise "not to bewitch people" anymore and warning that if another of his family takes ill he will regard it as the sorcerer's doing.

In this text, the "infliction of harm by the shaman" happens unintentionally ("I was guilty of it"—acknowledges the shaman—"but it couldn't be helped. . . . Out of spite, when I asked for the reindeer, and you didn't give it, I swallowed it without even noticing. He was sitting directly opposite" [Dolgikh, 1962, p. 187]); and an ordinary man comes away with the "victory." But there are many legends attributing to a particular shaman the regular practice of devouring people's souls, sending a cattle plague, and the like. Here again we may observe the tendency for these accounts to revolve around a certain personality, not only a particular famous shaman of the past, but frequently also a narrator's contemporary.

In a certain sense, these legends may be regarded as the *source of popular beliefs* as to the existence of black shamans, raising the question of whether we should distinguish these beliefs from the classification of shamans (e.g., among the Yakut and Buryat) as "white" and "black" in the ritual itself. White shaman functions among these peoples usually coincide with the activity of the priest, or rather the leader of an entire clan's prayers; while seances, during which a shaman *portrays* dealings with spirits, enter into the functions of black shamans. It is the latter who engage in therapeutic ritual activity (in the broad sense, including not only the cure proper, but also general rectification of an unfavorable situation), and therefore such "black shamanism" in no way involves doing harm.[8]

The classification of shamans as black or white is occasionally made according to the world—nether or upper—conjured by a shaman. This also, however, is based not on an opposition of "evil" and "good" shamans, but an opposition between the "bright" upper and the "dark" nether world. Thus, belief in the existence of evil (black) shamans is rooted not so much in rituals (acts of baleful magic can be performed by anyone, not just shamans, although of course they are attributed greater aptitude in this respect; in such case, however, they appear not in the role of mediator, but in the role of an "evil" individual), as in the popular beliefs about the propensity of shamans to send misfortune.

The folkloric nature of these beliefs becomes obvious given the peculiarity of plot variation just considered: the possibility of reducing one of the syntagmatic structural blocs even to the extent of total discarding. In legends about miracles, a shaman punishes his offender "in response" to insult. In legends of shamans who bring harm, this element is often omitted; in its place, the opening piece is a "doing of damage" with no plot motivation, and the story unfolds by depicting actions of "response" undertaken against this evil shaman. But if such development does not occur, then instead of tripartite fabulate composition we have the composition of a belief story, comprising only two blocs: in the present case, the "doing of damage" and the "outcome of doing the damage." The character playing the part of the evil shaman may be a certain shaman ancestor who was known for his harsh manners when alive, or a shaman belonging to the storyteller's generation and suspected of misdeeds for certain reasons. In either case, they come within the scope of current belief and it is possible to perform protective ritual actions against them.

Legends and beliefs about evil-doing shamans can also be contrasted with legends and beliefs about wonder-working shamans in a somewhat different light, associating the positive and negative value of the basic predicates ("help/doing of harm") with the hero's *change in perspective*. In reality, stories about a shaman who performed various wonders while alive and who after death protects his descendants from oppressors, revenging their enemies and guarding against evil spirits, often revolve around a given ancestral figure venerated by a particular group: the shamans tracing their genealogy from him add him to the number of their helping spirits, and sometimes he is even held to be the spirit-owner of the locality where he is buried. A person belonging to the clan under his protection generally becomes the main character in the many mini-histories about the miracles of his relics.[h]

Accounts of evil-doing shamans can also be presented as descriptions of a conflict between them and the narrator, or as legends in which the hero entering into battle with a malicious shaman is a person belonging to the narrator's clan (this may be a *bogatyr*, a brave young man, a blacksmith, or a legendary wonder-working shaman who protects his descendants, i.e., figures endowed with certain preternatural abilities). Therefore, even in such cases when the relations between the shaman and "his" group remain outside the plot and, thus, a story is created from the vicissitudes of the combat between two shamans, the heroes of these legends usually appear as "good" (friendly) and "evil" (foreign).

This welding of the text to its narrator emerges more clearly in those legends where shamans engage in battle because one of them has done harm not to his adversary proper, but to one of his family. If, however, the conflict arises exclusively from their rivalry, then we are dealing with the next link in the chain of transformations between plots—legends of shamanic contests in strength, or the duels between shamans [Popov, 1937, pp. 51–57; 59–62; Dul'zon, 1972, no. 77; Ergis, 1960, nos. 184, 185; Ksenofonotov, 1929b, pp. 74–75; Dolgikh, 1961, pp. 64–67; Okladnikov, 1949, p. 96; Khudiakov, 1969, pp. 304–5; see Vasilevich, 1936, no. 41, and many others].

The motive for such conflicts, again, is commonly an insult given to one by the other, although a motivation may also be absent here: it is replaced by the mere description of one of the antagonists as a sorcerer, a ravenous shaman (i.e., one who devours souls), an evil shaman, and the like. The central bloc of the plot, however, involves not just a demonstration of might (as in the above-considered examples, where lack of confidence in the shaman is expressed and he works a wonder to prove his strength), but a "combat" between the two antagonists. The development of this central bloc occurs here by inclusion of such motifs as "deception," "trickery," "wiles," "magical flight," making use of articles that change into insurmountable obstacles; the shamans skirmish in the form of animals or change shape during the duel, becoming various animals, birds, or objects. Such "transformations" are sometimes similar in form to the ritual of black magic: one of the antagonists places the soul of his rival in a substitute image and attacks him by magical means. The outcome of the battle (the third bloc) explains the elevation of one of the antagonists, while the etiological ending associates the conflict resolution with the origin of hallowed places where the venerated shaman or his adversary is buried (in customary accounts and clan traditions), landscape features, or elements in the cosmology (in the toponymic legends and myths).

We present a short text recorded by I. A. Khudiakov among the Yakut:

> Once a certain powerful shaman for some reason desired to kill a sorceress, so she fled from him, jumped across the Indigirka, landed on a mountaintop and drilled straight through the bare rock. *And ever since*, in memory of this, people point to the opening, six feet high, made by the sorceress in the rock lying far to the east of the Indigirka, along the road from Zhigansk to Russkoe Ust´e [Khudiakov, 1969, p. 304] [my emphasis—E.N.].

A similarly constructed but more developed myth concerning a battle between the legendary shaman Al´ba and the evil Khosedam was recorded by A. P. Dul´zon among the Ket [see Dul´zon, 1972, pp. 89–90, no. 77], which explains the origin of the Yenisei (it is cut out by the shamanic sword of the *bogatyr* Al´ba), the Great Red Mountain below the village of Vorogov, near an offerings site (it is the body of a giant, wounded by Al´ba), the Osinovskie Rapids (made from reindeer and elk when Al´ba glanced at them), rock outcroppings to the east of the Yenisei (Al´ba himself turned into this), and finally, the origin of death (foreordained by Khosedam, since in the end Al´ba could not defeat her).

The etiological endings of these stories are an operator linking the result of the competitions described therein with the present state of affairs. The mere inclusion of etiological motifs in the fabric of the story clearly demonstrates, first, the universality of the logic of interaction (underlying both narrative plot conflicts and rituals on various levels), and second, the relative independence of the narrative from the ritual structure: the third syntagmatic bloc of the story contains not only the direct resolution of the conflict between the characters, but also the outcome with a bearing on the present condition of the world. Let us recall that, even in the seance—this most developed of ritual forms, mimicking not only the provocative actions of the celebrants, but also the "responding" reactions of the addressee—the last element in the chain of the plot is usually only an "elimination of a need," while full "elimination of ill fortune" (regaining health, success in the hunt, birth of offspring, and the like) will occur only in the future, even though also described as the result of a successful seance.

Thus, the syntagmatic structure of even such a laconic account as the above Yakut toponymic legend is more wide-ranging in the sweep of its events than that of the seance. As for plot structure itself, it is in fact much more narrow than that of the seance, due to reduction of almost all intermediate elements: the story is based on a conflict between only two characters.

Legends of shamanic duels offer an interesting range of personalities playing the part of the rivals. These may be two quarreling persons, one of whom is the narrator himself (a true story of such kind has been recorded by I. A. Khudiakov from a Yakut blacksmith, whom a shaman tried to destroy; it concludes with the following words: "And so, I live *to this day*, while he died in three weeks' time" [see Khudiakov, 1969, pp. 360–61]). In the customary accounts or true stories it may be a question of two warring shamans of the present or recent past, one of whom—the good one—generally belongs to the group of the narrator, while the other—the evil one—to a "foreign" clan or ethnic group. The outcome of the contest explains the prosperity (or decline) of "his" clan. But if the account concerns a conflict between great shamans of the past, it usually explains the origin of worshipped (or banned) places and sacred precincts, while the etiological ending stresses the details of rituals to be performed in honor of these shamans, now the object of worship. And finally, in the myths where the gods and culture heroes appear, their shamanic feats and duels explain the origin of cosmological points and cultural institutions.

The last group of texts, i.e., the shamanic legends in which the adversary of the shaman is not a member of the community (even one endowed with preternatural qualities, such as a sorcerer or a hostile shaman), but an evil spirit, a spirit of disease, or the like—i.e., a part of the religious system, leads to the next element of the original structure: the relation "shaman—evil spirit." The plot is based on a conflict that also constitutes the central bloc in the seances. It might be expected that these accounts would follow a seance pattern most faithfully, since the distribution of roles among the characters is the same. However, we have already seen that this is not so, that even in the memorate the outward form of the ritual generally receives very little attention, while models of traditional prose often do not dwell on it in the least, or employ the elements of the ritual to arrange their own plot structures.

For example, one Buryat legend tells how a famous white shaman, sitting on the bank of a river, caught sight of an evil spirit or *anakhai*. Spitting beneath the feet of the latter, the shaman froze the *anakhai* to the ice and began to beat him. The *anakhai* begged the shaman for mercy, promising not to appear in his village; but he lied, and one day entered the house where the shaman was *naizhe* [guardian of the children]. Attempting to strike the *anakhai* with a saber, the shaman missed and cut off the head of a child, after which he slept for three days, so that his soul could catch and kill the evil spirit. But he also failed in this; the *anakhai* outwitted the shaman and was able to take protection under his *tengrii* [Zatopliaev, 1890, p. 3].

In other accounts of the same type, the shaman is victorious:

In olden times, the calves began to disappear from some of the villagers. They summoned a shaman, who hid and waited for the calf-*abaasy* [evil spirit]. In the evening, after it was dark, a boy wearing a calf-skin jacket appeared in the cowshed, mounted one of the calves, and began to roll his head from side to side, while the calf bleated furiously. The shaman crept up and grabbed the *abaasy* by the hair. The spirit screamed, broke free, and vanished forever. Ever since then, no more calves were lost [Popov, 1949, p. 318].

In a Chukotkan legend, a shaman of the village of Neten, learning that a plague was drawing near, warns the residents of the arrival of *ke-l'et* spirits and orders them to hide in their homes and wait until they are called, while he himself goes out of the *yaranga* [tent], sits down in the snow, and when the *kele* arrive, presents himself as a wayfarer whom they will not let inside (cf. the above Buryat legend where the shaman pretends to be one of the *ada* in order to entice them into the pitcher, but where the story plot also included the ritual motif of invitation of the shaman by the hosts of the house). By a series of deceptions, the shaman manages to kill first the dog of the *kele*, then his wife, and finally, with the help of the villagers responding to his call, he captures the *kele* itself [Menovshchikov, 1972, no. 77].[7]

As we notice, plot conflicts in shamanic legends gradually displace specific circumstances of an "incident" from the text and concentrate on the mere encounter of opposing forces.

By speaking of a "narrative prism," I deliberately forego using the term "conceptualizations," which invariably occurs in this context, since I believe that the latter themselves depend in large measure on the arsenal of how events are symbolically recorded. One such means is in fact the plot-organized account, based on a description of the interactions between personages and allowing the fullest possible presentation of the occurrence, including the perspectives of both antagonists.

Instructive in this respect is a legend published by Iu. B. Simchenko [Simchenko, 1976, p. 49]. The scene is set at the end of the latter century, and the hero is the grandfather of the narrator.

> Once there was unbearable heat in the summer, the rivers dried up and the reindeer began to die. The hero of the story—Syry'a, a shaman by profession—tells his people that the heat is the result of Kadiu'o-Thunder, who is sitting on the tent poles and cannot move away, because his elder brother has been wounded during a fight with mythological beings [*nerymsy*] (this motif is a kind of citation of the myth concerning the battle between the god of thunder and the god of cold, Kodu). Kadiu'o-Thunder proposes that the shaman cure his brother, and a seance is performed. "He shamanized for three days, and then said: 'I have cured Kadiu'o-diuntu'o. In three days time, *argish* [rain clouds] will gather.' Three days passed and it rained. The streams began to move and there was water. The ground became moist. All the reindeer got to their feet and lived."

The plot of this legend arises from inverting perspectives with a corresponding redistribution of roles: the beneficial deity, usually bringing warmth and light, appears here in a destructive role, causing a heat wave; yet the shaman, considering the circumstances, does not enter into battle with him, but renders him a service, curing his brother, and in thus allowing them to move on, saves his people from destruction.

However, the shaman's "service" may also be false, if the antagonist is not an unintentional malefactor, as in the incident just cited, but an evil spirit.

> As a complement to the legends where the shaman pretends to be an outside party offended by those whom the spirits plan to assail, we present one more, in which a clairvoyant meets three evil spirits and goes off with them hunting for a human soul. Along the way, the spirits notice that the grass is trampled beneath the feet of their new companion, but the hero reassures them, saying he has only just died and has not yet learned how to move properly. After they capture the soul of a sick man, the four of them continue on their way, and the human begins asking the spirits what they fear the most. "The spirits replied that they fear most of all the dog rose and the hawthorn. 'And

what did you fear the most when you were alive?' ask the spirits. 'When I was alive, I feared fatty meat the most,' answers the crafty Buryat. Again, the spirits believe him. They proceed further. The Buryat coaxes the spirits: 'Give me the soul, I will carry it, you are tired.' The spirits give him the captured soul. Encountering a dog rose and a hawthorn along the way, the Buryat runs there with the soul and lies down among the prickly shrubs. The spirits cannot even come close to the hawthorn and dog rose and vainly try to force the Buryat out of the shrubs. Finally, they hit upon the idea of throwing fatty meat into the bushes. The Buryat cries out: 'I am afraid, I am afraid,' but eats up the meat. Seeing their failure, the spirits go away, and the Buryat comes out of the bushes and returns the soul to the sick man, for which he is rewarded'' [Khangalov, 1958, pp. 398–99].

The pretended transformation of the hero into one of the evil spirits, making it easier to open contact with them, is further supplemented in the story with a pretended service and a clever ruse, making it possible to provoke the adversary into admissions and actions favorable to oneself.

But the entering into contact, as has been said, may itself develop into a syntagmatic chain of events, where instead of the ''transformation'' we have the (isofunctional) ''translation'' of the shaman into the world of the spirits.

Here, then, we arrive at the next element in the transformation between plots—the legends of the shamanic journeys, which hold a central place in both shamanic folklore and shamanic rituals. As in the previous group of legends about the shaman's combat with evil spirits, the point of ''inviting'' the shaman-mediator may also be omitted here. Often, for example, the shaman himself is the bereaved, having lost a son or one of his relatives during his absence, and he sets out in quest of the soul without resorting to any intermediaries [see, e.g., Bogoraz, 1900, no. 78 and others; Dul′zon, 1972, no. 76; Menovshchikov, 1972, no. 76].

The plot begins with the ''absence'' of the shaman, opening the way to ''misfortune.'' The cause of the latter is ascertained by the hero in conformity with a familiar scheme: the death of a person is the result of an evil spirit ''capturing'' the soul. The ''discovery'' of which spirit has committed the ''misdeed'' is expanded in certain legends into a long chain of episodes, repeating these attempts until the shaman succeeds in finding the realm where the soul of the deceased is located. Then comes the ''transporting'' of the shaman into the spirit's presence, which (again) may be reduced to the declaration of a single action (''he flew away,'' ''he rushed there straightaway''), or be elaborated into a lengthy description of his journey, assuming the form of a cumulative chain where the shaman successively overcomes several obstacles, or (finally) may be set forth in hierarchically organized sequences including a number of ordeals, each ensconced in another. Thus, the method of transport may be a "transformation" (into a bird, a steed), but this "transformation" itself often degenerates into a "fabrication" of a means of transport or an "acquisition" of such from the guardian spirits of the border, and the appearance of these personages entails new sequences of conflict/contact with them (e.g., "request—granting" of a vehicle, rendering of a "service" to the sentries, "deception," "battle," and so forth).

However, the predicate "transporting" may be not only reduced or expanded, but also omitted altogether: the story can focus on only the moment of the shaman's "arrival" at the spirits.

Such, for example, is a Yakut legend, published by Ksenofontov [Ksenofontov, 1930, pp. 94–95]. The shaman's battle with a spirit who has stolen a girl's soul is presented here from the perspective of the young shaman, who is still "lying in the nest," i.e., is being brought up by the chief of the upper spirits [abaasy], Uluu toion. The story has neither a portrayal of the seance in the tent of the sick girl, nor a description of the shaman's journey: the initiate watches from his nest as the son of Uluu toion comes up from the floor of the yurt and sits in the corner silently. After this, a "shaman of earth" flies into the yurt and asks Uluu toion to return the stolen soul. The master pleads ignorance, while the son does not respond to the shaman's questions and sits with his head on his knees. Then the shaman, turning into a wasp, stings the son, thus forcing him to show his face, and flies up his nose. A silver female ornament—the soul of the victim—falls out of his nostrils, the shaman-wasp grabs it and flies down to earth. A version of this legend [ibid., pp. 98–100] has another etiological ending: an old woman who is bringing up the souls of future shamans on a bed in her house plasters their eyes shut with the excrement of children, and "ever since then" there have been no such great shamans on earth as are capable of resurrecting the dead.

Such a change in perspective on an event is yet another very important technique for varying the plot, as it opens the fundamental possibility of presenting an occurrence *from the viewpoint of the spirit itself.* This was done in rituals as well, especially in seances, which are wholly devoted to mimicking the dialogic relations between people and spirits. But while in the seances this contact is achieved along lines of "exchanges" (of power, information, valuables), in the narrations these direct approaches are supplemented by a broad range of deceptive, concealing actions, the occurrence of which is likely due to just such a possibility (and necessity) of a deeper level of mimicking an adversary's thinking processes. Along with characteristic ritual gifts to spirits, the open clashes or negotiations about receiving a desired item of value, shaman vogage legends also deal with clever ruses, deceptive transformations, and hypocrisy, to which both parties resort.

For example, after entering the world of the dead a shaman "seizes" a girl in the tent of the dead, which leads to her sickness. Here we are dealing with actions that are a mirror reflection of a characteristic situation in shamanic beliefs, explaining sickness as the result of contact with a being from another world. Yet the hero does this not merely to occasion harm to the spirits, but to compel them to act in a way favorable to himself: the dead call to the sick girl "their own" shaman, who discovers the newcomer (the other dead do not see him) and proposes to give him, as reward for releasing the girl, either the item of value on whose quest "our" shaman is engaged, or a certain intermediate item of value (e.g., a demon), with whose help the hero can achieve final success [see Dolgikh, 1976, pp. 86–87].

Thus, we have here not only direct conflicts, negotiations, and exchanges, but also inverted actions, which mimic behavior that is *seemingly advantageous* to the adversary. In the present case, it is not a question of the opposition of direct and deceptive actions, but the opposition of direct deception and deception concealed as assistance, i.e., a "tricking," a "pretended service," a "pretended kinship" with the adversary, and the like.[8]

We may also regard as an inversion of perspectives and, thus, a simulation of the reasoning of the adversary, the appearance here of such typically folkloric motifs as "making the worst choice," based on the circumstance that everything is reversed in the other world and therefore "what is bad here" will be "good in one's own world" (compare with the "proper" choice, signifying the simple finding of a concealed object); the motif of hide and seek and blind man's bluff, a game involving the task of seeing the invisible; the ban on eating and sleeping in the world of the spirits, violation of which provides the adversary the possibility of the hero's "adaptation," thus depriving him of the ability to return to his own world, and so forth.

Granted, such deflecting of plot lines into a motif is characteristic not so much of shamanic legends as of fables, but it occurs quite frequently in our material as well; still, it is secondary to plot variation using either the positive or the negative value of a function, as already mentioned.

Whereas such variation in the legends considered above led to the formation of plots concerning "good" and "evil" shamans, saving their kinsmen or bringing harm to strangers (i.e., again a result of determining who is the hero), accounts of shamanic voyages deal with the possibility/impossibility of the shaman "arriving," "achieving," or "returning."

The outcome of the voyage to the world of the spirits may also be successful or unsuccessful here, unlike the ritual, where there is a natural tendency to pattern a positive result.

The dependence of goal attainment on the degree of simulation of the adversary's reasoning may be illustrated by the example of legends that describe parallel actions of two shamans, one of whom achieves success, while the other comes to grief.

At the start of the chapter we presented examples where the role of the shaman-mediator was played by several personalities. In the Enets customary account, featuring at first one shaman whose efforts did not help the patient, and then a second shaman who was able to defeat the evil spirit, there was a simple repetition of the function of "inviting an intermediary" (corresponding, incidentally, to ritual practice itself, where a second shaman is invited after one whose seance does not bring the desired result). In the Nganasan legends describing how an old shaman tried to revive his daughter by appealing to a young shaman, who was able to cross the river separating the world of the living from the world of the dead and obtain the heart of the girl, the figure of the old shaman is duplicated by that of the young one, i.e., one of the two shamans is relegated to the role of the "requestor." In the legends that will now be discussed, both shamans arrive in the land of the spirits, but one of them behaves "properly" there and achieves success, while the other commits blunders and experiences failure or even death. Whereas in legends about competitions between two shamans the emphasis was placed on their rivalry, and the plot was molded by their confrontations, their role as mediaries—successful and unsuccessful—between humans and spirits is now at the center of the story, i.e., there is no mere repetition of the function of "calling an intermediary" with reduplication of the personalities performing it, nor a redistribution of roles in connection with a reversal of predicates, but a proper or improper performance of a function.

Curiously, outside the context of the account, these actions in themselves are often indistinguishable. For example, if a shaman arriving in the other world produces sickness in a girl simply from inadvertence or while pursuing the goal of satisfying his lust, such behavior is regarded as improper and results in death [see Dolgikh, 1976, no. 31]. But the same action when performed merely as a provocation, i.e., intending a subsequent "deliverance" of the girl from the sickness, results in obtaining the desired item of value in gratitude for this "service" and is therefore regarded as proper [ibid., no. 22]. The "causing of harm" here is merely a means of placing the adversary in a helpless condition, compelling him to search for "his own" means of redemption, thus facilitating the path to the shaman's goal. The fact that the role of the adversary is played by several personages (the dead, the girl taking sick from contact with the newcomer, the shaman who discovers the newcomer and offers him ransom) does not alter the situation, but only brings out the complexity of the hero's tactics, who finds the weak spot in the enemy's clan and a mediating shaman with whom to bargain.

It must be pointed out that accounts of a seance in the spirit world are not always tied to the figure of a shaman. Frequently the hero of this widespread plot is an ordinary person, accidentally arrived in the world of the spirits [see, e.g., Vasilevich, 1936, pp. 33, 34; Popov, 1949, pp. 256-60, and many others]. The picture of the seance in these legends is rendered almost as a mirror image: the outsider is invisible to the inhabitants of that place, his voice is perceived as the crackling of the fire, his touch causes pain, and only "their" shaman is able to discover him and help him return to earth.

That this mirroring is due to a change in perspective and an intensification of reflection is witnessed by the text recorded by Dolgikh [Dolgikh, 1976, no. 33], in which there is a twofold reversal of the picture: first, in accordance with the universal pattern, one of our kind accidentally enters the other world, is discovered there by a "great" shaman and driven back, but upon returning to "our" world and noticing that, instead of a reindeer as steed, which he requested, the shaman has dispatched him on a wooden reindeer, he turns himself and his comrades into spirits of sickness. Concerning this latter motif, Dolgikh mentions in his commentary that the idea of a person arrived in the land of the dead turning into a spirit of sickness is not typical of the Nganasan [ibid., p. 323].

Actually, the return of the hero from the world of the dead more often has the effect of turning him into a shaman, while the dual contrasting of the upper and lower worlds results in the idea that the inhabitants of the "upper" world are spirits of sickness for those of the "lower," and *vice versa*. But in our example, where the actions of the shaman expelling the outsider are regarded as improper (the "service"—return to earth—is coupled with a "deception"—handing over a wooden, instead of a live reindeer), they consequently entail a hostile move in retaliation (transformation of the hero into a spirit of sickness), located in the etiological ending, which, incidentally, is also delivered in the person of the one who has become a spirit of sickness [ibid., p. 129].

This example confirms once more that beliefs themselves are largely conditioned by the storytelling possibilities, i.e., they are based on plot-organized folkloric texts (of course, such rare technique as the double mirroring of the present text has no direct parallels in the sphere of religious ideas).

As in the ritual practice, where the purpose of the seance may be not only a cure, but also the assurance of economic prosperity, so too in the shamanic legends the voyages of the shamans are often dedicated to "acquisition" of success in the hunt, food, happiness, spirits of children, and so on. The material considered above allows a conjecture as to the direction in which these seances will be refracted in the narratives.

Customary accounts (for example, how the shaman solicits from the spirits the soul of a child for childless parents) may describe a ritual framework: the invitation of the shaman, his preparations for the seance, the approach to the deity, dialogues with it, and so forth [see, e.g., Ksenofontov, 1930, pp. 92–94; Ksenofontov, 1977, no. 108; Ergis, 1960, p. 255, and others], but much more often all these ritual features are omitted and the plot is based on the vicissitudes of the shaman's journey, his successful or unsuccessful confrontations with the spirit-owners, his proper or improper behavior in the world of the spirits, leading to a positive or negative outcome.

The figure of the requestor is also frequently omitted here. For example [see Popov, 1937, pp. 58–59], it is told how two shaman-brothers, having gone off hunting in a year of famine, become lost and cannot find game even with the help of their spirits. When they at length track down two wild reindeer but are not able to overtake them, the elder brother in vexation utters three loud cries (an action tantamount to violating the ban of ritual silence during the hunt), which results in the death of the reindeer and the wrath of the deity Aiyy. In another part of the story, it is the younger brother who does wrong: taking vengeance on a wolf for damage done, he magically lures him to within shooting distance and himself makes the kill, instead of appealing to Aiyy for help. As punishment, the deity curses the shaman's descendants, dooming them to poverty.

This Dolgan legend, enforcing the necessity of supplicatory seances as the basis of prosperity (with a proof by contradiction), involves the figures of the shamans in only a purely outward manner: the impropriety of their actions consists in the fact that they conjure Aiyy only after having themselves tried to succeed, thereby violating ritual rules with respect to animals.

As an example interpreting the seasonal seances tied to calendrical festivals, we may cite the very common plot of the flight of shamans to the country of the geese or their transformation into fish. Such stories were common among the Ket, Dolgan, Enets, Nganasan, Yakut, and Evenk. Their substantive relationship with seasonal supplicatory seances appears with special clarity in those variants where the voyage of the shaman is prompted by the desire to assure a successful hunt to his fellow clansmen (B. O. Dolgikh has recorded a similar legend among the Enets, directly incorporated into a customary account of how the Enets celebrated the pure tent festival). But in other versions, they represent stories that merely demonstrate the might of the shamans, who are able to turn into birds or fish. In either case, however, the plot describes a parallel journey of two shamans, one of whom is well prepared for the flight (he has provided himself with new clothing, alerted his clansmen as to the necessary preparations for his return, and so forth), while the other has "forgotten" to do this [see, e.g., Dolgikh, 1976, no. 16]; the one crosses an obstacle improperly—reviling an old woman seated at the hole leading to the land of the geese and not recognizing in her the Owner of the Universe—while the other flies quietly past her [Popov, 1937, pp. 54–57]; the one chooses a flowing river to shed his feathers, while the other stays on the lake and is killed by hunters [Vasilevich, 1936, p. 255; Dolgikh, 1976, no. 16; Popov, 1937, pp. 54–57, and others].

A Nganasan text involves the figures of shamans from two clan groups—Ngamtuso (who perished because of his mistakes) and Linanchera (who managed to return) and directly explains the relationship between the prosperity of the clan and the results of their voyage: "Ngamtuso shaman has lost his life. There in the ground the geese ate him. And here in the tundra, thus, there is no food at all. The people of

Ngamtuso shaman this year were hungry all summer and ate nothing. The people of Linanchera shaman are not hungry, they all eat plenty— they catch the wild reindeer, they catch the geese, they catch every kind of food'' [Dolgikh, 1976, p. 61].

But, as we see, in contrast with the seances, whose plot unfolds as a "going" of the shaman to the spirit-owners, a "handing over" of gifts to them, and a "receiving" of the souls of game animals from them, here only the mere fact of a successful or unsuccessful voyage is recorded, while all other plot confrontations of the ritual are reduced and displaced by the description of the events motivating this success or failure as the result of the personal attributes of the shamans themselves. But even in those legends that do describe how the shaman obtains items of value from the spirit-owners, direct correspondences with ritual are extremely infrequent.

> The closest to the scheme of the seance is the Nganasan legend, telling how a shamaness "in a dream" goes underground to Nily-nguo (the "god of happiness" or "god of life") so that "the people may live easily," "in order to arrange a happy life." Arriving at the tent of the gods, the woman is subjected to a triple ordeal: she must find the owner of the tent as he hides from her.[9] Three times the heroine of the story finds the old man in hiding, and he gives her reindeer wool, fish scales, and dog hair.
>
> But on the return trip, when the shamaness was crossing the river dividing the world of the spirits from the world of people, "a little blood and something white" stuck to her parka: "this blood means that humans will die of blood, of murder; the white means that humans will die of alcohol intoxication." Despite such obviously late touches, the etiological ending assigns the entire action of the story not to the calendar festival of the start of a new annual cycle, but to "beginning" times, when the prevailing order was established: "And people began to live as we live today. This proves that gods indeed exist somewhere. Verily, it is said, this happened long ago," concludes the narrator [see Dolgikh, 1976, no. 19].

In connection with such an etiological ending, the question also arises: who is in fact the hero of the legend? The narrator herself at first wavered in her decision: "Nily-nguo, the god of happiness, helps everyone. They say he was a small boy, seven years old, or a woman." In this beginning of the legend, three personages are mentioned at once—one of the major spirit-givers of the Nganasan pantheon, the deity Nily-nguo (Dolgikh considers this a later transformation of Nily-niami—the Mother of Life), who is first identified by the informant with the figure of a small boy (perhaps there is a reference here to the chief culture hero of the Nganasan—the orphan Döiba-nguo), but afterwards with the figure of the shamaness-woman who obtains "fortune" and "misfortune" from Nily-nguo himself. Thus, the role of the spirit-giver is split up here, being duplicated by a chain of intermediaries "giver > helper > procurer > shamaness" (recall that such development took place both in the rituals and in the above-given examples, where the figure of the "requestor-receiver" breaks down into the series "spectator > requestor > shaman"), warranting our regarding the entire text as a myth reporting the process of interaction between humans and spirits from the perspective of these latter, and not from the perspective of humans, as in the seances; therefore the correspondence between their plot schemes is the result of a refracted mirroring of the underlying structure of the ritual, and not a direct reflection of the latter in the narrative.

Thus, we have now reached the shamanic myths, in which the culture hero—this central figure of mythology—is depicted as a great shaman-procurer, while the plot records his contacts/confrontations with spirit-owners, the givers or original custodians of cultural and natural objects. The just-mentioned account of a shamaness's journey to Nily-nguo may be compared with the myth of Döiba-nguo himself [Dolgikh, 1976, no. 2], who obtains from Mou-niamy (the Earth Mother) "a sapling and a willow," so that vegetation appeared on earth, from Nilulemy-mou-niamy (the Mother of the Life on Earth or the Mother of Wild Reindeer) a reindeer and a doe, and from Kou-niamy (the Mother of the Sun) a sunbeam so that the snow would melt.

The common structure of both stories becomes evident if we consider the isomorphism of the threefold repetition of the trials of the shamaness by the gods (the task of finding the old man in hiding) and the threefold repetition of the journeys of Döiba-nguo (Mou-niamy sends him to Nilulemy-niamy, and she to Kou-niamy); moreover, the myth of Döiba-nguo is even closer to the plot scheme of the seances, especially those confined to the calendrical festivals, during which the shaman visits all the major spirit-owners in turn. However, although the plot of this myth does concur in this segment with the plot of the seance, it develops quite independently of the ritual scheme proper and may be regarded as one of the elements in the chain of transformations of the creation myths, in which the formation of the world is described as the result either of "procuring" the natural objects by the cultural hero from their original custodians, or of their "engendering" by the creator, or of "fabrication" by a demiurge [see Meletinskii, 1976, pp. 195–96].

In the myth in question, Döiba-nguo "procures" from the sun god not only warmth, but also a wife, with whom he "generates" the first people ("the Nganasan, to be sure" notes the narrator), i.e., the predicates "procuring" and "generating" stand in a consecutive, and not only a paradigmatic relationship, which in turn leads to episodes encountered in the shamanic initiations, but totally foreign to the seances, these ordinarily employing only the first of these predicates. And finally, in other variants of this Nganasan myth [Dolgikh, 1976, no. 1], Döiba-nguo "procures" nothing whatsoever, but in fact "generates" (and not with a wife obtained from the spirits, but with the owner of earth, Mou-niamy, herself) a grass-child, a reindeer-child, the first human twins, or even "sends" helper-birds beyond the earth to the bottom of the sea [ibid., no. 4 and 5], i.e., he behaves as a true demiurge-sender, and not as a shaman-procurer. In a purely syntagmatic sense, of course, the creator's "generating" and "sending" of his helper-birds are comparable with the shaman's "making" and "sending" of his helper-spirits with certain errands, i.e., in both cases there is a hierarchically organized plot, resulting from introduction of extra mediator-personages.

As a result, the culture hero not only merges with the creator-demiurge, but the latter, being relegated to the role of a passive "sender," is sometimes directly identified with the "requestor," or the object of procurement is delivered directly to him by the mediator.

Thus, in another Nganasan myth [see ibid., no. 14], the bird-*dia-maku* during a heavy frost asks a certain "old man" to forge her iron wings, beak, and talons, so that she may fly to the god of warmth; the old blacksmith, living alone in a small tent (a personage in whom we may easily identify the familiar culture hero-demiurge and patron of initiation), grants her request, and the bird flies to the south, finds the seven daughters of the god of warmth, who are guarding seven sacks with clouds, makes them drowsy and undoes one of the sacks. Upon returning, she sees that it has become warm on earth, and the "grandfather" who forged her wings is walking about his tent without a coat. One other element is worthy of attention in this text. The "procuring" here is accomplished not by means of the predicate "obtaining of an item of value" from a spirit-giver, as is characteristic of the ritual scheme, but by "theft," i.e., once again a change of perspective takes place: entering into contact with the giver of warmth to facilitate the "obtaining" is replaced by putting the daughters to sleep (i.e., avoiding contact), which facilitates the "theft."

And finally, in yet another Nganasan myth, Döiba-nguo himself appears in the role of "helper," and what is more, a helper of both "your kind" and "our kind" [ibid., no. 20]. He is presented here as the son of one of three gods of the hunt, into whose abode a hunter inadvertently wanders (the episodes describing the man's entering into the world of these spirit-owners contain features allowing them to be interpreted as a highly fanciful recoding of the shamanic initiations, but we shall not dwell on them). The greedy owners of the hunt carefully lock the "guarding ones" on their river, so that the fish and the beasts cannot come to earth; the bodies of those who die of hunger float to the spirits and become their "prize." The whole picture of the interaction between humans and spirits is given here in reversed form, but still obeys the same logic: the seizing of items of value by one of the partners (spirits) leads to the destruction of the other partner (humans), but at the same time the *talan* [success in the hunt] of the gods is also "bad," since they get only the skinny, famished fish-people. Döiba-nguo (in the text he is termed the Man in the White Soku) tries to rectify the situation by breaking the "guarding ones" and thus freeing the animals of the hunt, but the gods curse him for this, calling him a thief and threatening to kill him. Döiba-nguo then shifts the blame for the broken gates onto the human arrived in their midst, but at the same time arranges the escape of the latter with his sister (she is also called the "mother of shamans," and Dolgikh is inclined to identify her with Mou-niamy, the Earth Mother [see ibid., p. 318]).

Nganasan folklore, as we see, offers examples in which plot variation occurs since the culture hero, Döiba-nguo, appears now in the role of sender-requestor, now in the role of shaman-procurer, now in the role of helper, combining in himself the features of demiurge, first ancestor, and trickster—a phenomenon characteristic of the myths of other peoples as well, including other Siberian peoples (see the monograph of E. M. Meletinskii on the paleoasiatic Raven [Meletinskii, 1979]).[i]

The very fact that all these roles are played by an identical character—namely, the culture hero of a particular ethnos—may be examined in two ways. In the realm of folklore proper, this has the effect of grouping stories of different plot type around the figure of the very same hero, which under certain conditions (if the grouping takes on a biographical nature) will give rise to a scheme characteristic of the heroic myth, and then the *bogatyr* fable, the heroic epos, or the magical fable. But if we confine ourselves to a more narrow viewpoint, analyzing only the mechanics of plot generation, it emerges that the ability of the culture hero to change roles is conditioned by a change of predicates, and this in turn derives from a narrative in which views of both interacting parties are fixed and presented.

The culture hero as first ancestor ("orphan," "first human," and so on) doubtless is a model for society in its relationship with the natural surroundings, a model that in turn is reflected by spirits of the different levels. But the very same culture hero as trickster, deceiver, and thief represents a picture of the society rendered (as it were) from the perspective of the spirits themselves. Such shifting of perspective may also result in the fact that the figure of the culture hero is assigned both to the pantheon of spirits (cf. the word *nguo*, i.e., "god," appearing in the name of this same Nganasan Döiba) and to society. In the plot, this dual view is expressed in the culture hero being endowed with the qualities of a trickster, in motifs such as the hero's celestial, "divine" birth, in his descent to earth to organize it (such are the Mansi Ekva-pyrishch or the son of Turum Pairakht'-Bear), and many accounts of marriage between a celestial man and an earth woman, or the like. By reduction of these themes, the motifs of "abandonment" (celestial parents abandon the child), "solitude," and "orphanhood" of the culture hero arise, receiving further justification by the fact that he is the first man on earth. But the mediating status of the culture hero is established not only on the level of theme or motif, but also on the plane of realities— by his zooanthropomorphic nature, his transgressions (the accounts of incest between the founders of the clan are perhaps a plot development of the latter), his androgynism, or his being one of twins, and so on.

Returning to the shamanic legends, we observe that the theme of "procuring" and, in a broader context, the cultural achievements of the shaman-mediator in a final productive result lead to the last bloc of our original scheme—the "transferral" to the requestor of valuables procured by shamans. Whereas in the seances this bloc is implied by all previous elements, in the narratives it is either replaced by the etiological ending, connected only in a kind of account collision by its explanation of a logical conclusion, but not in terms of plot; or it is entirely abstracted from the blocs of the original structure, creating a basis for its own thematic group of shamanic legends. This leads to the situation (already familiar from the other groups), whereby the entire plot of a legend elaborates one particular element of the original structure by varying the relations between a pair of characters, in the present instance the shaman and those persons on whose behalf he is performing (or trying to perform) the seance.

As in the examples considered above, the plot text arises here in those cases where the ritual is violated in some manner. Such is the widely distributed Yakut legend, telling how a shaman ascended into the sky and attempted to cut the fixtures of the stars in the constellation Pleiades, in order to produce warmth on earth. The shaman forbade his clansmen to leave their houses and look at the sky, but one curious woman disobeyed and came out to watch the sparks dropping from the sky as the shaman cut the fixture with a hatchet. He immediately stopped his work, but had managed to cut only two of the nine stars; therefore, it only became a little warmer on earth [Kulakovskii, 1923, p. 12] (compare [Ksenofontov, 1929b, pp. 94-96], where a similar occurrence is presented in a positive, normal aspect, being therefore one of the legends about the shamans who are able to perform great deeds). We cite additional themes of similar structure: because of a faithless wife, a shaman who has flown off with the eaves is unable to return to his previous form [Khudiakov, 1969, p. 310] (note that this text does not contain episodes describing the actual voyage of the shaman with the birds, in contrast with the above-given legends where the death of the shaman was explained by his own mistakes in the land of the geese); the lack of attention of the people gathered for the seance has the result that an ancestor spirit summoned by the shaman—a great shaman of the past who had successfully fought against smallpox during his earthly existence—does not receive a proper reception and goes away, while his tribe perishes from smallpox [Ksenofontov, 1930, pp. 18-19]; a lazy fisherman goes out to meet a shaman, transformed into a fish, with a torn net, and thus the shaman dies [Popov, 1937, p. 57]. The last text also has an etiological ending: after trying to return his kin, a new shaman "said during the incantations that the owner of the river will not release those coming into his grasp, and so let shamans no longer descend into the water." We find a similar account among the Nganasan [see Dolgikh and Fainberg, 1960, p. 60], but here the hero is a shaman of the ancient tribe *nia*, and the etiological ending links him to one of the lakes, i.e., it becomes a toponymic legend.

## Editor's Notes

a. Syntagmatic is used here to describe systematic relationships within ritual, that is, aspects of ritual that follow logically. It is different from the more grammatical (structural) term "syntactical."

b. This was mentioned on page 95 of the original book.

c. The term potlatch refers to the ritual feasting and dancing traditional in Northwest Coast American cultures, involving elaborate displays and exchange of wealth on the basis of carefully defined social ranks and categories. The structural correlation of potlatching with the bear festival and shamanism is not far-fetched, given Northwest Coast traditions of shamanism and reverence for certain animals and birds (including the bear and raven).

For classic descriptions of the potlatch see Franz Boas, *The Kwakiutl of Vancouver Island, Memoirs of the American Museum of Natural History*, 8, pp. 307–515 (New York, 1909); Frederica de Laguna, *Under Mt. Saint Elias: The History and Culture of the Yakutat Tlingit, Smithsonian Contributions to Anthropology*, 7, 1972. For comparison of bear festivals in Siberia and North America see A. Irving Hallowell, "Bear Ceremonialism in the Northern Hemisphere," *American Anthropologist*, 1926, vol. 28, pp. 1–175. A recreation of an Amur River bear festival was sponsored and filmed in 1987 by the Nivkh ethnographer Chuner M. Taksami of St. Petersburg. Section of the Institute of Ethnography in Leningrad).

d. The importance of the bear in northern traditions is further emphasized here. See Boris Chichlo, "L'Ours chamane," *Etudes Mongoles*, 1981, vol. 12, pp. 35–112. Note also the recent story, told in the introduction, of revenge taken by a bear on a Sakha (Yakut) hunter.

e. The Buryat yurt is a traditional round house (referring both to nomadic felt tent styles and to semisubterranean housing); *salamata* is a kind of porridge; *domb* is a wooden dish. M. N. Khangalov was a well-respected Russian-educated Buryat ethnographer, active around the turn of the century.

f. The issue of determining death was not so clear, according to Khanty who told me in 1976 that shamans occasionally were summoned to revive "dead" patients by shamanizing alone with them for as long as five days.

g. Note Novik's awareness of the potential of shamans to cure their patients, through psychological therapy, social manipulation, and perhaps other means. This is debated among Soviet and post-Soviet scholars; see the introduction here.

h. Women as well as men are revered as such ancestral shamans, and are worshipped, for instance among the Khanty, in traditional sacred groves where images of ancestors have been kept. See also M. Mandelstam Balzer, "Rituals of Gender Identity, " *American Anthropologist,* 1981, vol. 83, no. 4, pp. 850-67.

i. On the widespread trickster hero see also Ann Chowning, "Raven Myths in Northwestern North America and Northeastern Asia," *Arctic Anthropology*, 1962, no. 1, pp. 1–5. E. M. Meletinskii's analysis is summarized in "The Epic of the Raven among the Paleoasiatics," *Diogenes*, 1980, vol. 110, pp. 98–133.

j. This was at the start of chapter 5 in the original book.

## Notes

1. On time scale as a basis for distinguishing the RS levels see Ivanov and Toporov, 1965, p. 122.

2. See, for example, Dolgikh, 1962, pp. 73–79, where the course of an Enets funerary rite is set forth, involving a shaman of the *sabode* category, who conducts the soul of the deceased to *dia-sie*, the "Hole in the Earth"; pp. 96–103, where the narrator recalls how the Enets held the pure tent festival; the account regarding a Yakut

ritual for arousing sexual passion, *dzhalyn*, recorded by Ksenofontov [see Ksenofontov, 1930, pp. 95–97], and many others.

3. That the legends themselves may become, in turn, a program for ritual, see below.

4. We shall see hereafter that the etiological ending of the shamanic legends often serves as a justification for ritual operations, and therefore it may be that the very custom of "taking girls" in return for shamanizing is based on folkloric texts of such type.

5. Thus, these beliefs have, as their source, not ritual, and not even a social institution or "conceptualization," but epic.

6. We shall not discuss here the issues in plot formation pertaining to an explanation of the principles of such grouping.

7. As for this account, a quite ordinary treatment is in fact possible, instead of a ritual one: V. G. Bogoraz mentions a similar legend of the invasion of a tribe that kept dogs and used them to hunt down the Chukchi. The tribe (probably the Yukagir, who employed dogs in their livelihood) is called *kel'et* [evil spirits] in the legend, "which expresses (as Bogoraz notes) only a difference in origin, especially since the Chukchi call only themselves people [*opawedat*]" [Bogoraz, 1900, p. x]. Yet even this "reality," refracted through the narrative prism, is cast in a traditional scheme: the story about the conflict between the members of the community and the foreign tribe is portrayed as a battle between their shaman and the *kele* spirit.

8. Compare the animal story, where such motifs serve as the main plot-forming clichés [see Meletinskii, 1979; Permiakov, 1972].

9. This "difficult task," owing to the fact that the spirits (dwellers of other worlds) are invisible to ordinary mortals and can be detected only by shamans, is intended to test the shamanic might of the heroine, but at the same time resembles the details of the seance during the pure tent festival of the Nganasan, when the shaman, in order to secure prosperity for his fellow clansmen, is supposed to find, blindfold, the amulets symbolizing "health," "increase," and the like, at the instance of the visiting spirits.

Translated by Ronald Radzai

# Part III.

# A Final Tribute

# The Evenk *Alga* Ritual of Blessing

## Matriona Kurbeltinova in Action

Nadezhda Ia. Bulatova

This paper presents an account of a shamanic rite (Russian *kamlanie*) performed by Matriona Petrovna Kurbeltinova, an Evenki shaman woman. I myself recorded her shamanic songs in the summer of 1987 along with colleagues from Yakutsk, Dr. A. N. Myreeva, and Dr. G. I. Varlamova. Today, Kurbeltinova is the only Evenki shaman able to present such valuable and unique material.[a] She was about ninety years old at the time of the recording. She lived with her relatives in the taiga (Siberian forests) and had been nomadizing with them. She enjoys great respect among her kinsmen. This rite was performed on the occasion of our arrival and is called *alga*, which means "blessing," "wishing [someone] well."

Evenki ritual folklore is a complex and multifaceted phenomenon. With its social basis largely destroyed, much of it has been lost. Nevertheless, ritual ceremonies are still held in places where traditional types of households are not altogether things of the past. These rituals are a facet of the spiritual life of the Evenki on which no precise research has been done to date. No complete texts in the original language have been published, though many of the rites have been described in the ethnological literature. We were the first to record a complete version of one type of *alga* rite.

Structurally, the rite can be divided into two parts: the first began at sunset and lasted for three hours; the second began at sunrise and lasted for about one hour.

The ritual began with preparations: a *salama* (a white, heavy rope about six meters long) was prepared beforehand for everyone. We were told to tie our ropes [onto the] *khulgaptïn* (colored pieces of cloth tied together), sweets, cigarettes (for those who smoke) and [other]

---

© 1992 N. Ia. Bulatova; from the journal *Shaman*, 1992, vol. 2, no. 2, pp. 167–172.

adornment. The grandson of the shaman, Terenty, her constant helper during her shamanic activities, prepared a *turu* for us. A *turu* is a ritual name for a larch symbolizing the shamanic tree. Through the *turu* our souls would travel to the upper world. Three *turu* were put up in the eastern part of the tent. This row of larches is called *darpe*. Terenty tied a long belt to the upper horizontal pole of the tent. He held one end of this belt during the shamanic activities; the other end was tied to Matriona Petrovna. This belt connects the shaman with the Upper World, the world of birds, and Heaven. A [portable iron] stove was brought in and a fire lit in it. All those present took part in the preparation. The grandmother let her hair down, sat by the fire and said: "We shall look at their future." Then she took a spoon containing alcohol and presented it to the fire with the following words: "Inhale and say if it is possible to perform shamanic activities." The fire flared up with a whoosh, which meant that permission to perform the ritual had been given. The kinsmen brought her *archi*, juniper used for fumigating during the shamanic ceremony. The shaman put on a gown, an apron, fur and chamois shoes; she tied herself to the belt, put on a special hat, and asked the juniper to burn. The grandmother was given a drum. The juniper burned, the entrance to the tent was closed, and the first sound of the shamanic drum was heard—the ceremony of blessing had begun.

It started with an appeal to the spirit helpers and with a call for them to come down from the Upper World. The first of the helpers to be mentioned is the cuckoo and the hooper [wild swan], whom she summons by imitating their voices: *ko-ko-ko, tut-tut.* The Evenki consider the cuckoo to be a sacred bird; according to their belief, it was once a human being who was turned into a bird by a shaman from the Kuktï clan. Even today, meeting a cuckoo in the forest is considered to be a sign of good luck and happiness. For the ceremony, the shaman also needed the help of a *barkanatkan*, a small stuffed animal figure, a bear. The Evenki are known to have preserved the bear cult. The shaman called to the river near which we were camped:

"Oh, Mulemkën-river,
I ask for good from your flow,
Only for good I ask!"

Then she appealed to Heaven and to the Mother-Elk, which is her soul and her spiritual double:

"Mother-Elk, Mother-Elk,
Receptacle of my soul,
Tell us only good things!"

She explained to all of them the reason for her present shamanic activities, and asked them to help her.

After calling the spirit helpers, the shaman appealed to those who give her physical strength. First was the fire, which symbolizes life. The drum gives strength to her legs, which is why she beat herself on the joints with the drum. She asked to be given water, to partake of the power *mukhun*, which is the spirit-host of all the natural phenomena: water, wind, mountains, rivers, and so forth.

Then she ordered us to bring her our *salama*, and said the words of blessing sanctifying them, sprinkling them with wine and fumigating them with juniper. After sanctification, the *salama* are the bearers of our souls.

At that point, the shaman saw a mystic vision of the river that passes through three worlds: the Upper World, the Middle World, and the Lower World, and ordered the *salama* to carry us to Heaven. The grandmother appealed to the bird protectors:

On the occasion of the arrival of three women,
On the occasion of the arrival of three women
We send you *salama* to Heaven as blessing,
*Salama* to Heaven we are sending as blessing,
In the beautiful sacred place *malu* I pronounce my words,
Wish and say only good,
Wish only good,
Distant Heaven, distant Heaven!"

Then she sprinkled us with wine, and gave some to the fire. Her helper Terenty greeted us by touching our hands, and told us that our *salama* was flowing safely down the river.

The shamanic ceremony continued with the shaman spinning around at a great speed and the drum thundering loudly. The grandmother watched our *salama* and helped her birds to carry them to Heaven. Suddenly during the journey, birds resembling a deaf cuckoo [image] began to peck this cuckoo. The sound of the drum grew louder. "Spread your feathers and fly higher," advised the shaman, and asked for the little bell, brought it to her mouth, and pronounced

shamanic ritual words. Then she tied it to the drum in order that she
and her helpers might have more strength for the flight. The sound of
the drum died down. Matriona Petrovna tended the fire, sat down, and
began fortune-telling [fate-telling], speaking of the fulfillment of everything she wished for us.

Matriona Petrovna told each of us to take nine needles, thread all the
needles, connect them, and hold the threads in our hands. The number of
needles is determined by the shaman's strength. One can tell someone's
fortune on three, seven, or nine needles. The more needles, the stronger
the shaman is. She chanted that we should squat on the left side of the tent
and explained that if the thread on the needles broke, there would be evil;
if they were intact, everything would be all right. We gave her our needles
one by one for her to take in her mouth. The shaman, smacking her lips,
sucked the needles into her mouth. We held the threads tightly and did not
let them go. Then she was given scissors, and bit it. Then everyone
examined the needles and the scissors. They were intact; this was a good
sign. The tension was released; everyone was satisfied. We tied our needles to our *salama*. Then she told our fortunes with a beater (a special
shaman's club) called a *gekhik*. A *gekhik* is made of wood that has been
hit by lightning. Its handle is narrower than the part that beats the drum.
The latter has a *bulge* covered with bear's fur and with skin from deer or
elk antlers. During the fortune-telling, the shaman throws up the club; the
side it falls on determines whether her fortune-telling will come true. If it
falls on the *bulge*, the desired future will come true; if it falls *bulge* side
up, it will not. The assembled inform her of positive results with the word
*teveche*, which means "it caught," "it took"; they say *eche* ("no") when
the beater shows a negative prognosis. Matriona Petrovna told our future,
speaking of our health, our work, and our children; then she told the
future concerning herself and her kinsmen. Then she lowered her hands
into a cup of water in order to gather new strength, and began to sing
again, imitating the cuckoo. This was her way of speaking with her spirit
helpers. She stood near the *salama*, put the *gekhik* to her forehead, looked
ahead, and conjured with the following words:

Do not yield to anybody,
Do not yield to anybody,
Safely bring the *salama* to Heaven,
My drum, my drum like the fire sparkles

Then she asked to be given reindeer's blood and sprinkled our *salama* with it. The first part of the *alga* rite was drawing to an end. She continued:

> When the Sun-Mother rises,
> When the Sun-Mother rises,
> Go and tie the *salama*,
> Tie it tight, not to break away
> If anybody tears it away,
> There will be evil.
> When the wind blows,
> It may break away.
> When the wind blows,
> It may break away.
> Even if it is so,
> Let everything be well!
> Let everything be well!
> People with shameless eyes
> May harm, may harm.
> Protect from such people,
> Protect from such people.
> The deer may take it away
> On their horns unintentionally.
> Tie it tight . . .
> May the good I have told come true.
> Heaven, say your word,
> Say your word.
> To those coming from distant lands
> Wish what is good, wish what is good.
> To these plains, to these plains,
> To the rivers, to the rivers say
> Let everything good come true . . .

Again she told the future with her beater. By and by Terenty let the belt tied to her waist loosen. The grandmother sat down and people gave her water. She washed her hands and face with water. People took off her hat and put a scarf on her head. Then they took off her fur shoes and put another pair of shoes on her feet. Then she took off her gown. The shaman's costume and ritual objects were put into a special bag (*inmek*). Here the first part of the *alga* rite ended.

The next morning, at sunrise, Matriona Petrovna put on her shamanic costume, asked people to bring her water, and washed her hands. Sitting on the *malu*, she began to sing, and asked us to repeat it after her. Shamanizing, she went outside, and went up to the *darpe* saying words of blessing. Then she sprinkled it with wine, and rubbed her side against each *turu*. An animal [image with antler] fell (*barkanatkan*) was tied to each larch. Then she collected the *salama*, returned to the tent, and fumigated it with juniper's smoke. Dancing and shamanizing, she and Terenty tied our *turu* together, putting *salama* between them. Matriona Petrovna went around the *turu* several times, blessing and shaking the fell *barkanatkan*. Asking the spirits if everything was all right, she again told fortunes with the beater. Then she addressed the hearth with words of blessing. She drank some water, washed her face and hands, and finished her fortune-telling with the words: "And now I have told your fortune and blessed you at your request." Terenty took the *salama* and *turu*, went off in the direction of the sunrise, and tied both *salama* and *turu* to a larch in the forest. With this the *alga* rite was over.[b]

## Editor's notes

a. Unfortunately, Matriona Kurbeltinova passed away in 1996, well after this text was written. While she has some possible successors, no one can fully take her place.

b. Continuity of the blessing is ensured through this further forest ritual. See also articles by G. M. Vasilevich and A. F. Anisimov in Henry N. Michael, ed., *Studies in Siberian Shamanism*, trans. Stephen P. Dunn and Ethel Dunn (Toronto: University of Toronto Press, Anthropology of the North, 1963, 4).

Translated by Sergei Muravev and Piers Vitebsky

# Bibliography

## Acronyms

*AN*. Akademiia nauk [Academy of Sciences]

*IE AN SSSR*. Institute etnografii AN SSSR im. N. N. Miklukho-Maklaia [Institute of Ethnograpy]

*IVSORGO*. *Izvestiia Vostochono-Sibirskogo otdela Russkogo geograficheskogo obshchestva*, Irkutsk [Proceedings of the Eastern Siberian Section of the Russian Geographic Society]

*RGO. Russkoe geograficheskoe obshchestvo* [Russian Geographic Society]

*SMAE. Sbornik muzeia antropologii i etnografii Akademii nauk SSSR* [Collection of the Museum of Anthropology and Ethnograpy]

*TIE. Trudy Instituta etnografii Akademii nauk SSSR* [Transactions of the Institute of Ethnograpy]

*AIaKGO. Zapiski Iakutskogo kraevogo geograficheskogo obshchestva* [Notes of the Yakut Regional Geographic Society]

Abramzon, S. M. *Kirgizy i ikh etnogeneticheskie i istoriko-kul'turnye sviazi*. Leningrad: Nauka, 1971.

Ackerknecht, E. "Psychopathology." *Bulletin of the History of Medicine*, 1943, no. 14, pp. 30–67.

"Aktual'nye voprosy ideologicheskoi, massovo-politicheskoi raboty partii." *Materialy Plenuma Tsentral'nogo Komiteta KSPP. 14–15 iiunia 1983 goda*. Moscow: Politizdat. 1983.

Alekseenko, E. A. *Shamanstvo u Ketov. Problemy istorii obshchestvennogo soznaniia aborigenov Sibiri*. Leningrad: Nauka, 1981.

———. *Shamanizmy tiurkoiazychnikh narodov Sibiri*. Novosibirsk: Nauka, 1984.

Alekseev, N. A. "Obriad posviashcheniia v kuznetsy u iakutov." *Iz istorii Iakutii v XVII-XVIII vv*. Yakutsk: "Iakutsk" izdat., 1965.

———. "Materialy o religioznykh verovaniiakh iakutov kak istoriko-etnograficheskii istochnik." *Sovetskaia etnografiia*, 1966, no. 2.

———. "Traditsionnye religioznye verovaniia iakutov v XIX-XX vekakh." Candidate's dissertation. Moscow, 1967.

———. "Kul't aiyy—plemennykh bozhestv, pokrovitelei iakutov." *Etnograficheskii sbornik*, issue 5. Ulan-Ude: Nauka, 1969.

————. *Traditsionnye religioznye verovaniia iakutov v XIX-nachale XX v.* Novosibirsk: Nauka, 1975.

————. "Obshchee v rannikh formakh religii iakutov i tuvintsev." *Etnografiia narodov Altaia i Zapadnoi Sibiri.* Novosibirsk: Nauka, 1978a.

————. "Religioznye verovaniia tiurkoiazychnykh narodov Sibiri i nekotorye voprosy ikh etnogeneza." *Vsesoiuznaia sessiia, posviashchennaia itogram polevykh etnograficheskikh i antropologicheskikh issledovanii 1976–1977 gg. (Tezisy dokladov).* Erevan: Armiansk. AN, 1978b.

————. "K voprosy datirovki etnokul'turnykh kontaktov tiurkoiazychnykh narodov Sibiri." *Literaturovedenie i istoriia. Tezisy dokladov i soobshchenii III Vsesoiuznoi tiurkologicheskoi konferentsii.* Tashkent: Uzbek AN, 1980a.

————. *Rannie formy religii tiurkoiazychnykh narodov Sibiri.* Novosibirsk: Nauka, 1980b.

————. "Mif o dukhe-khoziaike zemli v iakutskom geroicheskom epose." *Fol'klor narodov RSFSR.* Ufa: Bashkir. Universitet, 1980c.

————. "Deiatel'nost' V. M. i M. N. Ionovykh po izucheniiu etnografii i iazyka iakutov." *Ocherki istorii russkoi etnografii, fol'kloristiki i antropologii.* Issue 9. Moscow: Nauka, 1982a.

————. "Problemy metodiki polevogo izucheniia shamanstva u narodov Sibiri." *Tezisy dokladov Vsesoiuznoi sessii po itogam polevykh etnograficheskikh issledovanii 1980–1981 gg. posviashchennoi 60–letiiu obrazovaniia SSSR.* Nal'chik, 1982b.

————. *Shamanizm tiurkoiazychnykh narodov Sibiri.* Novosibirsk: Nauka, 1984.

Anisimov, A. F. *Religiia evenkov v istoriko-geneticheskom izuchenii i problemy izucheniia pervobytnykh verovanii.* Moscow/Leningrad: Nauka, 1958.

Anisimov, A. F. *Religiia Evenkov v istoriko-geneticheskom izuchenii i problemy proiskhozheniia pervobytnykh verovanii.* Moscow/Leningrad: Akademiia Nauk, 1958.

Ankudinov, N.; Dobriev, A.; and Sergeeva, K. S. *Shamany obmanshchiki.* Leningrad: Glavsemorputi, 1939.

Anokhin, A. V. *Materialy po shamanstvu u altaitsev, sobrannye vo vremia puteshestvii po Altaiu v 1910–1912 gg. po porucheniiu Russkogo komiteta dlia izucheniia Srednei i Vostochnoi Azii.* SMAE, vol. 4, issue 2. Leningrad, 1924.

————. "Dusha i ee svoistva po predstavleniiu teleutov." *SMAE*, vol. 8. Leningrad, 1929.

Antonov, N. K. *Materialy po istoricheskoi leksike iakutskogo iazyka.* Yakutsk: "Iakutsk" izdat., 1971.

Anuchin, V. I. *Ocherk shamanstva u Eniseiskikh Ostiakov. SMAE*, vol. 2, issue 2. St. Petersburg, 1914.

Atkinson, Jane Monnig. "Shamanisms Today." *Annual Review of Anthropology*, 1992, no. 21, pp. 301–30.

Austerlitz, Robert. "Shaman." *Ural-Altaic Yearbook*, 1986, no. 58, pp. 143–44.

Avrorin, V. A., and Lebedeva, E. P. *Orochskie skazki i mify*. Novosibirsk: Nauka, 1967.

Bakhtin, Mikhail M. *Rabelais and His World*. Cambridge: MIT Press, 1965.

———. *The Dialogic Imagination*. Austin: University of Texas Press, 1981.

Balzer, M. Mandelstam. "Rituals of Gender Identity." *American Anthropologist*, 1981, vol. 83, no. 4, pp. 850–67.

———. "Doctors or Deceivers?" In *The Anthropology of Medicine*. New York: Praeger, 1982.

———. "Behind Shamanism." *Social Science and Medicine*, 1987, vol. 24, no. 12, pp. 1085–93.

———. "Shamanism." In *Encyclopedia of Cultural Anthropology*. New York: Henry Holt for Human Relations Area Files, 1996a, pp. 1182–90.

———. "Flights of the Sacred: Symbolism and Theory in Siberian Shamanism." *American Anthropologist*, 1996b, vol. 98, no. 2, pp. 305–18.

Basilov, V. N. *Izbranniki dukhov*. Moscow: Nauka, 1984.

Baskakov, N. A. *Tiurkskie iazyki*. Moscow, 1962.

Beebe, John Fred. See Jakobson, Roman.

Belenkin, I. F. See Gurvich, I. S.

Black, L. " The Nivkh (Gilyak) of Sakhalin and the Lower Amur." *Arctic Anthropology*, 1973, vol. 10, no. 1, pp. 1–110.

Boas, Franz. "The Kwakiutl of Vancouver Island." *Memoirs of the American Museum of Natural History*, 8, pp. 307–515. New York, 1909.

———. "The Religion of the Kwakiutl." *Columbia University Contributions to Anthropology*, 1930, vol. 10, no. 2.

Bogoras, W. See Bogoraz, V. G.

Bogoras, W., and Jochelson, W. *Jesup North Pacific Expedition, American Museum of Natural History Memoirs* (1904–1909), nos. 11 & 13.

Bogoraz, V. G. (Bogoras, Waldemar). "The Chukchee." *Memoirs of the American Museum of Natural History*, 1989, 11 (part 2).

———. "Lamuty. Iz nabliudenii v Kolymskome krae." *Zemlevedenie*, 1900a, vol. 7, no. 1.

———. *Materialy po izucheniiu chukotskogo iazyka i fol'klora, sobrannye v Kolymskom okruge*. St. Petersburg, 1900b.

———. "K psikhologii shamanstva u narodov Severo-Vostochnoi Azii." *Etnograficheskoe obozrenie*, 1910, 84–95 (1–2).

———. "The Shamanistic Call and the Period of Initiation in Northern Asia and Northern America." *Proceedings of the 23rd International Congress of Americanists*, 1930, pp. 441–44.

Bolo, S. I. *Proshloe iakutov do prikhoda russkikh po predaniiam Iakutskogo okruga.* Issue 4. Moscow/Yakutsk: "Iakutsk" izdat., 1937.

Bromlei, Iu. V. *Etnos i etnografiia.* Moscow: Nauka, 1973.

Brown, David. "Traditional Healing Returns to Tuva." *Washington Post Health*, 18 July 1995, pp. 10–11.Budegechi, Tamara (ed.). *Shamanizm v Tuve.* Kyzyl: Gosudarstvennyi litsei respubliki Tuva, 1994.

Campbell, C. *The Way of the Animal Powers.* New York: Alfred Van Der Mark, 1983.

Castenada, Carlos. *The Teachings of Don Juan, a Yaqui Way of Knowledge.* Berkeley: University of California, 1968.

Chadwick, N. "Shamanism Among the Tatars of Central Asia." *Journal of the Royal Anthropological Institute*, 1936, 66, pp. 75–112.

Chanchibaeva, L. V. "Religioznye perezhitki u altaitsev i voprosy ateisticheskoi raboty." Candidate's dissertation. Leningrad, 1978.

Chichlo, B. "K probleme kul'ta predkov i totemizma u narodov Sibiri." *Problemy arkheologii i etnografii*, 1977, vol. 1, pp. 130–40.

———. "La Fête de l'ours aujourd'hui chez les Ougriens de Sibérie." *Études mongoles*, 1980, no. 11, pp. 47–62.

———. "L'Ours chamane." *Études mongoles*, 1981, vol. 12, pp. 35–112.

Chowning, Ann. "Raven Myths in Northwestern North America and Northeastern Asia." *Arctic Anthropology*, 1962, no. 1, pp. 1–5.

Clark, Katerina, and Holquist, Michael. *Mikhail Bakhtin.* Cambridge: Harvard Press, 1984.

Comaroff, Jean. "Medicine, Symbol and Ideology." In *The Problem of Medical Knowledge. Examining the Social Construction of Medicine*, eds. P. Wright and A. Treacher. Edinburgh: Edinburgh University Press, 1982, pp. 49–65.

Crandon, Libbet (ed.). "Beyond the Cure: Anthropological Inquiries in Medical Theories and Epistomologies." *Social Science and Medicine*, 1987, vol. 24, no. 12, pp. 997–1118.

Crane, F. "Jew's (Jaw's? Jeu? Jeugd? Gewgaw? Juice?) Harp." *VIM*, 1982, vol. 1, pp. 29–41.

Czaplicka, A. M. *Aboriginal Siberia.* Oxford: Oxford University Press, 1914 (reprinted 1969).

Davidenkov, S. N. *Evol'iutsionno-geneticheskie problemy v nevropatologii.* Leningrad: Nauka, 1947.

Day, Jane. See Seamans, Gary.

D'iakonova, V. P. "Pokhorony po-lamaistski" and "Shamanskii pogrebal'nyi obriad." In Potapov, L. P., *Ocherki narodnogo byta tuvintsev.* Moscow: Nauka, 1969.

———. *Pogrebal'nyi obriad tuvintsev kak istoriko-etnograficheskii istochnik.* Leningrad: Nauka, 1975.

———. "Religioznye predstavleniia altaitsev i tuvintsev o prirode i cheloveke." *Priroda i chelovek v religioznykh predstavleniiakh narodov Sibiri i Severa.* Leningrad: Nauka, 1976.

————. "Religioznye kul'ty tuvintsev." *Pamiatniki kul'tury narodov Sibiri i Severa (vtoraia polovina XIX-nachalo XX v.). SMAE*, vol. 33. Leningrad, 1977.

————. (Djakonova, V). "The Vestments and Paraphernalia of Tuva Shamaness." *Shamanism in Siberia*. Budapest: Akadémiai Kiadó, 1978.

————. "Predmety k lechebnoi funktsii shamanov Tuvy i Altaia." *Material'naia kul'tura i mifologiia. SMAE*, vol. 37. Leningrad: Nauka, 1981a.

————. "Tuvinskie shamany i ikh sotsial'naia rol' v obshchestve." *Problemy istorii obshchestvennogo soznaniia aborigenov Sibiri (Po materialam vtoroi poloviny XIX-nachala XX v.)*. Leningrad: Nauka, 1981b.

Diószegi, V. *Shamanizmus*. Budapest: Akadémiai Kiadó, 1962a.

————. "Tuva Shamanism." *Acta Etnografiia*, 1962b, vol. 11, pp. 143–90.

————. *Tracing Shamans in Siberia*. New York: Humanities [1960] 1968a.

———— (ed.). *Popular Beliefs and Folklore Tradition in Siberia*. Bloomington: Indiana University Press, Ural-Altaic Series, 57, 1968b.

Diószegi, V., and Hoppál, M. (eds.). *Shamanism in Siberia*. Budapest: Akademiai Kiado, 1978.

Dmitrieva, L. V. "Arkhivnye materialy V. M. Ionova." *Uchen. zap. In-ta vostokovedeniia AN SSSR*, 1958. vol. 16.

Dobriev, A. See Ankudinov, N.

Dolgikh, B. O. (ed.). *Mifologicheskie skazki i istoricheskie predaniia entsev*. Moscow: Nauka, 1961.

————. *Bytovye rasskazy entsev*. Moscow: Nauka, 1962.

————. *Mifologicheskie skazki i istoricheskie predaniia nganasan*. Moscow: Nauka, 1976.

Dolgikh, B. O., and Fainberg, L. A. "Taimyrskie nganasany." *Sovremennoe khoziaistvo, kul'tura i byt malykh narodov Severa*. Moscow: Nauka, 1960.

Dul'zon, A. P. "Ketskie skazki i drugie teksty." *Ketskii sbornik. Mifologiia, etnografiia, teksty*. Moscow: Nauka, 1969.

————. *Skazhi narodov Sibirskogo Severa*, vol. 1. Tomsk, 1972.

Durrant, Steve. See Nowak, Margaret.

Dyrenkova, N. P. "Poluchenie shamanskogo dara po vozzreniiam turetskikh plemen." *SMAE*, 1930, vol. 9.

————. *Shorskii fol'klor. Zapisi, perevod, vstupitel'naia stat'ia i primechaniia N. P. Dyrenkovoi*. Moscow/Leningrad: Nauka, 1940.

————. "Materialy po shamanstvu u teleutov." *SMAE*, 1949, vol. 10.

Dzhuliani, Iu. "O Iakutakh." *Syn Otechestva*, vol. 101, no. 28. Moscow, 1836.

Eliade, Mircea. *Shamanism. Archaic Techniques of Ecstasy*. Princeton: Princeton University Press, 1972.

Emsheiner, E. "Eine sibirische Parallele zur lappishen Zaubertrommel." *Ethnos*, Stockholm, 1948, bd. 13, no. 1–2.

Engels, F. *Origin of the Family, Private Property and the State*. London:

Lawrence and Wishart, 1940. (In Russian: Marx, K., and Engels, F. *Sobranie sochineniia.* Moscow; original 1884.)

Ergis, G. U. *Sputnik iakutskogo fol'klorista.* Yakutsk: Gosizdat IaASSR, 1945.

——— (ed.). *Istoricheskie predaniia i rasskazy iakutov,* vol. 2. Moscow/Leningrad: Nauka, 1960.

———. *Ocherki po iakutskomu fol'kloru.* Moscow: Nauka, 1974.

———. "O nauchnoi deiatel'nosti i rukopisnom arkhive G. V. Ksenofontova." *Ocherki istorii russkoi etnografii, fol'kloristiki i antropologii.* Vol. 102, issue 8. Moscow: Nauka, 1978.

Fainberg, L. A. See Dolgikh, B. O.

Funk, D. A. *Teleuty.* Moscow: Rossiiskaia Akademiia Nauk, 1992, 2 vols., in series "Narody i Kul'tury," XVII).

——— (ed.). *Shamanizm i rannie religioznye predstavleniia.* Moscow: Rossiiskaia Akademiia Nauk, 1995.

Furst, Peter (ed.). *Flesh of the Gods: The Ritual Use of Hallucinogens.* London/New York: Praeger, 1972.

———. *Stones, Bones and Skin: Ritual and Shamanic Art.* Toronto: Arts Canada, 1977.

Geertz, Clifford. *Islam Observed.* Chicago: University of Chicago Press, 1968, p. 1.

Gellner, David N. "Priests, Healers, Mediums and Witches: The Context of Possession in the Kathmandu Valley, Nepal." *Man,* 1994, no. 29, pp. 27–48.

Gmelin, I. G. *Reise durch Sibirien von der Jahre 1733–1743.* Bd. 11. Götigen, 1752.

Gogol, N. "May Night or the Drowned Woman." *Collected Tales and Plays of Nikolai Gogol.* New York: Random House, 1969. (In Russian: *Sobranie sochinenii.* Moscow, 1966–67.)

Gogolev, A. I. *Istoricheskaia etnografiia Yakutov: Narodnye znaniia i obychnoe pravo.* Yakutsk: "Iakutsk" Gosudarstvennyi Universitet, 1983.

Gogolev, A. I., et al. (eds.). *Shamanizm kak religiia (Tezisy dokladov mezhdunarodnoi nauchnoi konferentsii).* Yakutsk: "Iakutsk" Gosudarstvennyi Universitet, 1992.

Goodman, Felicitas D. *Where the Spirits Ride the Wind: Trance Journeys and Other Ecstatic Experiences.* Bloomington: Indiana University Press, 1990.

Gorokhov, N. S. "Iuriung Uolan. Iakutskaia skazka." *IVSORGO,* 1884, vol. 15, issue 5–6.

Gracheva, G. N. "Shamany u nganasana." *Problemy istorii obshchestvennogo soznaniia aborigenov Sibiri.* Leningrad: Nauka, 1981.

Grim, J. *The Shaman: Patterns of Siberian and Ojibway Healing.* Tulsa: University of Oklahoma Press, 1994.

Grumm-Srzhimailo, G. E. *Zapadnaia Mongoliia i Uriankhanskii krai.* Vol. 3. Leningrad: RGO, 1926.

Gumilev, L. N. *Drevnie tiurki.* Moscow: Nauka, 1967.
Gurvich, I. S. "Kozmogonicheskie predstavleniia i perezhitki totemicheskogo kul'ta u naseleniia Olenekskogo raiona." *Sovetskaia etnografiia,* 1948a, no. 3.
———. "Okhotnich'i obychai i obriady naseleniia Olenekskogo raiona IaASSR." *Sbornik materialov po etnografii iakutov.* Yakutsk: "Iakutsk" izdat., 1948b.
———. "Otmiranie religioznykh verovanii u narodnostei Sibiri." *Voprosy preodoleniia religioznykh perezhitkov v SSSR.* Moscow/Leningrad, 1966.
———. *Kul'tura severnykh iakutov-olenovodov. K voprosy o pozdnykh etapakh formirovaniia iakutskogo naroda.* Moscow: Nauka, 1977.
———. "Ot redaktora." In Alekseev, N. A.: *Rannye formy religii tiurkoiazy-chnykh narodov Sibiri.* Novosibirsk: Nauka, 1980.
Gurvich, I. S., and Belenkin, I. F. "Mitskevich kak etnograf. Ocherki istorii russkoi etnografii, fol'kloristiki i antropologii." *TIE AN SSSR,* 1978, 107, issue 8.
Halifax, Joan. *Shamanic Voices.* New York: Dutton, 1979.
———. *Shaman: The Wounded Healer.* New York: Crossroads, 1982.
Hallowell, A. Irving. *The Role of Conjuring in Salteaux Society.* Philadelphia: University of Pennsylvania Press, 1942.
Hamayon, Roberte. "Des chamanes au chamanisme." *Etnographie,* 1982, vol. 87–88, pp. 13–48.
———. *La chasse à l'âme: Esquisse d'une théorie du shamanisme sibérien.* Nanterre: Société d'etnologie, 1990.
Hallowell, A. Irving. "Bear Ceremonialism in the Northern Hemisphere." *American Anthropologist,* 1926, vol. 28, pp. 1–175.
Harner, Michael. *The Way of the Shaman: A Guide to Power and Healing.* New York: Bantam, 1982.
Harner, Michael (ed.) *Hallucinogens and Shamanism.* London: Oxford University Press, 1973.
Holquist, Michael. See Clark, Katerina.
Hoppál, Mihály. "On the Origin of Shamanism and the Siberian Rock Art." *Studies on Shamanism.* Helsinki: Finnish Anthropological Society; Budapest: Akademiai Kiado, 1992,, pp. 132–49.
———. See Diószegi, V.
———. See Kim, Tae-gon.
———. See Siikala, A.-L.
Hoppál, Mihály, and Howard, Keith (eds.). *Shamans and Cultures.* Budapest: Akademiai Kiado, 1993.
Howard, Keith. See Hoppál, Mihály.
Hultkranz, Åke. *Shamanic Healing and Ritual Drama: Health and Medicine in Native North American Religious Traditions.* New York: Crossroad, 1992.

————. "Introductory Remarks on the Study of Shamanism." *Shaman*, 1993, vol. 1, no. 1, pp. 3–14.

Humphrey, C. *The Karl Marx Collective: Economy, Society and Religion in a Siberian Collective Farm*. Cambridge: Cambridge University Press, 1983.

————. "Theories of North Asian Shamanism." In *Soviet and Western Anthropology*. New York: Columbia University Press, 1980, pp. 243–54.

Humphrey, Caroline, and Thomas, Nicholas (eds.). *Shamanism, History and the State*. Ann Arbor: University of Michigan, 1994.

Humphrey, Caroline, with Onon, Urgunge. *Shamans and Elders: Experience, Knowledge and Power Among the Daur Mongols*. Oxford: Oxford University Press, Clarendon, 1995.

Hunt, Eva. *The Transformation of the Hummingbird: Cultural Roots of a Zinacantecan Mythical Poem*. Ithaca: Cornell Press, 1977.

Hüttl-Worth, Gerta. See Jakobson, Roman.

Iakovlev, E. K. *Etnograficheskii obzor inorodcheskogo naseleniia doliny iuzhnogo Eniseia i ob''iasnitel'nyi katalog etnograficheskogo otdela muzeia*. Minusinsk, 1900.

*Iakutskii fol'klor*. Leningrad, 1936.

Iastremskii, S. V. "Ostatki starinnykh verovanii u iakutov." *IVSORGO*, 1897, vol. 28, issue 4.

Iokhel'son, V. I. (Jochelson, Waldemar). *Materialy po izucheniiu iukagirskogo iazyka i fol'klora, sobrannye v Kolymskom okruge*. Ch. 1. St. Petersburg, 1900.

————. "Magicheskoe begstvo kak obsherasprostranennyi skazochnomifologicheskii episod." *Sbornik v chest' 70–letiia D. N. Anuchina*. St. Petersburg, 1913.

Ionov, V. M. "Orel po vozzreniiam iakutov." *SMAE*, 1913, issue 16.

————. "K voprosy ob izuchenii dokhristianskikh verovanii iakutov." *SMAE*, 1918, vol. 5, issue 1.

*Istoricheskie predaniia i rasskazy iakutov*. 1960, pt. 1–2. Moscow/Leningrad: Nauka.

Ivanov, V. F. *Istoriko-etnograficheskoe izuchenie Iakutii XVII-XVIII vv*. Moscow: Nauka, 1974.

Jakobson, Roman; Hüttl-Worth, Gerta; and Beebe, John Fred. *Paleosiberian Peoples and Languages: A Bibliographic Guide*. New Haven: Human Relations Area Files Press, 1957.

Jochelson, W. See Bogoras, W.

————. See Iokhel'son, V. I.

Kalachev, A. "Poezdka k telengitam na Altai." *Zhivaia starina*, 1896, issue 3–4.

Kan, S. (ed.) Special issue on Christianity in the North. *Arctic Anthropology*, 1987, vol. 24, no. 1.

Karjalainen, Kustaa F. *Die Religion der Jugra-Volker*. Porvoo: Finnish Academy of Sciences, 1927.

Karunovskaia, L. E. "Predstavleniia altaitsev o vselennoi." *Sovetskaia etnografiia,* 1935, no. 4–5.

Katanov, N. F. "Poezdka k karagasam v 1890 gody." *Zapadnoi otdeleniia etnografii RGO,* 1891, vol. 17, issue 2.

———. *Otchet o poezdke, sovershennoi c 15 mai po 1 sentiabria 1896 g. v Minusinskii okrug Eniseiskoi gubernii.* Kazan, 1897 (Otd. ottisk, izd. UZKU za 1897 g.).

———. *Otchet o poezdke v Minusinskii uezd Eniseiskoi gubernii letom 1899 g.* Kazan, 1900.

———. *Obraztsy narodnoi literatury tiurkskikh plemen, izdannye V. Radlovym.* Pt. 4. *Narechiia uriankhatisev (soiotov), abakanskikh tatar i karagasov. Teksty sobrannye i perevedennye N. F. Katanovym.* St. Petersburg: Nauka, 1907.

Kendall, Laurel. *Shamans, Housewives, and Other Restless Spirits: Women in Korean Ritual Life.* Honolulu: University of Hawaii Press, 1985.

———. "Korean Shamans and the Spirits of Capitalism." *American Anthropologist,* 1996, vol. 98, no. 3.

Kendall, Laurel, and Lee, Diana. "An Initiation, *Kut* for a Korean Shaman" (in video format, distributed by Honolulu: University of Hawaii Press, 1991.

Khangalov, M. N. *Sobranie sochinenii.* Vol. 1. Ulan-Ude: Buriat. izdat., 1958.

———. *Sobranie sochinenii,* vol. 1, Ulan-Ude, 1958; vol. 2, Ulan-Ude, 1959.

Kharuzin, N. N. *Etnografiia: Lektsiia chitanniia v Imperatorskom Moskovskom Universitet.* St. Petersburg, 1905.

Khlopina, I. D. "Iz mifologii i traditsionnykh religioznykh verovanii Shortsev." *Etnografiia narodov Altaia i Zapadnoi Sibiri.* Novosibirsk: Nauka, 1978.

Khomich, L. V. "Shamany u Nentsev." *Problemy istorii obshchestvennogo soznaniia aborigenov Sibiri.* Leningrad: Nauka, 1981.

Khudiakov, I. A. *Kratkoe opisanie Verkhoianskogo okruga.* Leningrad: Nauka, 1969.

Kim, Tae-gon, and Hoppál, Mihály (eds.). *Shamanism in Performing Arts.* Budapest: Akademiai Kiado, 1995.

Kleinman, Arthur. *Patients and Healers in the Context of Culture.* Berkeley: University of California Press, 1979.

Klements, D. A. "Minusinskaia Shveitsariia i bogi pustyni." *Vostochnoe obozrenie,* 1884, no. 5.

———. "Zametki o tiusiakh." *IVSORGO,* 1892, vol. 23, issue 4–5.

Kliashtornyi, S. G. "Stelly Zolotogo ozera. (K datirovke eniseiskikh runicheskikh pamiatnikov.)" *Turcogogica (K 70–letiiu akad. A. N. Kononova).* Leningrad: Nauka, 1976.

Kon, F. Ia. "Fiziologicheskie i biologicheskie dannye o Iakutakh." *Byloe i nastoiashchee sibirskikh inorodtsev. Materialy dlia ikh izucheniia.* Issue 1. Minusinsk, 1899.

————. "Predvaritel'nyi otchet po ekspeditsii v Uriankhaiskuiu zemliu." *IVSORGO,* 1903–1904, vol. 34, no. 1.

————. *Predvaritel'nyi otchet o poezdke v Soiotiiu.* Leningrad, 1934.

————. *Za piat'desiat let.* Leningrad, 1936.

Konstantinov, I. V. *Material'naia kul'tura iakutov XVIII veka.* Yakutsk: "Iakutsk" izdat., 1971.

————. "Proiskhozhdenie iakutskogo naroda i ego kul'tury." *Iakutiia i ego sosedi v drevnosti.* Yakutsk: Iakutsk Filial AN, 1975.

Kornilov, I. "Obriad posviashcheniia kuznetsa i Kydai-Bakhsy. Kak stanoviatsia shamanami." *IVSORGO,* 1908, vol. 39.

Kosokov, I. N. *K voprosy o shamanstve v Severnoi Azii.* Moscow: Bezbozhnik, 1930.

Krader, L. "A Nativistic Movement in Western Siberia." *American Anthropologist,* 1956, vol. 58, pp. 282–92.

Kreinovich, E. A. *Nivkhgu. Zagadochnye obitateli Sakhalina i Amura.* Moscow: 1973.

Ksenofontov, G. V. *Legendy i rasskazy o shamanakh. Prilozhenie k "Ocherkam izucheniia Iakutskogo kraia."* Issue 2. Irkutsk, 1928.

————. *Kul't sumasshestviia v uralo-altaiskom shamanizme.* Irkutsk. 1929a.

————. *Khrestes. Shamanizm i khristianstvo.* Irkustsk: 1929b.

————. *Legendy i rasskazy o shamanakh u iakutov, buriatov, i tungusov.* Moscow, 1930.

————. "Soshestvie shamana v preispodniuiu." *Voinstvuiushchii ateizm,* 1931, no. 12.

————. *Elleiada. Materialy po mifologii i legendarnoi istorii iakutov.* Moscow: Nauka, 1977.

————. *Shamanizm: Izbrannye trudy.* Yakutsk: Sever-Iug, [1928–29] 1992.

Ksenofontov, G. V., and Zherebina, T. V. *Religioznyi synkretizm.* Aftoreferat. Moscow, 1983.

Kulakov, P. E. See Kuznetsov, A. A.

Kulakovskii, A. E. "Materialy dlia izucheniia verovanii iakutov." *ZIaKGO,* bk. 1, 1923, Irkutsk.

————. "Materialy dlia izucheniia verovaniia iakutov." Kulakovskii, A. E.: *Nauchnye trudy.* Yakutsk: "Iakutsk" izdat., 1979.

Kulemzin, V. M. *Shamanstvo Vasiugansko-Vakhovskikh Khantov. Iz istorii shamanstva.* Tomsk: Universitet, 1976.

Kuznetsov, A. A., and Kulakov, P. E. *Minusinskie i achinskie inorodtsi.* Krasnoiarsk: Eniseisk. gubernsk. statistichesk. komiteta, 1898.

Laderman, Carol, and Roseman, Marina (eds.). *The Performance of Healing.* New York: Routledge, 1996.

Laguna, Frederica de. *Under Mt. Saint Elias: The History and Culture of the Yakutat Tlingit, Smithsonian Contributions to Anthropology,* 1972, 7.

Larsen, Stephen. *The Shaman's Doorway: Opening Imagination to Power and Myth.* New York: Anchor, Station Hill, [1976] 1988.

Laufer, Berthold. "Origin of the Word Shaman." *American Anthropologist*, 1917, no. 19, pp. 261–78.

Lebedeva, E. P. See Avrorin, V. A.

Lee, Diana. See Kendall, Laurel.

Lenin, V. I. "Sotsializm i religiia." *Polnoe sobranie sochinenii*, vol. 12.

Lepekhin, I. *Dnevnye zapiski puteshestviia po raznym provintsiiam Rossiiskogo gosudarstva*, ch. 4. St. Petersburg, 1805.

Leroi-Gourhan, André. *The Dawn of European Art*. New York: Cambridge University Press, 1982.

Lévi-Strauss, Claude. *Structural Anthropology*. New York: Anchor, [1958] 1967.

———. *The Raw and the Cooked*. New York: Harper and Row, 1975.

Levin, M. G., and Potapov, L. P., eds. *Narody Sibiri*. Moscow/Leningrad: Nauka, 1956.

Lewis, Ioan M. *Ecstatic Religions: An Anthropological Study of Spirit Possession and Shamanism*. Middlesex: Penguin, 1971.

Lindgren, E. J. *Notes on the Reindeer Tungus of Manchuria. Their Names, Groups, Administration, and Shamans*. Cambridge, Ph.D. thesis, 1935.

Lommel, Andreas. *Shamanism: The Beginning of Art*. New York: McGraw-Hill, 1967.

Lönngvist, Bo. "Problems Concerning the Siberian SHaman Costume." *Ethnologia Fennica*, 1976, no. 1–2.

Maak, P. *Viliuiskii okrug Iakutskoi oblasti*. Pt. 3. St. Petersburg, 1887.

Malov, S. E. "Neskol'ko slov o shamanstve u turetskogo naseleniia Kuznetskogo uezda Tomskoi gubernii." *Zhivaia starina*, 1909, issue 2–3.

———. "Predislovie k trudu A. V. Anokhina *Materialy po shamanstvu u altaitsev.*" *SMAE*, 1924, vol. 4, issue 2.

Marx, K. "Gogentsollernskii obshchii plan reforma." Marx and Engels, *Sochineniia*, 2nd ed., vol. 6.

Maskarinec, Gregory G. *The Rulings of the Night: An Ethnography of Nepalese Shaman Oral Texts*. Madison, WI: University of Wisconsin Press, 1995.

Matarasso, Michel (ed.). "Chamanes et chamanisme au seuil du nouveau millénnaire." *Diogène*, 1992, no. 158, pp. 1–163.

Meletinskii, E. M. *Proiskhozhdenie geroicheskogo eposa. Rannie formy i arkhaicheskie pamiatniki*. Moscow, 1963.

———. "Mif i skazka." *Fol'klor i etnografiia*. Leningrad, 1970.

———. *Poetika mifa*. Moscow, 1976.

———. *Paleoaziatskii mifologicheskii epos. Tsikl Vorona*. Moscow, 1979.

———. "The Epic of the Raven Among the Paleo-Asiatics." *Diogenes*, 1980, vol. 110, pp. 98–133.

Menovshchikov, G. A. *Mestnye nazvaniia na karte Chukotki. Kratkii toponimicheskii slovar'*. Magadan: Magadanskoe knizhnoe izdatel'stvo, 1972.

Michael, Henry N. (ed.). *Studies in Siberian Shamanism*, trans. Stephen P. Dunn and Ethel Dunn. Toronto: University of Toronto Press, Anthropology of the North, 4, 1963.

Middendorf, A. F. *Puteshestvie na sever i vostok SIbiri*. Pt. 2. St. Petersburg, 1896.

Mikhailov, T. M. *Iz istorii buriatskogo shamanizma (s drevneishikh vremen po XVII v.)*. Novosibirsk: Nauka, 1980.

———. *Buriatskii shamanizm: istoriia, struktura i sotsial'nye funktsii*. Novosibirsk: Nauka, 1987.

——— (ed.). *Sovremennye problemy buddizma, shamanizma i pravoslaviia*. Ulan-Ude: Akademiia Nauk, 1980.

Mikhailovskiii, V. M. *Shamanstvo*. Moscow: Izvestiia Imperatorskogo obshchestva liubitelei estestvoznaniia, antropologiia i etnografii, 1892, 12.

———. "Shamanism in Siberia and European Russia, Being the Second Part of *Shamanstvo*." *Journal of the Royal Anthropological Iustitute*, 1894, 24.

Mistkevich, S. I. *Menerik i emeriachen'e—formy isterii v Kolymskom krae*. Leningrad, 1929.

Moerman, Daniel. See Romanucci-Ross, Lola.

Murphy, Jane M. "Psychotherapeutic Aspects of Shamanism on St. Lawrence Island." *Magic, Faith and Healing*, ed. Ari Kiev. New York: Free Press, 1964.

Myreeva, A. N. See Romanova, A. V.

Nagishkin, D. *Folktales of the Amur*. New York, 1980.

Neher, A. "A Psychological Explanation of Unusual Behavior in Ceremonies Involving Drums." *Human Biology*, 1962, vol. 34, pp. 151–60.

Noll, R. "Shamanism and Schizophrenia." *American Ethnologist*, 1983, vol. 10, no. 3, pp. 443–59.

Nowak, Margaret, and Durrant, Steve. *The Tale of the Nišan Shamaness*. Seattle: University of Washington Press, 1977.

Ohlmarks, A. *Studien zum Problem des Schamanismus*. Lund, 1939.

*Oirotsko-russkii slovar'*. Moscow: OGIZ. izdat. slovarei, 1947.

Okladnikov, A. P. "Istoricheskie rasskazy i legendy Nizhnei Leny." *SMAE*, 1949, vol. 11.

———. "Iakutiia do prisoedineniia k Russkomy gosudarstvu." *Istoriia Iakutskoi ASSR*. Vol. 1. Moscow/Leningrad: Nauka, 1955.

Oktiabr'skaia, I. V. See Sagalaev, A. M.

Onon, Urgunge. See Humphrey, Caroline.

*Osnovy nauchnogo ateizma*. Moscow: Gospolitizdat, 1962.

Ostrovskikh, P. "Etnograficheskie zametki o tiurkakh Minusinskogo kraia." *Zhivaia starina*, 1895, issue 3–4.

*Pamiatniki kul'tury narodov Sibiri i Severa (vtoraia polovina XIX-nachalo XX v.)*. *SMAE*, vol. 33. Leningrad: Nauka, 1977.

Pekarskii, E. P. "Materialy po iakutskomy obychnomu pravu." *SMAE*, 1925, vol. 5, issue 2.

————. *Slovar' iakutskogo iazyka.* Vols. 1–3. Moscow: Nauka, 1959.

Pekarskii, E. P., and Vasil'ev, B. N. "Plashch i buben iakutskogo shamana." *Materialy po etnografii Possii.* Vol. 1. St. Petersburg: Russk. muzeia, 1910.

Pekarskii, E. P., and Popov, N. N. "Sredi iakutov. Sluchainye zametki." *Ocherki po izucheniiu Iakutskogo kraia.* Issue 2. Irkutsk, 1928.

Pentikainen, J. (ed.). *Shamanism and Northern Ecology.* Berlin/New York: Mouton de Gruyter, 1996.

Peters, L. G. *Ecstasy and Healing in Nepal: An Ethnographic Study of Tamang Shamanism.* Los Angeles: Undena, 1981.

Peters, L. G., and Price-Williams, D. "Towards an Experiential Analysis of Shamanism." *American Ethnologist,* 1980, no. 7, pp. 98–418.

Petri, B. E. *Promysli karagas.* Irkutsk. 1928.

Pomerantseva, E. V. *Mifologicheskie personazhi v russkom fol'klore.* Moscow, 1975.

Popov, A. A. *Materialy dlia bibliografii russkoi literatury po izucheniiu shamanstva severoaziatskikh narodov.* Leningrad: izd. In-ta narodov Severa TsIK SSSR, 1932.

————. "Tavgiisty." *Trudy Instituta antropologii i etnografii.* Vol. 1, issue 5. Moscow/Leningrad, 1936a.

———— (ed.) *Iakutskii fol'klor.* Moscow, 1936b.

———— (ed.) *Dolganskii fol'klor.* Moscow, 1937.

————. "Poluchenie /shamanskogo dara' u viliuiskikh iakutov." *TIE,* 1947, vol. 2.

————. *Naganasany.* Leningrad: Nauka. 1948.

————. "Materialy po istorii religii iakutov b. Viliuiskogo okruga." *SMAE,* 1949, vol. 11.

————. *Nganasany: sotsial'noe ustroistvo i verovaniia.* Leningrad, 1984.

————. "How Sereptie Djarouskin of the Nganasans (Tavgi Samoyeds) Became a Shaman." *Popular Beliefs and Folklore Tradition in Siberia.* Ural-Altaic Series 57. Bloomington, Indiana, 1968.

Popov, G. A. *Ocherki po istorii Iakutii.* Yakutsk. 1924.

Potanin, G. N. *Ocherki Severo-Zapadnoi Mongolii.* 4 vols. St. Petersburg, 1881–83.

————. *Neskol'ko voprosov po izucheniiu poveriu, skazanii, suevernykh obychaev i obriadov u Sibierskikh inorodstev.* St. Petersburg, 1888.

Potapov, L. P. "Okhotnich'i pover'ia obriady y altaiskikh turkov." *Kul'tura i pis'mennost' Vostoka.* B. 5. Baku. 1929.

————. "Luk i strela v shamanstve u altaitsev." *Sovetskaia etnografiia,* 1934, no. 3.

————. "Sledy totemisticheskikh predstavlenii u altaitsev." *Sovetskaia etnografiia,* 1935, no. 4–5.

————. "Obraid ozhivleniia shamanskogo bubna u tiurkoiazychnykh plemen Altaia." *TIE,* 1947, vol. 1.

————. "Buben teleutskoi shamanki i ego risunki." *SMAE*, 1949, vol. 10.

————. "Materialy po etnografii tuvintsev raionov Mongun Taigi i Kara-Kholia." *Trudy Tuvinskoi kompleksnoi arkheologo-etnograficheskoi ekspeditsii.* Vol. 1. Moscow/Leningrad, 1960.

————. "Ocherki etnografii tuvintsev basseina levoberezh'ia Khemchika." *Trudy Tuvinskoi kompleksnoi arkheologo-etnograficheskoi ekspeditsii 1959–1969 gg.* Vol. 2. Moscow/Leningrad, 1966.

————. *Ocherki narodnogo byta tuvintsev.* Moscow: Nauka, 1969a.

————. *Ethnicheskii sostav i proiskhozhdeni altaitsev. Istoriko-etnograficheskii ocherk.* Leningrad: Nauka, 1969b.

————. "K semantike nazvanii shamanskikh bubnov u narodnostei Altaia." *Sovetskaia tiurkologiia,* 1970, no. 3.

————. "Kon' v verovaniiakh i epose Saiano-Altaia." *Fol'klor i etnografiia. Sviazi fol'klora s drevnimi predstavleniiami i obriadami.* Leningrad, 1977.

————. "K voprosu o drevnetiurkskoi osnove i datirovke altaiskogo shamanstva." *Etnografiia narodov Altaia i Zapadnoi Sibiri.* Novosibirsk: Nauka, 1978.

————. "Shamanskii buben kachintsev kak unikal'nyi predmet etnograficheskikh kollektsii." *Material'naia kul'tura i mifologiia. SMAE,* vol. 37. Leningrad: Nauka, 1981.

————. "Die Herstellung der Samanentrommel bi den Sor." *Mitteilungen des Seminars für orientalische Sprachen zu Berlin, Ostasiatische Studien,* 1924, vol. 27, no. 1.

————. See Levin, M. G.

Price-Williams, D. See Peters, L. G.

Priklonskii, V. P. "O shamanstve iakutov." *IVSORGO,* 1886, vol. 15, no. 1–2.

————. "Pokhorony u iakutov v severnoi chasti Iakutskoi oblasti." *Sibirskii sbornik.* Issue 1. Irkutsk, 1890.

————. "Svedeniia o iazycheskikh verovaniiakh u obychaiakh prezhnikh iakutov." *Iakutskie eparkhial'nye vedomosti,* 1893, no. 22.

Pripuzov, N. P. "Svedeniia dlia izucheniia shamanstva u iakutov Iakutskogo okruga." *IVSORGO,* 1884, vol. 15, no. 3–4.

*Priroda i chelovek v religioznykh predstavleniakh narodov Sibiri i Severa.* Leningrad: Nauka, 1976.

Prokof'eva, E. D. "Shamanskie bubny." *Istorko-etnograficheskii atlas Sibiri.* Moscow/Leningrad: Nauka, 1961.

————. "Shamanskie kostiumy narodov Sibiri." *Religioznye predstavleniia i obriady narodov Sibiri v XIX-nachale XX v. SMAE,* vol. 27. Leningrad: Nauka, 1971.

————. "Materialy po shamanstvu sel'kupov." *Problemy istorii obshchestvennogo soznaniia aborigenov Sibiri.* Leningrad: Nauka, 1981.

Propp, V. Ia. *Istoricheskie korni volshebnoi skazki.* Leningrad, 1946.

————. *Russkii geroicheskii epos.* Moscow/Leningrad, 1953.

————. *Morphology of the Folktale.* Bloomington: Indiana University Press, 1968.

————. "The Historical Bases of Some Russian Religious Festivals." In *Introduction to Soviet Ethnography,* eds. Stephen P. Dunn and Ethel Dunn. Berkeley: Highgate Road Social Science Research Station, 1974), pp. 367–410.

Purevzhav, S. "K voprosu o stadiiakh razvitiia ideologicheskoi kontseptsii drevnemongol'skogo shamanizma." *Trudy mongol'skikh istorikov (1960–74).* Ulan-Bator, 1975.

Putilov, B. N. "Epos i obriad." *Fol'klor i etnografiia. Obriady i obriadovyi fol'klor.* Leningrad, 1974.

Radin, Paul. *Primitive Religion: Its Nature and Origin.* New York: Viking, 1937.

Radlov, V. V. (Radloff, W.). *Aus Sibirien. Zose Blätter ausd meinem Tagebuch.* 2nd ed. Leipzig, 1893, no. 1–2.

————. *Opyt slovaria tiurkskikh narechii.* Vol. 3, pt. 1. St. Petersburg, 1905.

Raikov, M. I. "Otchet o poezdke i verkhov'iam reki Eniseia, sovershennoi po porucheniiu Russkogo geograficheskogo obshchestva." *Izvestiia RGO,* 1898, vol. 34, issue 4.

Revunenkova, E. V. "O lichnosti shamana." *Sovetskaia etnografiia,* 1974, no. 3, pp. 104–11.

Romanova, A. V., and Myreeva, A. N. *Fol'klor evenkov Iakutii.* Leningrad, 1971.

Romanova, E. N. *Yakutskii prazdnik ysyakh: istoki i predstavleniia.* Novosibirsk: Nauka, 1994.

Romanucci-Ross, Lola; Moerman, Daniel; and Tancredi, Lawrence (eds.), *The Anthropology of Medicine.* New York: Bergin and Garvey, 1991.

Roseman, Marina. See Laderman, Carol.

Rouget, G. *La Musique et la trance.* Paris: Gallimard, 1980.

Sagalaev, A. M.; and Oktiabr'skaia, I. V. *Traditsionnoe mirovozrenie tiurkov Iuzhnoi Sibiri. Znak i ritual.* Novosibirsk: Nauka, 1990.

*Sakha fol'klora (Iakutskii fol'klor).* Yakutsk, 1947.

Salomon, Frank. "Shamanism and Politics in Late-Colonial Ecuador." *American Ethnologist,* 1983, vol. 10, no. 3, pp. 413–28.

Satlaev, F. A. *Kumandintsy. (Istoriko-etnograficheskii ocherk XIX-pervoi chetverti XX vv.).* Gorno-Altaisk: Gorno-Altaiskoe otd. Altaisk. izdat., 1974.

Seamans, Gary, and Day, Jane (eds.). *Ancient Traditions: Culture and Shamanism in Central Asia and the Americas.* Denver: University of Colorodo, and Denver Museum of Natural History, 1994.

Sergeeva, K. S. See Ankudinov, N.

Seroshevskii, V. L. (Sieroszewski, W. L.). *Iakuty. Opyt etnograficheskogo issledovaniia.* Vol. 1. St. Petersburg: RGO, 1896.

————. "Du chamanisme d'après les croyances des Yakoutes." *Revue de l'histoire des religions.* Paris, 1902, vol. 46.

Shcherbak, A. M. *Grammaticheskii ocherk iazyka tiurkskikh tekstov X-XIII vv. iz Bostochnogo Turkestana.* Moscow, 1962.

Shchukin, N. S. *Poezdka v Iakutsk.* St. Petersburg, 1833.

Sherstova, L. I. *Altai Kizhi v kontse XIX–nachale XX v.* Aftoreferat. Leningrad: Nauka, 1985.

———. "Shamanizm i Burkhanizm: Dinamika vzaimootnoshenii." In Gogolev, A. I., et al. (eds.), *Shamanizm kak religiia (Tezisy dokladov mezhdunarodnoi nauchnoi konferentsii).* Yakutsk: "Iakutsk" Gosudarstvennyi Universitet, 1992.

Shimkevich, P. P. "Materialy dlia izucheniia shamanstva u Goldov." *Zapiski Priamursk. otd. RGO*, vol. 1, issue 2. Khabarovsk, 1896.

Shirokogorov, S. M. (Shirokogoroff). "Opyt issledovaniia osnov shamanstva u tungusov." *Uchenye zapiski istoriko-filologicheskogo fakul'teta Vladivostokskogo Universiteta.* Vladivostok, 1919.

———. *Social Organization of the Manchus.* Shanghai: Royal Asiatic Society, 1924.

———. *Social Organization of the Northern Tungus.* Shanghai, 1929.

———. *Psychomental Complex of the Tungus.* London: Routledge & Kegan Paul, 1935.

Shternberg, L. Ia. "Giliaki." *Etnograficheskoe obozrenie*, 1904, 1; 2; 4.

———. "Die Religion der Gilyaken." *Archiv für Religionswissenschaft*, 1905, vol. 8, pp. 244–73 (Leipzig).

———*Pervobytnaia religiia v svete etnografii.* Leningrad: Nauka, 1936.

Shvetsov, S. *Gornyi Altai i ego naselenie.* Vol. 1. *Kochevniki Biiskogo uezda.* Barnaul, 1900.

Siikala, A.-L. *The Rite Technique of the Siberian SHaman.* Helsinki: Academia Scientiarum Fennica, 1978.

Siikala, A.-L., and Hoppál, Mihály. *Studies on Shamanism.* Helsinki: Finnish Anthropological Society; Budapest: Akademiai Kiado, 1992.

Silverman, J. "Shamans and Acute Schizophrenia." *American Anthropologist*, 1967, vol. 69, pp. 21–31.

Simchenko, Iu. B. *Kul'tura okhotnikov na olenei Severnoi Evrasii.* Moscow: Nauka, 1976.

Sleptsov, A. "O verovaniiakh iakutov Iakutskoi oblasti." *IVSORGO*, 1886, vol. 17, no. 1–2.

Smirnov, Veniamin. "Samoedy mezenskie." *Vestnik Russkogo geograficheskogo obshchestva*, 1855.

Smoliak, Anna V. *Ulchi.* Moscow: Nauka, 1966.

———. *Shaman: Lichnost', funktsii, mirovozrenie (narody nizhnego Amura).* Moscow: Nauka, 1991.

Sofronov, D. D. " 'Tainy' Shamanov." *Poliarnaia zvezda,* Yakutsk, 1972, no. 1.

Soilov'ev, F. "Ostatki iazychestva u iakutov." *Sbornik gazety Sibiri.* Vol. 1. St. Petersburg, 1876.

*Soveshchanie po problemam razvitiia khomeiia.* Kyzyl: Ministerstvo kul'tury, 1988.

Sukhov, A. D. *Filosofskie problemy proiskhozhdeniia religii.* Moscow: Mysl', 1967.

Sukhovskii, O. V. "O shamanstve v Minusinskom krae." *Izv. O-va arkheologii, istorii i etnografii pri Kazanskom Universitete,* 1901, vol. 17, issue 2–3.

Suslov, I. M. "Shamanstvo i bor'ba s nim." *Sovetskii Sever,* 1931, no. 3–4.

Suzukei, V. Iu. "Shamanizm i muzykal'nyi fol'klor Tuvintsev." In Gogolev, A. I., et al., eds., *Shamanizm kak religiia (Tezisy dokladov mezhdunarodnoi nauchnoi konferentsii).* Yakutsk: "Iakutsk" Gosudarstvennyi Universitet, 1992, pp. 57–58.

Taksami, Ch. M. "Shamanstvo u Nivkhov." *Problemy istorii obshchestvennogo soznaniia aborigenov Sibiri.* Leningrad: Nauka, 1981.

Tancredi, Lawrence. See Romanucci-Ross, Lola.

Taussig, Michael. *Shamanism, Colonialism and the Wild Man.* Chicago: University of Chicago Press, 1987, p. 237.

Thomas, Nicholas. See Humphrey, Caroline.

Tokarev, S. A. "Shamanstvo u iakutov v XVII v." *Sovetskaia etnografiia,* 1939, no. 2.

———. *Ocherk istorii iakutskogo naroda.* Moscow, 1940.

———. "Perezhitki rodovogo kul'ta u altaitsev." *TIE,* 1947, vol. 1.

———. *Rannie formy religii i ikh razvitie.* Moscow: Nauka, 1964a.

———. *Religii v istorii narodov mira.* Moscow: Politizdat, 1964b.

———. *Istoriia russkoi etnografii (dooktiabr'skii period).* Moscow: Nauka, 1966.

———. "Religion As a Social Phenomenon" and his critics' responses: *Soviet Anthropology and Archeology,* Winter 1979–80–Spring 1982 (vols. 20–22).

Tolstov, S. P. "Osnovnye teoreticheskie problemy sovremennoi sovetskoi etnografii." *Doklady sovetskoi delegatsii na VI Mezhdunarodnom kongresse antropologov i etnografov.* Moscow: Nauka, 1960.

Tret'iakov, P. I. "Turukhanskii krai, eto priroda i zhizn'." *Zapiski Russkogo geograficheskogo obshchestva (po otd. geografiia),* 1869, vol. 2.

Troitskaia, A. L. "Lecheniia bol'nykh iz gnaniem zlykh dukhov (*kuchuruk*) sredy osedlogo naseleniia Turkestana." *Biulleten' Sredne-Asiatskogo Gosudarstvennogo Universiteta,* 1925, 10.

Troshchanskii, V. F. "Evoliutsiia chernoi very (shamanstva) u iakutov." *Uchenye zapiski Kazenskogo Universiteta,* 1902–1904, vol. 70, bk. 4.

Turner, Victor. *The Ritual Process: Structure and Anti-Structure.* Ithaca: Cornell Press, 1977.

——— (ed.). *Celebration: Studies in Festivity and Ritual.* Washington, D.C.: Smithsonian Institution Press, 1982.

Vainshtein, S. I. *Tuvintsy-todzhintsy: Istoriko-etnograficheskie ocherki.* Moscow: Izdat. vost. lit., 1961.

———. "Tuvinskoe shamanstvo." *Doklad na VII Mezhdunarodnom kongresse antropologicheskikh i etnograficheskikh nauk.* Moscow: 1964.

———. "Etnograficheskie issledovaniia v Gornom Altae i Tuve." *Polevye issledovaniia Instituta etnografii. 1978.* Moscow: Nauka, 1980.

Vasil'ev, B. N. See Pekarskii, E. P.

Vasil'ev, V. N. "Shamanskii kostium i buben u iakutov." *SMAE*, 1918, vol. 1, issue 8.

Vasilevich, G. M. *Materialy po evenkiiskomu (tungusskomu) fol'kloru.* Leningrad, 1936.

———. *Evenki. Istoriko-etnograficheskie ocherki (XVIII-nach. XX v.).* Leningrad: Nauka, 1969.

Vcherashniaia, I. A. "Tuvinskie narodnye skazki." Candidate's dissertation. Moscow, 1955.

Vdovin, I. S. "The Study of Shamanism Among the Peoples of Siberia and the North." In *The Realm of the Extra-Human: Agents and Audiences.* The Hague: Mouton, 1976, pp. 261–73.

———. *Khristianstvo i lamaizm u korennogo naseleniia Sibiri (vtoraia polovina XIX-nachalo XX v.).* Leningrad: Nauka, 1979.

——— (ed.). *Problemy istorii obshchestvennogo soznaniia aborigenov Sibiri (po materialam vtoroi poloviny XIX-nachala XX v.).* Leningrad: Nauka, 1981.

Verbitskii, V. I. "Kratkie svedeniia ob Altaiskoi missii." *Tomskie eparkhial'nye vedomosti,* 1886, no. 22.

———. *Altaiskie inorodtsi.* Moscow, 1893.

Verbov, G. D. "Lesnye Nentsy." *Sovetskaia etnografiia,* 1936, no. 2.

Vitashevskii, N. A. "Materialy dlia izucheniia shamanstva u iakutov." *IVSORGO,* 1890, vol. 2, issue 2.

———. "Iz nabliudenii nad iakutskimi shamanskimi deistviiami." *SMAE*, vol. 5, issue 1, 1918.

Vitebsky, Piers. *The Shaman.* London: Macmillan, 1995.

Walsh, Roger. *The Spirit of Shamanism.* Los Angeles: Tarcher, 1990.

Wasson, R. G. *Soma: The Divine Mushroom of Immortality.* New York: Harcourt Brace Jovanovich, 1960.

Zatopliaev, N. I. "Nekotorye pover'ia alarskikh buriat." *Shamanskie pover'ia inorodtsev Vostochnoi Sibiri.* Irkutsk, 1890.

Zelenin, D. K. "Ideologiia sibirskogo shamanstva." *Izvestiia Akademii Nauk SSSR. Otd-nie obshchestvennoi nauk,* 1935, no. 8.

———. *Kul't ongonov v Sibiri. Perezhitki totemizma v ideologii sibirskikh narodov.* Issue 3. Moscow/Leningrad: Nauka, 1936.

Zherebina, T. V. See Ksenofontov, G. V.

Zhukovskaia, N. L. "Modernizatsiia shamanstva v usloviiakh rasprostraneniia budizma u mongolov i ikh sosedei." *Etnograficheskii sbornik,* 1969, no. 5. Ulan-Ude.

———. *Lamaizm i rannie formy religii.* Moscow: Nauka, 1977.

Zolotarev, A. M. *Rodovoi stroi i religiisa ul'chei.* Khabarovsk, 1939.

Archival references are in each individual chapter.